QADDAFI, TERRORISM, AND THE ORIGINS OF THE U.S. ATTACK ON LIBYA

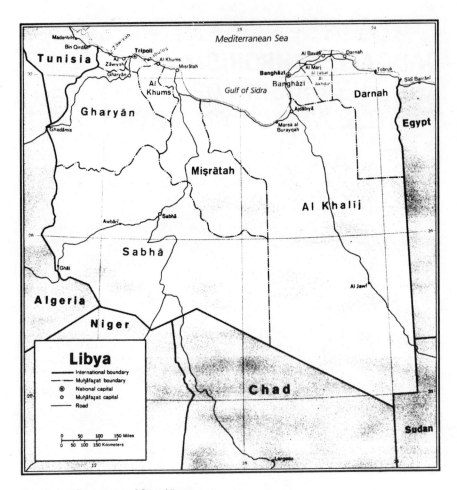

Source: U.S. Department of State Library.

QADDAFI, TERRORISM,
AND THE
ORIGINS
OF THE
U.S. ATTACK ON LIBYA

BRIAN L. DAVIS

PRAEGER

New York
Westport, Connecticut
London

Library of Congress Cataloging-in-Publication Data

Davis, Brian Lee.
    Qaddafi, terrorism, and the origins of the U.S. attack on Libya /
Brian L. Davis.
        p.   cm.
    Bibliography: p.
    Includes index.
    ISBN 0–275–93302–4 (alk. paper)
    1. United States—Foreign relations—Libya.   2. Libya—Foreign
relations—United States.   3. Libya—History—Bombardment, 1986.
4. Terrorism—Libya.   5. Quaddafi, Muammar.   I. Title.
E183.8.L75D38   1990
327.730612—dc20   89–16095

Library of Congress Catalog Card Number: 89–16095
ISBN: 0–275–93302–4

First published in 1990

Praeger Publishers, One Madison Avenue, New York, NY 10010
A division of Greenwood Press, Inc.

Printed in the United States of America

The paper used in this book complies with the Permanent
Paper Standard issued by the National Information Standards
Organization (Z39.48–1984).

10 9 8 7 6 5 4 3 2 1

Contents

Preface

The United States' military attack against Libya on April 15, 1986, was probably the most controversial discrete foreign policy action undertaken by the Reagan administration. I respect some of the arguments that have been made on both sides of this matter, and I do not see fit to endorse or decry the action. I cannot respect, however, the tendency to portray it as though it occurred in a vacuum, particularly where the foreign behavior of the Qaddafi regime is concerned. This book is written to give an account of the context of "Operation El Dorado Canyon," as much as of the event itself.

I wish to express thanks for the encouragement and assistance provided by the following members of the Department of Political Science at the University of Mississippi (in alphabetical order): Goberdhan Bhagat, Daniel S. Geller, Harold W. Kuhn, Jr., Raimond W. Lehman, and Chester L. Quarles. My gratitude also goes to those individuals who granted me interviews; to Don Campbell for his long and patient work typing the manuscript; to the staff of the John Davis Williams Library, particularly Elizabeth S. Buck, Sherrie Sam, Sharon L. Schreiber, and Martha E. Swan; and to those who enabled me to extend the grasp of my research, specifically Thomas and Victoria Jarmusik, John Haydon, S. D. Jayasuriya, Thomas A. Tarrants III, Robert Moeller, Z. Fadlallah, and the International Security Council. Needless to say, none of these bear responsibility for the deficiencies of the work.

Introduction

The U.S attack on Libya on April 15, 1986, marked the culmination of America's frustration over years of being attacked with impunity by international terrorists. It was simultaneously the culmination of a long downward course in U. S.-Libyan relations, a course that was related to the external policies of the dictator of Libya, Colonel Muammar al-Qaddafi, avowed friend of the Soviet Union, expansionist, archopponent of Middle East peace, archproponent of world terrorism and radical revolution, and head of a brazenly outlaw regime. The idea of engaging in military reprisal against terrorism had been circulating in the United States since the Tehran hostage crisis and had been endorsed by President Ronald Reagan in its aftermath. However, the political will to translate words into action had not emerged until the humiliation of the Beirut TWA hostage crisis of 1985, after which the Reagan administration began seriously looking for the right occasion to inflict a military blow against terrorism.

In light of this, there have been suggestions that the White House arbitrarily selected Libya as a target because of its weakness, and there have been insinuations that to justify itself, Washington manufactured a "Libyan threat" where there was none. To the contrary, Qaddafi very much brought his harsh punishment upon himself. The never-mild Libyan strongman had been taking on an increasingly belligerent posture since 1984. Apparently inspired by the success of Iranian-sponsored terrorism in Lebanon, he intensified his terrorist activities, particularly as directed against Americans. The most crucial aspect of Qaddafi's terrorist role during this period was his increasingly close relationship with the Palestinian "master terrorist" Abu Nidal, whose agents carried out the Malta hijacking of November 1985 and the Rome and Vienna airport massacres of December 1985. Libya was linked to both incidents, and together they brought the United States and Libya closer to a direct collision. The bombing of a West Berlin discotheque frequented by U. S. soldiers was the last straw, and it precipitated the April 15, 1986, air raids. This book traces the clash's origins in the years of Qaddafi's rule on up to the air raids.

Chapter 1 initially describes the domestic course of Libya under Qaddafi, an important factor considered by the Reagan administration in its Libya policies and in its ultimate decision to attack. How a country as small as Libya came to attract such attention from a superpower is made understandable by the next section, which delineates the astonishingly ambitious global activities of Qaddafi, almost all of which were inimical to the interests of the United States. A particular focus of attention for U. S. policymakers, covered in the third section of Chapter 1, is the personality and the motives of the Libyan who, if one of the least admirable, is one of the most interesting of contemporary leaders.

Chapter 2 reviews the gradual decline in U.S.-Libyan relations under the Nixon, Ford, and Carter administrations. This decline would become more precipitous in the last fourteen months of the Carter administration because of a number of events, which are described. The circumstances were propitious for the subsequently detailed watershed in Libyan policy under the Reagan administration, which was determined to force an end to the flaccidity of the international response to Qaddafi's various outrages. The new policy of confrontation with Libya, as well as contemplation of military retaliation against terrorism, ran counter to the advice of the mainstream Middle East experts. The book describes their elaborate rationale for a quiescent approach to both Libya and terrorism, a viewpoint that the governments of Western Europe found economically convenient to embrace and that framed the debate over the Reagan administration's policies in these areas.

Chapter 3 describes the collision course between the United States and Libya from 1983 to 1986, as terrorism provoked increasing concern in Washington and the Reagan administration slowly and with difficulty worked out its internal divisions over military response to terrorism, even while Libya pursued an increasingly aggressive course, especially in respect to terrorism. The Rome and Vienna massacres and the international crisis they precipitated are recounted in detail. Particularly analyzed is the refusal of the NATO allies of the United States to apply sanctions against Libya, a crucial factor in the eventual decision to attack Libya.

Chapter 4 describes Operation Prairie Fire, an exercise in which the Reagan administration sent naval vessels into the Gulf of Sidra, claimed by Libya but considered to be international waters by nearly all the world, in hope that Qaddafi would start a military conflict in which the firepower of the Sixth Fleet would teach him an intimidating lesson. Subsequently recounted are the international reaction to the Gulf of Sidra clash and the flurry of terrorist plotting that followed it, particularly by Libya. Chapter 5 covers the La Belle discotheque bombing, the subsequent U. S. decision to retaliate against Libya, the planning and preparations for the attack, and the calculations that underlay them. Chapter 6 recounts the April 15 air strikes and the international reaction to them, particularly the controversy between the United States and Western Europe and its resolution, and attempts to sort out the ramifications and lessons of the action.

QADDAFI, TERRORISM, AND THE ORIGINS OF THE U.S. ATTACK ON LIBYA

1

Muammar Al-Qaddafi, Leader of the Revolution

The country ruled by Colonel Muammar al-Qaddafi is strategically located in North Africa, with 1,100 miles of Mediterranean coastline. Its land area of 685,524 square miles (1,775,500 sq. km.) makes it the fifteenth largest country in the world, but it is hampered by having a population of only three and a half million people, about 90 percent of whom live in the fertile coastal strip. The people of Libya are 92 percent Arabs, and there are 4 percent and 2.5 percent minorities of Berbers and blacks respectively; 97 percent of the populace are Sunni Muslims. Ninety percent of Libya consists of desert (mostly rocky), and the land contains few natural resources, but the one major resource—oil—made possible Libya's ascent to international recognition.[1]

Prior to independence Libya was united only as an administrative subunit of the colonial empires of Turkey and Italy, respectively. The Italian conquest, begun in 1911, met fierce resistance conducted in the name of Islam and was completed only after twenty years of fighting. A commonplace of Libyan nationalism is that half the country's population, or about 750,000 people, died in the struggle; although that claim has been doubted by some, it is accepted that the Italians were guilty of great brutalities. They had begun implementing plans to make Libya a settler colony, exporting peasants to dispossess the natives, but their plans were cut short by Italy's defeat in World War II, after which the British and the French ruled Libya for eight years. The fighting on Libyan soil by contending European armies left the country with a heritage of a few million unexploded landmines. Obviously, the foundation for powerful anti-Western sentiment had been laid.[2]

King Idris, a traditional religious leader, presided from independence in 1951 over a regime that was autocratic but mild by the standards of the region. He pursued a relatively passive foreign policy, which was seen as subservience to the West in the Arab context of that era. Originally one of the poorest countries in the world, Libya's prospects changed dramatically with the discovery of oil in 1959. Great strides were subsequently made in social welfare, but unrest over the presence of British and U.S. bases and over massive corruption and the concentration of wealth in relatively few hands in the wake of the oil boom led foreign observers in the 1960s to believe that a coup d'etat in Libya was inevitable.[3]

The man who led the coup that overthrew King Idris on September 1, 1969, was Captain Muammar al-Qaddafi,[4] who claimed to be only twenty-seven years old. Qaddafi was the only son of a poor and illiterate tent-dwelling shepherd who had fought the Italians as a guerrilla under the renowned resistance leader Omar Mukhtar. Muammar was a scion of the Qadadfa, a small tribe possessing maraboutic, or saintly, status, claimants of descent from the prophet Muhammad, but abiding in servitude to larger tribes. At great sacrifice to his family, Qaddafi had been sent off at age ten to Quranic school in Surt, where he slept in the mosque at night and was looked down upon by his classmates as a poor desert Bedouin. From very early in his life he possessed a deep indignation against injustice and felt hostility toward the rich and powerful.[5]

At the age of fourteen, he had moved with his family to the oasis of Sebha, where he became enthralled by the radio broadcasts of the revolutionary Arab nationalist leader Gamal Abdel Nasser of Egypt, who became his lifelong idol. Qaddafi displayed remarkable leadership qualities and tenacity of purpose while still a teenager. In Sebha Preparatory School he befriended the men who are today his chief lieutenants and led them in demonstrations, in the adoption of an austere Islamic lifestyle, and in the formation of a secret revolutionary cell that inaugurated the ten-year conspiracy that eventually brought him to power through infiltration of the armed forces. In 1966 he was sent for a signals course to England, where he found the people cold and condescending, but he read with interest the writings of utopians and of anarchosyndicalists (an important source of terrorism several decades earlier).[6]

THE COURSE OF THE REVOLUTION IN LIBYA

Having carried out their well-planned coup as King Idris vacationed abroad, Qaddafi and his fellow officers established in September 1969 a Revolutionary Command Council (RCC) for unabashed rule by the suitably purged military, which was claimed to be the authentic representative of the Libyan people. The new regime immediately issued militant rhetoric on behalf of the pan-Arab and Palestinian causes and vowed to eliminate foreign dominance, which together with the old regime was held responsible for all of Libya's ills. The ownership of businesses by any other than "Arab Libyans" was outlawed; churches and synagogues were soon closed. By 1970 the British and U.S. bases were evacuated, and the Italian community and the ancient Jewish community had their property confiscated and were in effect expelled; even the bones from the Italians' cemeteries were unearthed and sent to Italy. A new emphasis on Islam was embodied in the closing of nightclubs and cafés, enforcement of Ramadan fasting and the prohibition of alcohol, and the public promise of the reinstatement of traditional Islamic law, the *shariah*.[7] According to Muslim world expert Daniel Pipes, Qaddafi's coup "more than any other single event marked the beginning of the Islamic revival. . . . Coming after decades of seemingly irreversible Westernization throughout Islamdom, his actions gave heart to [Muslim] legalists everywhere and attracted worldwide attention to the Shari'a."[8]

The RCC consciously endeavored to make its dominant member, the newly promoted Colonel Qaddafi, into a charismatic figure in the tradition of such Third World leaders as Nasser, Nkrumah, and Sukarno, an end that was greatly furthered by Qaddafi's successes in two areas. First, the revolutionary regime pressed demands upon the Western oil companies in a highly confrontational manner, determined to reverse perceived exploitation. Libya was in a strong bargaining position for a number of reasons and was able to obtain the raising of prices and taxation rates and eventually to nationalize about 70 percent of the oil industry. While practicing conservation in cutting output by more than half, the government was able to quadruple its oil revenues between 1970 and 1974, and Libyan oil went from being consistently underpriced to consistently overpriced. Furthermore, these successes touched off the phenomenon of "leapfrogging," as other oil-producers sought to match or surpass Libya's concessions (with an element of ideological competition between conservative monarchies and radical Arab regimes involved), leading to the companies' loss of control over the oil industry and to the period of OPEC dominance. Nonetheless, the settlement ultimately reached in Libya was mutually satisfactory to the government and to U.S. and other Western companies, and Western capitalists continued to be quite eager to do business with the man who would become one of the world's most notorious dictators.[9]

A second area of spectacular success for the RCC was economic redistribution, aided greatly by the huge increase in petroleum revenues. Under Qaddafi's so-called Quranic socialism, the minimum wage was raised, work terms were improved, and rents were lowered. Massive housing construction proceeded with the goal of providing a "decent home" for every family; the shanty towns of the capital city of Tripoli and the second largest city of Benghazi disappeared, along with the street populace of beggars, pimps, and pickpockets. The proportion of the population receiving education and the literacy rate increased. Free medical care already existed under the monarchy, but the numbers of doctors and hospital beds were increased under the Qaddafi regime, and nutrition was substantially improved. Libya came to have the highest per capita gross national product in Africa, and per capita income rose from $2,168 in 1970 to $9,827 in 1979, surpassing Great Britain, Italy, and Japan. Although it was eventually dissipated by his foreign policies, a considerable amount of esteem in the Third

World accrued to Qaddafi as a result of his successes in confrontation with the oil companies and in economic redistribution.[10]

In contrast to those two aspects, the revolutionary regime experienced failure in the realm of political mobilization. The economic measures and the emphasis on Islam and Arab nationalism had won Qaddafi popularity with the Libyan masses, but they were not emerging out of their traditional political apathy and conservatism into the revolutionary zeal he sought. An attempt to build an Arab Socialist Union in Libya in imitation of Nasser foundered; Qaddafi openly expressed his dismay over popular apathy. These frustrations, as well as frustrations in foreign policy, stimulated Qaddafi to frequent threats of resignation and depressed retreats into the desert to brood and meditate. However, it was during these periods in the desert, while administration was left in the hands of his alter ego Major Abdel Salem Jalloud, that Qaddafi synthesized the ideology that he would attempt to implement in Libya and in the world.[11]

The "Third Universal Theory" that Qaddafi began to articulate in 1972 was definitively set forth in the three slender volumes of the *Green Book*, his counterpart of Mao Zedong's *Little Red Book*. In the volumes, published in 1975, 1977, and 1978, he elaborated his views on government, economics, and social organization respectively. The *Green Book* shows a wide range of influences, including Bedouin culture, Islam, Marxism, Fascism, anarchosyndicalism, and Rousseau,[12] and has been termed "a mishmash of half-baked ideology and romantic idealism."[13] Indeed, many of its contents are embarrassingly sophomoric; nonetheless, Qaddafi has declared that it is "the new gospel" that will sweep the world.[14]

Under his Third Universal Theory, Qaddafi rejects capitalism and communism, constitutions and man-made law, political parties and parliamentary democracy; representation is viewed as inherently undemocratic. Instead there must be "direct democracy" through "popular congresses and committees" in which consensus substitutes for election, a concept with some Quranic basis; however, Qaddafi in the *Green Book* justifies his own position[15] by inserting the observation that "realistically the strong always rule."[16] In the realm of economics he declares that every person is entitled to a house, a vehicle, and an income, but no one should own extra houses to rent to others. Money should be abolished; the wage system is a form of slavery, and the workers must be made partners. Rather than calling for a world government, Qaddafi exalts nationalism,[17] although he makes the admission, ironic for him, that "national fanaticism is essential to the nation but at the same time it is a threat to humanity."[18]

Serious efforts by Qaddafi to implement his ideology in Libya began with his speech of April 15, 1973, in which he rebuked the people for their lack of revolutionary zeal and announced a "cultural revolution" in Libya to include the suspension of all existing laws, struggle against clandestine political parties, purging of the bureaucracy and the universities, and the call for the people to assume power themselves, which subsequently entailed the carefully manipulated though raucous establishment of "people's committees" in neighborhoods, villages, workplaces, schools, and public enterprises. After continuing reorganization, in 1977 Libya's official name was changed to the "Socialist People's Libyan Arab Jamahiriyah" (a neologism translated as "state of the masses") as the nation's government purportedly ceased to exist, with all power being handed over to the people in what the official press hailed as the greatest event in history. Nonetheless, a conventional government structure remained in place, subject to interference from the newer system of people's committees and congresses, with the end result being a system whose components had overlapping authority and clashes to an extent far beyond that normal in governments, a system described by some as government by anarchy. The problem of the immaturity and amateurishness of Libya's political elite caused by the purge of the prerevolutionary elite (and probably as well by the eccentric tone set by Qaddafi) was compounded by the reorganization.[19]

The new system described by Qaddafi as democracy was a classic example of the leftist regime device of highly elaborate "orchestrated political participation" that "provides mechanisms of social control and produces the illusion of popular support."[20] (Although Qaddafi and his RCC colleagues formally resigned official positions in 1979, the colonel managed to increase his power in Libya with the restructuring of the late 1970s.) All Libyans were supposed to participate in "basic people's congresses," which featured speeches, endlessly repetitive chanting of slogans and waving of upraised fists (which resulted in a condition termed "Qaddafi arm"), and circumspect debate and voting by show of hands. Delegates from these and various other congresses and committees were elected to the theoretically sovereign body of Libya, the General People's Congress (GPC), whose deliberations were tightly controlled.[21]

From 1978 on, Qaddafi undertook a series of radical economic reforms in conformity with his *Green Book* precepts. Ownership of more than one home or car by a family was forbidden; rental properties were seized with payment of compensation. Bank accounts were frozen, and a limit of $34,000 in holdings was set. Libya's mixed economy came to an end as private wholesale trade, retail trade, and commerce were abolished and privately owned companies (as well as most public enterprises) were turned over to workers' committees. Even so, the politically well connected in the Jamahiriyah were able to obtain special economic dispensations, including ownership of excess property, and corruption flourished.[22]

These measures inevitably bred opposition among the propertied and educated classes in Libya and contributed to the instability that had plagued the revolutionary regime from the beginning. The first coup plot against the RCC had been discovered only three months after the September 1969 takeover, and several more unsuccessful plots had followed in the early 1970s. In 1975, a time of falling oil revenues, RCC member Omar Meheishi was disturbed by continuing expenditures on terrorism and huge amounts of Soviet arms while social programs to benefit Libyans were being cut. He launched an effort with other RCC members to oust Qaddafi; nearly one hundred army officers were supposedly involved.

Though it was quickly suppressed, the colonel was greatly shaken by the Meheishi affair.[23]

Qaddafi was disquieted not only by fear of enemies but by the masses' continued lack of revolutionary fervor in the face of his "people's power" projects, and his rule in the late 1970s increasingly took the form of tyranny. In late 1977 he introduced the revolutionary committees, his own counterpart of Mao's Red Guards. The revolutionary committees were rifle-toting bands of young zealots existing in every neighborhood, factory, and government office, assigned the tasks of spying on the Libyan people and keeping them from going ideologically astray. The committees were empowered to judge property disputes, issue decrees, close down shops without warning, and execute suspected opponents of the regime. In concert with the committees was an efficient domestic intelligence service run by East German advisers, who bugged the country's telephones and telexes with the latest West German equipment. Libyans lived in dread of government informers and even feared denunciation by their own relatives.[24]

Rigid indoctrination in the Third Universal ideology and a network of labor camps were implemented in Libya. Killings of political dissidents began in 1976, and a later decree introduced capital punishment for criticism of Qaddafi or the Libyan revolution. A particularly heavy surge of repression occurred in 1980 as a decision to "liquidate the middle class" was announced; over two thousand people were arrested and eight hundred executed for political offenses. Political dissidents were tried by popular committees without defense or appeal, but many times they simply disappeared. Reportedly thousands of them languished in prisons, where torture became so common that Amnesty International listed Libya as one of its five leading practitioners in the world; death under torture was common. In addition to carrying out secret execution, the Qaddafi regime sought to terrorize the populace through frequent televised hangings of dissidents. Beyond overt brutality, the government forbade unauthorized public gatherings, closed cafés, and at certain junctures even suspended theatrical and sporting events in order to deprive Libyans of opportunities to congregate outside government supervision.[25] Qaddafi indeed established what one analyst termed "one of the most efficient totalitarian states in the world today."[26]

Proficiency in repression did not carry over into economic policies, however. Under Qaddafi agricultural production declined, and misguided development policy resulted in little genuine industrial development outside the petroleum sector, leaving Libya, despite its wealth, as one of the least industrialized countries in the Arab world. The work ethic of Libyans declined;[27] they were "onlookers in their own land,"[28] as foreign workers made up more than half of the managerial and professional work force and much of the skilled and unskilled work force. Moreover, in the 1980s, the prosperity that Libya had long enjoyed began to fade for two major reasons. One was the collapse in world petroleum prices, which affected Libya more severely than most oil-producing countries; oil revenues fell from $22 billion in 1980 to $5 billion in 1985. The second reason for Libya's economic difficulties was Qaddafi's own *Green Book* policies, which crushed the private sector. Severe shortages of housing, foods, and consumer goods became typical; the new government-run supermarkets had numerous aisles of empty shelves. Development projects lay idle, yet Qaddafi defied expectations by maintaining his expenditures on terrorism and massive amounts of Soviet weapons, thereby compounding the difficulties.[29]

Economic austerity brings political peril for Third World regimes of every sort, and the Qaddafi regime was no exception: the loss of ability to buy public support with oil largesse greatly accelerated the piecemeal decline of the colonel's popularity, which had been waning since his early years in power. During the 1970s Qaddafi's various policies had alienated royalists, tribal leaders, the intelligentsia, the religious establishment, Islamic fundamentalists, businessmen, traders, professionals, bureaucrats, and substantial numbers of university students. In the 1980s it was clear that, though helpless to oppose him, most Libyans had grown disenchanted with Qaddafi's rule. Beyond the economic travails, factors responsible for his unpopularity were his absolutism and repression, especially the thuggery of the revolutionary committees; increasingly massive corruption; the fact that by all accounts Qaddafi had made Libya a very dull place; and mandatory universal military training, even for elderly women, as the colonel made his nation one of the most militaristic countries in the world.[30]

Libya suffered a tremendous brain drain as from fifty thousand to one hundred thousand of its people, including most of the intelligentsia and the technocrats, left to reside abroad. From the mid–1970s, formal opposition groups began to emerge in the expatriate community. They covered the broadest possible ideological spectrum and were able to attract apparently retaliatory support from victims of Qaddafi's subversion, including Saudi Arabia, Sudan, Morocco, Egypt, Iraq, Tunisia, and reportedly even Algeria and the Yasir Arafat-led Fatah organization within the Palestine Liberation Organization (PLO). The most prominent of such exile organizations was the National Front for the Salvation of Libya (NFSL), founded in 1981 and led by a former Libyan auditor-general, Muhammad Yusuf al-Mugarieff.[31]

Qaddafi often exhorted his people to sacrifice themselves in the struggle against such enemies of the revolution and against "imperialism," and some did so, but far more impressive was the willingness of Libyan military officers to sacrifice themselves in a steady stream of mutinies, coup attempts, and attempts to assassinate Qaddafi.[32] Disaffection in the Libyan military was long been known to be great, and its sources included (in addition to those mentioned concerning the general public) disapproval of Qaddafi's military interventions in Uganda and Chad, his open avowal of intentions to replace the regular military forces with a people's militia (an idea he had espoused since the early 1970s), and fear of the consequences for Libya of Qaddafi's foreign policies. The most dramatic attempt to unseat the colonel was an assault on May 8, 1984, upon the Bab al-Aziziyya barracks, the seat of the Libyan government and the chief headquarters of Qaddafi and the military. It was staged by NFSL infiltrators and sympathetic soldiers and resulted in a five-hour gun battle; a savage months-long orgy of murder and repression by the government followed. Qaddafi had already been obliged to rely for protection against such plots on members of his now-privileged Qadadfa tribe and on two hundred East German security experts.[33]

By the mid–1980s an aura of twilight hung over Qaddafi and his regime. The strongman who had once wrought remarkable accomplishments in his country now promulgated "reforms" that seemed increasingly foolish and displeasing to the general public. The leader of the people's revolution was becoming increasingly isolated from the people. He was reduced by fear to living behind the protection of a fifteen-foot wall and tanks, rarely staying more than one night in any of his several residences, keeping his movements a secret (even from close advisers), riding in a convoy of armor-plated cars, employing identical decoy convoys and decoy airplanes, wearing a bullet-proof vest even at home, and employing tasters to prevent poisoning. Many experts considered his downfall a likely prospect, his dying naturally a remote possibility (all of which was a factor in the Reagan administration's calculations as it sought to oppose him). Frustrations in foreign affairs and his continuing inability to convert his people into utopian revolutionaries rankled Qaddafi, and the boundless optimism of his youth had departed.[34]

FOREIGN POLICY OF THE BEDOUIN "WORLD LEADER"

Youthful optimism had manifested itself early in Colonel Qaddafi's rule in a foreign policy of breathtaking scope and of ambition worthy of a superpower; almost every aspect of it was inimical to the interests of the superpower at the head of the Western world. Pipes pointed out that Qaddafi has been a figure of much more than regional importance (indeed, the Libyan media tout him as the "world leader"): he made Libya a "global ministate" exercising much greater clout in international affairs than Japan, for example. The key factors enabling a young state with no industrial base and a small, unskilled population to be active on a global scale were petroleum and willpower stemming from the fanatical sense of mission of Qaddafi,[35] who was permanently "on the offensive . . . more interested in changing the world than in safeguarding his oil fields, . . . not fearing for his regime, but instead, eager to take the fight to the enemy's camp."[36] Libya's petroleum gave it substantial immunity from the consequences of its actions for many years and provided the funds needed for lavish aid to a variety of governments and nongovernmental organizations. Libyan foreign policy goals were also pursued by hiring foreigners to perform a wide variety of tasks, from piloting jets to training terrorists to invading neighboring states to preaching militant Islam on Third World mission fields.[37]

From the day he seized power Qaddafi trumpeted the magnificence of the Arab nation, sometimes to chauvinistic extremes, and he became the foremost advocate of unifying the Arab world. Immediately after his coup Qaddafi had offered Libya to Nasser, but the Egyptian leader hesitated, having grown cautious in his final years. Soon afterwards Libya entered into union agreements with

Egypt, Sudan, and Syria, but, like all such Arab compacts since the 1958–61 United Arab Republic, they were mere formalities that never developed into real mergers. Qaddafi did not, however, lose his enthusiasm for such agreements: he entered into an abortive compact with Tunisia in 1974 and sought unsuccessfully to unify with a number of other Arab countries. He became so enamored of mergers that he also sought to join Libya with the Roman Catholic island state of Malta, the landlocked African state of Burkina Faso, and the People's Republic of China;[38] his most notorious merger project would be with Chad.

Qaddafi was from the first the most implacable antagonist of Israel among Arab heads of state,[39] and in May and June of 1970 he toured Arab capitals with a plan for launching a war of annihilation against the Jewish state. Other leaders were unresponsive, finding Qaddafi's idea naive. The colonel therefore found three alternative methods of opposing Israel—terrorism, propaganda (insisting on attacking Israel in every international forum, no matter how inappropriate) and diplomacy. Qaddafi sought energetically to use Libyan economic clout to isolate Israel, even to the point of pressuring Nepal to break diplomatic relations in exchange for his gift of $50,000 in disaster relief. Using promises of aid, he was largely responsible in 1972–73 for the severing of black African diplomatic ties with Israel. Furthermore, according to his former colleague, Mugarieff, Qaddafi continually expressed the need for Libya to acquire nuclear weapons and declared that his dream was to drop a nuclear bomb on Tel Aviv.[40]

Economic assistance also served as a tool to promote Islam. Reception of Libyan aid by Third World countries was typically contingent upon the signing of cultural cooperation agreements through which Tripoli set up Islamic centers, schools, and mosques. In 1970 the regime set up the Association for the Propagation of Islam, which sent forth hundreds of mostly non-Libyan missionaries. Black Africa was a particular target: Qaddafi insisted on a halt to the spread of Christianity and that Africans must accept Islam and learn Arabic. Qaddafi's own personal proselytizing was continuous, sometimes with offers of bribes, and he converted two African dictators, Omar Bongo of Gabon and Jean-Bédel Bokassa, the Central African "Emperor." The colonel had success in pressuring governments such as those of Pakistan and Mauritania to adopt more strongly Islamic policies. In these matters Libya's efforts often ironically intersected with those of conservative Saudi Arabia, and, in the view of Pipes, the two countries played a significant role in fueling Islamic resurgence.[41]

Qaddafi, however, was chronically unable to get along with his brother Arab leaders, a situation that was exacerbated by disagreements surrounding the Yom Kippur War of 1973.[42] The colonel and his RCC colleagues held the Arab monarchies (which they termed "feudal" and "reactionary") and other pro-Western Arab regimes in unconcealed abhorrence. Qaddafi engaged in an unparalleled pattern of harsh public vituperation of other Arab leaders, including calls for their overthrow or even assassination. Often after such outbursts he would within months seek a reconciliation with the object of his denunciation; more often than not, his overtures would be accepted, perhaps out of fear, but only fragile surface rapprochements would result. Qaddafi's behavior was such that even leftist Arab regimes, such as that of Algeria, privately distrusted him, and the usually taciturn Saudis declared that he "afflicted the Arabs like the plague."[43]

Not just the Libyan dictator's rhetoric but also his actions provoked other Arab governments, for he imitated his deceased hero Nasser in widespread fostering of destabilization in the Arab world. In addition to launching assassination plots against leaders of Jordan, Saudi Arabia, Tunisia, Morocco, Egypt, and Sudan,[44] he at one time or another sponsored subversive plots or insurgent groups against apparently every government in the Arab world except (perhaps) that of South Yemen. After his efforts to unite Libya with Egypt collapsed in 1973, he began a permanent campaign of terrorism and subversion against that country. The regime of Jaafar Nimeiry in Sudan, once embraced by Qaddafi, incurred his wrath particularly by allying with Egypt and the United States; the colonel sent a Libyan plane over Khartoum in July 1976 in the most dramatic of his numerous coup attempts against Nimeiry. Qaddafi never forgave Tunisia for reneging on the 1974 union agreement: its anniversary was commemorated by skyjackings for a number of years, and a Libyan-created armed Tunisian opposition group kept permanent headquarters in Tripoli despite frequent Libyan-Tunisian rapprochements.[45]

Supporting terrorism was one of the Libyan strongman's earliest foreign policy decisions. In 1969 he began to financially support Fatah and the Popular Front of the Liberation of Palestine (PFLP) led by George Habash. In 1971 he resolved to help the Irish Republican Army (IRA) fight "British colonialism," and about the same time he welcomed the establishment of PLO terrorist training camps in Libya. A larger network of terrorist training camps subsequently emerged there,[46] sometimes giving training for specific upcoming attacks.[47] Among the instructors were some Libyans, but the majority were from a variety of foreign nationalities, including Palestinians, Cubans, East Germans, Bulgarians, Czechs, Iranians, Syrians, North Koreans, Russians, Britons (mercenary military veterans), and Americans (renegade former CIA agents and Green Berets lured by Libyan lucre). In pursuit of his interest in subversion, Qaddafi provided guerrilla warfare training under the aegis of a Bureau for the Export of the Revolution that he had established (thereby discarding the public posture of nonintervention normal for radical regimes) and created a fund for the support of "world revolution."[48] He expressed his views thus: "One should not consider the traditional outdated excuse about interference in the internal affairs of others."[49]

By the mid–1970s, Libya had come to be viewed pervasively as the model of a state devoted to international terrorism. In January 1986, Paul Wilkinson, the leading British terrorism expert, wrote: "If there were a Nobel Prize for terrorism, Gadaffi would surely be the obvious candidate."[50] Beyond training as many as seven thousand to eight thousand terrorists and guerrillas in a single year, the Qaddafi regime provided terrorists with rent-free offices, headquarters, and villas in Libya; generous and invaluable weapons supplies and funding—in

1981 alone $100 million worth of arms and financial disbursements were granted to Palestinian terrorists in particular; sharing of intelligence; transportation aboard Libyan airliners; false passports; and even safe houses in Europe. Libyan financial support for terrorists enormously surpassed that of any other terrorism-supporting country except Iran in the mid-and late 1980s. Not only did Qaddafi make contributions for the regular operating expenses of terrorist organizations; he also awarded large bonuses for successful operations such as the Munich Olympics massacres. Several press reports indicated that Libya had a fixed scale of payments to terrorists or their survivors for operations ranging from hand grenade attacks to suicide missions. Libyan diplomatic privileges were notoriously abused: supplies and information were delivered to terrorists in diplomatic pouches and secret cables, and Libyan embassies and consulates served as centers for weapons storage, planning, command and control, and communications for terrorists. On a number of occasions Libya hosted so-called "terrorist conventions," which were valuable in furthering international cooperation among terrorist groups.[51]

Libyan support extended to terrorist and guerrilla organizations across the globe. In the Middle East, virtually all of the Palestinian terrorist groups were Libyan beneficiaries. Tripoli paid the salaries of some of their major leaders and also supported Muslim extremists in Egypt and Turkey, ASALA (anti-Turkish Armenian terrorists), and Kurdish rebels in Iraq, among other subversive groups. Libyan-backed guerrillas in Morocco launched attacks in 1973 on U.S. Information Service installations and on the American consulate, in addition to Moroccan government establishments. Despite his misgivings about an independent Western Sahara, Qaddafi openly relished the further opportunity to destabilize the pro-Western regime of King Hassan II of Morocco through his role (up until 1983) as the principal supplier of arms to the Polisario guerrillas by sea and by a land route that became known as the "Qaddafi trail." He also sent mercenaries to fight with Polisario and for tactical purposes financed a successful diplomatic campaign with Algeria for Third World recognition of the hypothetical "Saharan Arab Democratic Republic."[52]

Libya sustained a permanent involvement in Lebanon, maintaining missile batteries there and from 1972 on stationing soldiers there. At one point they clashed with Syrian troops during tension over Syria's willingness to engage in peace negotiations; in 1976 Libyan soldiers participated in the infamous massacre of inhabitants of the Christian village of Damour. Qaddafi poured millions of dollars into support for most of the country's Muslim and leftist militias, keeping intimate ties with some of them (particularly the Nasserites) and strongly backing the "Left" coalitions of 1975–76 and 1983–84. Lebanese Muslims as well as Christians came to hate him for helping to destroy rather than build their country.[53] Regarding Iran, the colonel was able to make a meaningful contribution to the overthrow of the Shah, whom he abhorred for his seizure of Arab islands in the Persian Gulf and for his ties with Israel and the United States. For a number of years he provided training, arms, financing, and transmitting facilities to the Mujaheddin Khalq (who particularly targeted Americans in Iran), the Fedayeen, and the Islamic revolutionary forces of the Ayatollah Khomeini.[54]

The notorious "Carlos" (AKA Ilich Ramirez Sanchez) worked in his heyday as a client of Qaddafi, from 1973 to 1977 or later, and was reported again in 1981 and 1984 to be operating out of Libya.[55] European terrorists of the extreme left, including Swiss and Greeks, the Red Brigades of Italy, the Red Army Faction (AKA Baader-Meinhof gang) of West Germany, Direct Action of France, and FP–25 of Portugal, received aid from Tripoli, as did neo-Nazi activists in Spain and right-wing terrorists in Italy and West Germany. The Jamahiriyah gave terrorist training to the Black Liberation Army from Britain and funded the Workers' Revolutionary Party (famous for the membership of actress Vanessa Redgrave) and allegedly as well the extreme-right British Movement and the National Front. Qaddafi's hostility toward Western governments was also manifested in support for the European pacifist groups that flourished in the 1980s, some of which were themselves cultivating associations with terrorist groups.[56] Perhaps because of his *Green Book* notions about nationalism, separatists seemed to have a special attraction for the Libyan leader: he assisted Scottish and Welsh movements; Sicilian, Breton, Corsican, Sardinian, and Canary Islands terrorists; the Basque ETA, which long afflicted Spain; and the Irish Republican Army as well as its splinter, the Irish National Liberation Army. Seemingly oblivious to the unfeasibility of the plan, Qaddafi also sought to foster separatism among blacks in the United States—including support for the terrorist group Republic of New Africa—and American Indians, as well as Australian aborigines.[57]

In Asia, the Libyan embassy in Kuala Lumpur was "considered a supply-and-command center for terrorists"[58] of that continent. Qaddafi had loudly begun his intervention there in 1972, sending arms and funds to the Muslim Moro rebels in the Philippines, aid that was crucial in preventing the insurgency from being crushed soon after it began. He later added support for the Japanese Red Army terrorists; the Kawthoolei Muslim Liberation Front in Burma; Muslim rebels in southern Thailand; Malaysian dissidents; terrorist groups opposing the Indonesian government, including Kommando Jihad and the South Moluccan separatists; the Muslim rebels of Afghanistan; Muslim autonomists in Nepal; the Al-Zulfikar terrorist group founded by the sons of Ali Bhutto of Pakistan; the Tamil rebels of Sri Lanka; armed opponents of President Hossain Mohammad Ershad of Bangladesh; Muslim rebels in Kashmir and, reportedly, the Sikh terrorists who tormented India.[59]

Libyan activities in Africa included subversion against many black regimes as well as support for black guerrillas fighting white minority rule in the Portuguese colonies, Namibia (South-West Africa), and Rhodesia, and for the Pan-Africanist Congress in South Africa. Training was provided for an anti-French terrorist group called the Movement for the Independence of Réunion. Before the Marxist coup in Ethiopia, Libya substantially supported the Eritrean guerrillas; after the coup it ceased such support and later became a backer and coordinator of a group operating against Ethiopia's archenemy Siad Barre—the

Somali National Salvation Front, whose leadership was even selected by Qaddafi at one point. In the 1980s Libyan intervention was even extending to the island states and colonies of the South Pacific, where Qaddafi's agents were engaged in long-term efforts to cultivate violent radicalism.[60]

In 1972 Qaddafi created a Palestinian terrorist group of his own, the National Arab Youth for the Liberation of Palestine (NAYLP), which committed some of the most brutal and indiscriminate actions in the history of Palestinian international terrorism. In 1975 he established a Special Intelligence Service for terrorist operations. Islamic charities and Libyan airlines and training companies were used as fronts for terrorist activities. Libya was well known in the 1970s as the principal sanctuary for skyjackers and sometimes gave heroes' welcomes to terrorists, which provoked observers in the United States and elsewhere. Tripoli frequently directly aided or initiated specific terrorist actions, including some of the most memorable ones. Qaddafi exercised considerable personal control over Libya's terrorist apparatus and was himself sometimes involved in the plotting of specific acts.[61]

Among incidents in which Libya had a role before the Reagan administration were the 1972 Munich Olympics massacre[62] and the March 1973 embassy seizure in Khartoum, in which three diplomats—two Americans and one Belgian—were murdered (Qaddafi had a strong connection with the Black September arm of Yasir Arafat's Fatah); a skyjacking that won the release of the surviving Munich terrorists; the NAYLP's Athens airport massacre, in which five persons, including Americans, were killed in August 1973; a plot to shoot down an Israeli El Al jetliner with SA–7 missiles in September 1973;[63] the NAYLP's December 1973 killing of thirty-two people (including ten American children) at a Rome airport and hijacking of an airliner to Kuwait, carried out under a Libyan diplomat's orders in substitution for a thwarted attempt on Henry Kissinger's life meant to prevent convening of the Geneva Middle East peace conference;[64] the NAYLP's blowing up of a TWA airliner in September 1974 over the Ionian Sea, killing all eighty-one persons aboard;[65] the December 1975 kidnapping of OPEC oil ministers by Carlos in Vienna; the Entebbe hijacking in 1976; a PFLP attack on El Al passengers at Istanbul airport, killing an aide to Senator Jacob Javits (R-N.Y.) and three others; the seizure of the Grand Mosque in Mecca in 1979; the bloody Kano religious riots that shook Nigeria in 1980; and a plot to shoot down Anwar Sadat's plane in the Azores that same year.[66]

Libya under Qaddafi became a vital part of the international terrorism network that developed in the 1960s and 1970s and flourishes today. The international terrorism network was not a centrally controlled or directed conspiracy, but rather, what leading terrorism expert Brian Jenkins has described as, "a semipermanent infrastructure of terrorism . . . the resilient web of political fronts, personal relationships, clandestine contacts, foreign connections, alliances with other groups, support structures, resources, and suppliers of material and services that sustain the terrorist underground."[67] PLO terrorist groups, particularly PFLP, did especially diligent work in the formation of this informal network, and indispensable was the role played by state supporters of terrorism: Algeria, Iraq,[68] Libya, Syria, South Yemen, Iran, Cuba, Nicaragua,[69] North Korea, and the Soviet Union with its Eastern European vassals, especially Bulgaria, Czechoslovakia, and East Germany.[70] It was no coincidence that each state involved in the network had highly cooperative relations with most of the others, and they were known to collude in supporting terrorism. For example, Libya financed training for terrorists in South Yemen, and the USSR, East Germany, and Cuba all sent instructors; North Korea provided instructors for terrorist training in Iran and through its embassy in Austria reportedly worked with Libya in supporting local terrorist activities. Even before their establishment of diplomatic ties with each other, Libya and Cuba cooperated in the formation of the Revolutionary Coordinating Junta, an association of Latin American terrorist groups, in 1974.[71]

Qaddafi also made his country the worst violator of the hallowed Organization of African Unity (OAU) principle of inviolability of frontiers inherited from the colonial era. Libya claimed a portion of Chad known as the Aouzou strip on the dubious ground of an unratified Franco-Italian treaty of 1935, occupied it in two separate slices, and also annexed the smaller portion of the Aouzou strip belonging to Niger while obtaining a de facto control over that country's northernmost provinces. Some analysts related Libyan expansionism in these uranium-rich regions to Qaddafi's well-known quest for acquisition of nuclear weapons. A 1976 Libyan atlas portrayed those claims as well as a hypothetical claim to territory rich in oil and gas belonging to a far less feeble neighbor, Algeria. Libya also put forth claims to Egypt's western desert and quarreled with Tunisia and Malta over continental shelf economic rights. To the displeasure of the U.S. Navy, Qaddafi attempted expansion in a seaward direction in 1973, when he claimed the entire 150,000 square miles of the Gulf of Sidra as Libyan territorial waters; it was the most extensive claim to an indented coastline in the world and was untenable under international law. The gulf was immediately mined, resulting in the sinking of two foreign ships and the damaging of a third.[72]

As early as 1970, the RCC had shown a pragmatic openness to the Soviet bloc, importing Soviet tanks and East German military advisers for a variety of roles. Nonetheless, for several years Qaddafi and other Libyan spokesmen harshly reviled the USSR for its atheistic Communism and for dividing the Arabs, serving as an even worse enemy to them than the United States. In 1974, however, the visit of Major Jalloud to Moscow marked the formation of a significant Libyan-Soviet entente, the most important component of which was a $2.3 billion arms deal. The reasons commonly cited for Libya's about-face are the need to break out of the isolation the country found itself in after quarrels surrounding the Yom Kippur War; the desire to acquire advanced weaponry beyond what Western countries were willing to sell, at a time when Egypt was removing the weaponry it had lent Libya; and response to Egypt's opening to the United States and Israel, at a time when Libyan-Egyptian relations had sunk to the point where Qaddafi was seeking Sadat's overthrow.[73]

Another factor that probably facilitated the rapprochement was a shift in the attitudes of Qaddafi, whose thinking was gradually becoming influenced less by religion and more by leftist revolutionary ideals; the colonel even came to refer to his revolution as "neo-scientific socialism." Pedro Ramet has indeed argued that common support for revolutionary violence helped cement the Libya-Soviet relationship, and the two countries had some direct interaction in the realm of terrorism. The Soviets gave terrorist training to Libyans at a camp in the Crimea and sent instructors to terrorist camps in Libya; KGB agent Maurizio Folini coordinated deliveries of Libyan weapons to Italian terrorists. The governments of Egypt and Israel were both firmly convinced of Soviet involvement in a Libyan plot, detected by the Israeli intelligence service Mossad, to assassinate Sadat in 1977 with Palestinian hit men.[74]

By 1981 there were in Libya several thousand Soviet military advisers and many more from other Soviet bloc countries, including Cuba, in addition to over thirty-one thousand Soviet and Eastern European economic technicians. Libya became the Soviet Union's foremost arms customer, purchasing a staggering total of $20 billion worth of military hardware from the USSR and Eastern European countries up to 1983. Moscow even engineered the transfer of its weapons from Syrian and PLO stocks to Libya, and the building of an arsenal far beyond what the Libyan armed forces could ever use led to concern in the United States and elsewhere that a prepositioned stockpile for future Soviet military intervention was being created. The *Economist*'s *Foreign Report* stated that some of the arms stores in Libya were under the control of Soviet personnel. It is known that Qaddafi professed to be building an "arsenal of Islam" for the future annihilation of Israel and could transfer arms to other Arab countries in such an effort; that Libya transferred large amounts of Soviet weapons to terrorists (which was, of course, no secret to the Kremlin); that the stockpile proved useful in Libya's own interventions; and that, despite the lack of an indigenous arms industry, Libya became the sixth largest arms supplier among less-developed countries, with deliveries nine times greater than the more publicized Israeli arms exports.[75]

During the period of the Jimmy Carter administration, Qaddafi emerged as the most openly pro-Soviet non-Communist leader in the Third World. In 1978 the Libyan government began periodically proclaiming its evaluation of international politics to be identical with that of the USSR, and Qaddafi made the assertion, which would probably astonish most Muslims, that Marxism is closer to Islam than are Christianity and Judaism. Libyan diplomats took up the sometimes burdensome task of defending the Soviets regularly in Third World forums; Qaddafi even apologized for the Soviet invasion of Afghanistan and cut off aid to the Muslim rebels.[76] In 1983 he stated: "My third universal theory is not incompatible with Communism. Quite the contrary, we are both in a head-on collision with capitalism. Libya stands as the Arab world's principal guarantor of close relations with the Soviet Union on every level—military, political, economic, and ideological."[77] There were, however, limits to the relationship: while finding much agreeable in Qaddafi's policies, the Soviets considered him overly erratic and unpredictable and made no commitment to defend Libya; Qaddafi felt it necessary to preserve Libya's image of independence and refused the Soviets formal base rights.

According to Libya expert G. Henry M. Schuler, the Libyans had expected the Soviet Union's advisers to act as a trip wire in case of external attack; if so, they were disappointed at the absence of Soviet intervention when Sadat, tired of Libyan provocations, launched a brief military assault on the Jamahiriyah in July 1977. Toward Sadat later that year visiting Jerusalem and beginning the Camp David peace process, Libya's reaction was the most extreme in the Arab world. It was well typified when the Libyan national soccer team attacked the Egyptian team with clubs in the African Games the following year. Libya was the host for and a ringleader of the Steadfastness and Rejection Front, which also included Algeria, Syria, South Yemen, and the PLO. However, because he felt that Arafat was insufficiently intransigent, Qaddafi's relations with the PLO chairman fluctuated greatly and were mostly on the downside; at one point he reportedly offered $1 million for the assassination of Arafat by American mercenaries. Qaddafi was a consistent supporter of the rejectionist Palestinian factions, who performed most of the Palestinian terrorism and shared his opposition to Middle East peace; he offered bribes to Palestinians who would join the rejectionists and desert Fatah. He worked closely with President Hafez al-Assad of Syria in efforts to instigate Abu Musa's rebellion in 1983 and to use it to seize control of Fatah and, by implication, the PLO on behalf of rejectionists. Libyan troops participated in the siege of Arafat's forces at Tripoli, Lebanon.[78]

Qaddafi pursued a forward anti-Western policy in Africa generally harmonious with Soviet goals. Large landing strips were built in Libya's desert for Soviet and Cuban transit flights to Ethiopia, South Yemen, Angola, and Mozambique. Libya was a good friend to the "progressive" (i.e., leftist) regimes in black Africa, and he particularly supported its four worst tyrants in the 1970s: Francisco Macías Nguema in Equatorial Guinea; Jean-Bédel Bokassa in the Central African Empire; Idi Amin, favored for his efforts to impose Islam in Uganda; and Soviet protégé Haile Mariam Mengistu in Ethiopia. Qaddafi militarily intervened successfully to save Amin from Tanzania and Ugandan exiles in 1972 but failed miserably at the same task in 1979. Conventional operations in Africa such as the Uganda intervention and covert subversive efforts were both the work of Qaddafi's mercenary force, the Islamic Legion, many of whose members were foreign residents in Libya coerced into service; even Libyan agents abroad used press-gang tactics. The Jamahiriyah's subversive efforts in Africa north of the equator were intense, touching most of its countries. The Marxist government of Benin provided a base for such activities, which often included support for Muslim dissidents in states such as Nigeria. In addition to thwarted efforts, Libya had a role in successful coups in Niger in 1974, in Ghana in 1981, and in Upper Volta in 1980 and 1983, the latter upheaval bringing to power Thomas Sankara, a radical admirer of Qaddafi. Tripoli gave crucial support to the black insurgency that has raged in southern Sudan since 1983 spurred, ironically, by the imposition of Islamic law by Nimeiry.[79]

Chad had been torn by civil war for most of its history, and Qaddafi had been deeply involved from almost the beginning of his rule, but the Libyan role there finally attracted world attention in 1980 when, responding to pleas from the beleaguered President Goukouni Oueddei, Qaddafi's forces occupied the entire country, driving out Goukouni's rival, Hissen Habré. When Goukouni visited Tripoli in January 1981, a controversial joint communiqué, agreed to by the Chadians with obvious reluctance and perhaps under threat of violence, called for the realization of a "complete unity" between Libya and prostrate Chad. The Islamic Legion had also occupied portions of Niger. Qaddafi declared that he considered that country "second in line to Chad," and Libyan troops made frequent hot pursuit raids into Sudan. Widespread worries arose in Africa that Libya was acting as a proxy of Soviet expansionism and would use Chad as a base for further destabilization in Africa and that Qaddafi was pursuing a long-range plan to create a Libyan-dominated United States of the Sahel, based on the nomadic Muslim Saharan tribes. Credence was given to the latter idea by his calls for union of the Tuaregs (whom he claimed were Libyans) spread across the Sahel and his long-standing provision of military training to them and other nomadic tribes. To everyone's surprise, Qaddafi acceded to Goukouni's request in late 1981 for withdrawal of Libyan troops, but he quietly redeployed many of them in the far north of the country and launched a fresh invasion of Chad in 1983.[80]

The Western Hemisphere did not escape Qaddafi's attention, especially in the 1980s. Libya cultivated strong ties with Cuba and with the Marxist New Jewel regime on Grenada, providing an interest-free loan for the airport construction project over which Washington openly expressed worries. Qaddafi also sent missiles and other weaponry to Argentina in its 1982 war against his nemesis Great Britain. Libya's warmest relations in the area, however, were with the Sandinistas of Nicaragua, who had received Libyan training and arms as far back as the early 1970s in the context of their intimate ties with the Arab terrorist network. The Jamahiriyah supplied the Sandinista government with large loans and weaponry, invested in joint agricultural ventures, and sent advisers to help fight the *contras*, to assist in "interrogation techniques," and to train terrorists in Nicaraguan camps. The forging of close ties between Libya and the military regime in Suriname led to fears of more terrorist sanctuaries being established. Assistance in the form of arms, funds, and/or training was given by the Qaddafi regime to the M–19 guerrillas of Colombia; the Sendero Luminoso (Shining Path) and the Tupac Amaru Revolutionary Movement of Peru; the "Alfaro Vive, Carajo!" terrorists of Ecuador; Marxist guerrillas from El Salvador, Guatemala, Honduras, and Venezuela; terrorists from Uruguay, Chile, Costa Rica, the Dominican Republic, and Haiti; and leftist political groups in Panama, Antigua, Dominica, Saint Lucia, Saint Vincent, Jamaica, Barbados, and Trinidad and

Tobago. As in Oceania, in the Caribbean Libya was seeking to build a terrorist infrastruture for itself and was engaging in long-term efforts to convert nonviolent radicals to terrorist tactics. A terrorist organization titled the Caribbean Revolutionary Organization was put together with Libyan help in the French departments of Guadeloupe, Martinique, and French Guiana. High-ranking officials of Venezuela, Colombia, and Ecuador met in January 1986 to discuss their concern over these Libyan activities.[81]

An important factor in Libya's foreign policy in the 1980s was what Qaddafi called the "holy alliance" between Syria, Iran, and the Jamahiriyah. The catalyst for this Tripoli-Damascus-Tehran axis was the outbreak of the Iran-Iraq war in 1980, when, in opposition to other Arab states, Syria and Libya rallied to the side of Iran. Syria and even more so Libya were important suppliers of Soviet and other weapons to Iran, and both countries served as purchasing agents on behalf of Iran's armed forces. Syria received financial aid from Libya and discounted oil from Iran,[82] and in turn gave the other two states "a license to make mischief in Lebanon."[83] In spite of definite philosophical differences, the three countries' foreign ministers met regularly to coordinate Middle East policies, including support for the Soviet satellite South Yemen and opposition to Israel and to the United States (which top officials described in similar terms: the Ayatollah Khomeini branding America "the Great Satan," Qaddafi calling it the "devil," and the Syrian prime minister declaring it "the essence of evil").[84]

Another important area of cooperation between Libya, Syria, and Iran was in the realm of terrorism. Iran sent its Islamic Revolutionary Guards to train African terrorists in Libya; the Jamahiriyah reportedly provided Palestinian operatives for stepped-up training of Shi'ite terrorists in Iran starting in 1982; Tripoli aided efforts by Tehran to expand its terrorist contacts into Europe and Africa; and Syria and Libya cooperated closely in support and manipulation of the rejectionist Palestinian groups. Some terrorist groups received support from all three countries, including the Secret Army for the Liberation of Armenia (ASALA) and, for a period, Lebanese Shi'ite groups. Arab sources for the *Wall Street Journal* reported that in early 1985 the members of this state terrorism trio had agreed to cooperate in the exchange of intelligence, forging of passports for their terrorist operatives, and provision of financing and transport facilities for them, as well as ordering their embassies abroad to cooperate closely in these matters.[85] At least one terrorist attack has been found to involve participation by all three countries.[86]

No country in the period under review, not even Syria or Iran, matched the record of Libya under Qaddafi as an epitome of lawlessness and contempt for international norms. Beginning in 1972, the Qaddafi regime repeatedly expressed displeasure with foreign governments by having mobs "spontaneously" assault and sometimes burn their embassies or consulates. Hostage-taking in the form of arrests of foreigners in Libya for "espionage" was routine. Libya cultivated enduring ties with the Sicilian Mafia, was long involved in drug trafficking, and, despite signing the nonproliferation treaty (under Soviet pressure), contributed greatly to the Pakistani nuclear bomb project, providing funding, procuring equipment the West refused to sell to Islamabad, and both hijacking and purchasing "yellow cake" uranium from Niger for the effort. In the early 1980s Qaddafi was in some quarters expected to receive one or two bombs when the work was completed. In 1978 the leader of the Shi'ite community in Lebanon, Imam Musa Sadr, founder of Amal and related by marriage to the Ayatollah Khomeini, visited his patron Qaddafi as a guest of state. Sadr fell into quarrels with the colonel, and he and his two companions disappeared to be heard from no more.[87]

Furthermore, no regime was as brazen and arrogant in terrorist policies as Libya. Two Libyans were secretly expelled from Italy in 1982 for closely following the movements of President Sandro Pertini (whose outspoken indignation against terrorism had proved immensely popular with the Italian public). After a Libyan diplomat was expelled from Italy in 1985 for terrorist plotting, he was simply sent back to Rome in the role of employee of a Libyan government investment company and was eventually arrested. In early 1980 the Qaddafi regime began and loudly publicized a permanent campaign of poisoning, bombing, strangling, stabbing, and mostly shooting (sometimes in crowded public places) Libyan exiles, in locations ranging from Ogden, Utah, to Mecca (an enormous sacrilege). The antiexile hit squads concentrated particularly upon Western Europe, and their victims were hardly more likely to be anti-Qaddafi activists than Libyans simply known to disapprove privately of the colonel's rule. In many other instances the Libyan official media lauded specific terrorist acts, and, although he denied backing terrorists on many occasions, Qaddafi also often boasted of such backing and issued threats to inflict terrorism on foreign countries. He usually used euphemisms such as "liberation movements," "revolutionaries," and "suicide squads," but on a number of occasions he used the Arabic words for "terrorism" or "terrorists." He had first brashly announced his arming of the Irish Republican Army in a 1972 speech, and he later admitted backing the Red Brigades.[88]

The international response to Libya's various nefarious activities over the years was flaccid: several African countries severed diplomatic ties, and the European Economic Community (EEC) signed preferential trade and cooperation agreements with all Mediterranean Arab states except Libya, but Libya's economic ties with the West were still quite lucrative, and no meaningful penalties were inflicted upon the Qaddafi regime until the Reagan administration took office. There were several reasons for Third World governments' passivity, including genuine fear of potential Libyan assassination and subversive activities,[89] the immunity enjoyed by anti-Western governments due to pressures for Third World solidarity, and Qaddafi's skillful use of economic carrots—issuing development aid, selling discounted oil, buying the exports of politically cooperative countries and paying premium prices for them, and accepting their unemployed laborers—and sticks—threats of aid termination or oil embargoes and expulsion of foreign laborers, and the like.[90]

Western governments continued to sell arms to and expand economic ties with Libya even after its involvement in terrorism became public knowledge. The Western European governments more or less acquiesced in an open season on Libyan exiles in their countries; they occasionally engaged in the ineffectual measure of expelling individual Libyan diplomats while allowing their embassies, full of more terrorists, to remain open. France and reportedly Italy and perhaps other Western European countries made secret deals with Libya allowing free passage for terrorists in return for their own citizens not being targeted.[91] As one commentator stated, "European leaders often have seemed to take the view that Qaddafi's terrorist activities, his interference in their internal affairs, or his use of their major cities as bases of operation for terrorist attacks against third parties boil down to a cost of doing business with Libya."[92] The Tunisian foreign minister aptly remarked in 1981 that "Libya's strength is not her own power but the weakness of others."[93]

ANALYZING QADDAFI

Because Muammar Qaddafi's dominance over Libyan policy and especially foreign policy was so thorough, U.S. policymakers had to focus intensely on the colonel as an individual. It was said that he "thrives on crisis, and in quiet times he grows bored,"[94] and that "temperamentally he cannot endure tranquility. . . . [He] constantly creates turbulence . . . and revels in action for its own sake."[95] The Libyan leader is duplicitous and utterly devoid of scruples: an Egyptian commentator complained that the colonel would send a cordial emissary to Egypt whenever he was about to launch a terrorist attack in that country. Qaddafi is narcissistic, overbearing, scarcely able to endure not getting his own way, and childish, as exemplified by his insistence in 1986 that the Non-Aligned summit, scheduled for years to be held in Zimbabwe, should be shifted to Tripoli.[96] He is nonetheless clever and cunning and may possess good native intelligence; his skills at brinksmanship won the admiration of analysts. His level of wisdom, however, has seemed questionable; as Arabist Richard Parker stated, he has seemed "not to understand that he cannot ignore all the rules and still expect to have friends."[97] Qaddafi appears to regard himself as an intellectual giant, but his knowledge of the outside world is woefully deficient; much of his information about it is evidently filtered through the surreal prism of leftist propaganda. He was shocked when U.S. journalists told him in 1986 that President Reagan was very popular in the United States.[98]

In the 1980s the Western press, many academics, and reportedly even the CIA viewed Qaddafi as a "religious fanatic" and a "Muslim fundamentalist." Considering that two of Qaddafi's favorite pastimes have been trying to seduce foreign women (especially journalists) and plotting the demise of infidels and fellow Muslims alike, it is obvious that he does not possess the religious trait of willingness to bow before precepts that stand above one's own whims and attitudes. In his early years in power, the Libyan leader apparently was both doctrinally orthodox and fervent, but as the years passed, his Libyan revolution publicly emphasized religion less and less, and his supporters were noted as manifesting little concern with it. There was no actual implementation of amputation of limbs in Libya, and the Qaddafi regime was in reality responsible for a net diminishment of the role of the *shariah* in Libya. The *Green Book*, which did not mention Islam, replaced the Quran on Libyan television. Qaddafi enjoyed scant following among Islamic fundamentalists who did not receive his largesse, because of his emerging doctrinal heresies.[99] His Islam did not impart to him any moral restraint but did significantly provide him with a strong sense of self-righteousness and an intense partisan zeal: in spite of his doctrinal divergence from other Muslims, he felt a powerful identification with them.

Qaddafi's many opprobrious foreign policy actions are not mindless: he has a definite agenda with seven major motivations, which are to a large extent complementary and mutually reinforcing, although he has had to choose between them in numerous situations. First, there is the desire to preserve his regime, the cause of his war on Libyan exiles. Second, there is the desire to make great the once-forgotten country of Libya; this helps to spur his expansionism, but even if Qaddafi were successful in carving out the "Greater Libya" he seeks, that would not suffice to contain his ambitions. Third is Islam: he is said to regard Libya's oil wealth as a gift from God to be used in fighting the enemies of the faith. Fourth is pan-Arabism: he schemes against other Arab regimes because he sees virtually all of them as obstacles to Arab unity; he has not concealed his opinion that he would be a suitable leader for the Arab world and has compared himself to Garibaldi and Bismarck.[100]

Fifth, there is the Israel/Palestine issue: probably no passion in Qaddafi is greater than his hatred for the state of Israel, and the Palestinian cause is for him so surpassingly righteous that it serves not only as a motivation but as a rationalization for terrorism and other unsavory policies, such as propping up Idi Amin. It also plays a role in the sixth motivation: "anti-imperialism," that is, antagonism toward the West. Other factors in Qaddafi's hostility toward the West are his above-mentioned animus toward the rich and powerful; his professed revulsion for international capitalism (despite Libya's enthusiastic participation in the international capitalist system); the recent colonization of Libya and most of the Arab and Third Worlds; his acceptance of the popular myth that it was the West that divided the Arab world; and his obsession with the whole history of conflict between the West and the Arab/Islamic world, particularly the Crusades, which like many Muslims he somehow seems to treat as the initiation of that conflict. Finally, Qaddafi is motivated by his inveterate love of revolution and determination to upset the international status quo, which he sees as unjust;[101] although he insists that revolutionaries ought to follow the *Green Book*, his support for revolution in actual practice is essentially support for Marxists or Muslim fundamentalists.

Questioning of Qaddafi's sanity has long flourished, while Arabist academics have insisted that his actions are entirely explained by the just-mentioned motivations. Yet the idea that the colonel's kind of behavior—locking diplomats from North Yemen and South Yemen in a room until they reached an agreement for a unified Yemen modeled after revolutionary Libya, attempting to sink a passenger liner, and the most bizarre official rhetoric in the world, even including exhortation of Libyans to cannibalize their enemies—is simply to be expected from a resentful Arab nationalist strains credulity. There are unconfirmed reports of treatments for the Libyan leader at European sanitariums, and the idea that Qaddafi has some sort of drug abuse problem has found credence with serious observers.[102]

The truth about Qaddafi's mental condition may never be known. Whether or not he is psychotic, he is undoubtedly a fanatic. President Reagan and his administration's officials regarded Qaddafi as "crazy like a fox," and a 1985 CIA report said he appeared to be less like a madman than a "judicious political calculator." It can be pointed out that for a long time his perception that he could literally get away with murder abroad was substantially correct. One major key to understanding Qaddafi is undoubtedly how poorly informed he is.[103] Another probable key is the fact that, unlike other Arab leaders, he has never really been acculturated into the modern world. It has been noted that Qaddafi still considers himself a man of the desert and finds urban Arab society alien. Perhaps if he were the leader of a band of caravan-raiding desert tribesmen, his behavior would not seem so abnormal. No matter how inappropriate it may seem that an individual like Muammar Qaddafi should be the leader of a state in this day and age, five U.S. administrations spanning two decades have been forced to come to grips with him.

NOTES

1. *The Middle East*, 6th ed. (Washington, D.C.: Congressional Quarterly, 1986), p. 210; Aharon Levran and Zeev Eytan, *Middle East Military Balance, 1986* (Boulder, Colo.: Westview, 1988), p. 294 (hereafter cited as *MEMB, 1986*); Ronald Bruce St John, "The Determinants of Libyan Foreign Policy, 1969–1983," *Maghreb Review* 8 (May-Aug. 1983):96; John Wright, *Libya: A Modern History* (Baltimore, Md.: Johns Hopkins University Press, 1982), p. 260.

2. Wright, pp. 27–42, 222.

3. Ibid., pp. 93, 101, 107, 114, 272; Richard B. Parker, *North Africa: Regional Tensions and Strategic Concerns* (New York: Praeger, 1984), p. 66.

4. There are at least 648 ways to translate the Libyan leader's name into English (Wright, p. 130).

5. Ibid., pp. 124, 130: David Blundy and Andrew Lycett, *Qaddafi and the Libyan Revolution* (Boston: Little, Brown, 1987), pp. 33–35; John H. Cooley, *Libyan Sandstorm* (New York: Holt, Rinehart and Winston, 1982), p. 5; Lisa Anderson, "Qaddafi's Islam," in *Voices of Resurgent Islam*, ed. John L. Esposito (New York: Oxford University Press, 1983), p. 138–39.

6. Anderson, "Qaddafi's Islam," pp. 139–40; Wright, pp. 124–27; Cooley,

pp. 14–15; *New York Times* (hereafter cited as *NYT*), 11 Jan. 1986; Edward Schumacher, "The United States and Libya," *Foreign Affairs* 65 (Winter 1986/87):331.

7. Wright, pp. 132–35, 148–49, 154; *Washington Post* (hereafter cited as *WP*), 22 Apr. 1986; Anderson, "Qaddafi's Islam," p. 140; Cooley, pp. 132–33; Ann Elizabeth Mayer, "Islamic Resurgence or New Prophethood: The Role of Islam in Qadhdafi's Ideology," in *Islamic Resurgence in the Arab World*, ed. Ali E. Hillal Dessouki (New York: Praeger, 1982), p. 197. The task of driving out Libya's Jews had already been mostly accomplished by violence from the Arab majority from 1945 to 1967 (Wright, p. 75).

8. Daniel Pipes, *In the Path of God: Islam and Political Power* (New York: Basic Books, 1983), pp. 221, 298.

9. Cooley, pp. 42, 61, 66, 132–34; St John, p. 98; Wright, pp. 235–56.

10. Wright, pp. 184, 270, 272–73; Cooley, pp. 129–30; Parker, p. 19; U.S., Library of Congress, Congressional Research Service, *Conflict and Change in North Africa: Emerging Challenges for U.S. Policy*, by Ellen B. Laipson, Report No. 80–222F (Washington, D.C.: Government Printing Office, 1980), p. 19; Daniel Pipes, "Arab Influences in South Asia," *International Insight*, May-June 1981, p. 10.

11. Wright, pp. 135–37, 175, 179; Cooley, pp. 135–37, 274; *The Middle East*, p. 213.

12. Wright, pp. 183, 195; Cooley, p. 141; "An Anarchic and Naive Ideology," *Arabia: The Islamic World Review*, no. 34 (June 1984), p. 11; Schumacher, p. 332; Pipes, *Path of God*, p. 229.

13. Eduard Saab, quoted in Cooley, p. 141.

14. Anderson, "Qaddafi's Islam," p. 145.

15. St John, pp. 98, 100; Cooley, pp. 138–41; *The Middle East*, p. 213; Wright, p. 190.

16. Blundy and Lycett, p. 100.

17. Cooley, pp. 145, 149.

18. Ibid., p. 149.

19. Ibid., pp. 137–38, 141; *The Middle East*, p. 213; Pedro Ramet, "Soviet-Libyan Relations under Qaddafi," *Survey* 29 (Spring 1985):104; Wright, pp. 179–80, 191–92; Parker, pp. 75, 172; *Sunday Times* (London), 27 Apr. 1986. In an upheaval not untypical in the Qaddafi era, Libyan students in 1980 with the colonel's approval seized Libyan embassies and displaced incumbent professional diplomats, who were even threatened with being thrown out the window in East Berlin (*NYT*, 10 Apr. 1986).

20. Ramet, p. 97, following Robert C. Tucker, *The Soviet Political Mind* (New York: Praeger, 1963), pp. 7–9.

21. John W. Amos, "Libya in Chad: Soviet Surrogate or Nomadic Imperialist?" *Conflict* 5 (1983): 8–9; George Henderson, "Redefining the Revolution," *Africa Report* 29 (Nov.-Dec. 1984):37; David Blundy, "The Man We Love to Hate," *Sunday Times Magazine*, 2 Mar. 1986, pp. 30–31; *NYT*, 18 Jan. 1986; "Beyond the Barracks Gates," *Time*, 27 Jan. 1986, p. 31; Cooley, p. 145; St John, p. 100; Wright, p. 194. An illustration of how far Qaddafi was willing to go in fiction about the governance of Libya was his statement to an interviewer, "I have absolutely no power.... I do not have the power to sign any decision here in Libya or abroad" (*Foreign Broadcast Information Service, Daily Report*, Middle East & Africa [hereafter cited as FBIS-MEA], 25 Jan. 1985, pp. Q2–Q3).

22. Henderson, p. 38; Wright, pp. 196, 264–65; *WP*, 13 Apr. 1986.

23. *WP*, 13 Apr. 1986; Henderson, p. 38; Cooley, pp. 84, 86–100, 166–67, 281; Wright, pp. 139–40, 186–87.

24. Anderson, "Qaddafi's Islam," p. 135; Wright, p. 194; "An Anarchic and Naive Ideology," p. 11; *NYT*, 13 Jan., 14 June, 19 Jan., 7 Sept. 1986; Schumacher, p. 337; Henderson, pp. 38–39; "Instruments of Qaddafi's Repression," *Arabia: The Islamic World Review*, no. 34 (June 1984), p. 7; *WP*, 19 Jan., 13 Apr. 1986; Blundy, p. 31; "Beyond the Barracks Gates," p. 31; *Wall Street Journal* (hereafter cited as *WSJ*), 14 Apr. 1986.

25. Ramet, p. 107; Cooley, p. 277; Wright, p. 200; Mohamed A. El-Khawas, *Qaddafi: His Ideology in Theory and Practice* (Brattleboro, Vt.: Amana Books, 1986), p. 106; Oye Ogunbadejo, "Qaddafi's North African Design," *International Security* 8 (Summer 1983):159; "Amnesty International 1984–85: Mercy Is Rare," *Arabia: The Islamic World Review* 5 (Jan. 1986):30; Blundy, p. 31; Schumacher, p. 342; Bob Woodward, *VEIL: The Secret Wars of the CIA, 1981–1987* (New York: Simon & Schuster, 1987), p. 347; "Salvaging Victims of Torture," *Time*, 18 Feb. 1985, p. 86; *WP*, 13 Apr. 1986; Lisa Anderson, "Qadhdhafi and His Opposition," *Middle East Journal* 40 (Spring 1986):225.

26. Ronald Bruce St John [Nathan Alexander], "The Foreign Policy of Libya: Inflexibility amid Change," *Orbis* 24 (Winter 1981): 845.

27. Anderson, "Qadhdhafi and His Opposition," pp. 227–28; Henderson, pp. 39–40; Wright, p. 269; Parker, p. 80.

28. Terrell E. Arnold, "The Nine Lives of Muammar Qaddafi," *The World & I* 1 (June 1986):43.

29. Anderson, "Qadhdhafi and His Opposition," p. 228; Wright, p. 261; Henderson, p. 36; *NYT*, 2 May, 7 Sept. 1986; El-Khawas, p. 106; Blundy, p. 31; *WP*, 12 Apr. 1985, 15 Jan. 1986; *Los Angeles Times* (hereafter cited as *LAT*), 6 Apr. 1986; Blundy and Lycett, p. 31.

30. Schumacher, pp. 334, 341; *WP*, 15 Jan., 19 Jan., 13 Apr. 1986; Wright, pp. 136–37, 186, 188–89, 196–97; Cooley, pp. 274–77; El-Khawas, pp. 106–9; Ogunbadejo, p. 159; Parker, pp. 75–76; *Sunday Times* (London), 20 Apr. 1986; *NYT*, 19 Jan., 2 May 1986; "Havoc at Home, Too, for Gaddafi," *Time*, 14 May 1984, p. 44; *Times* (London), 23 Apr. 1986; "Instruments of Qaddafi's Repression," p. 7; *WSJ*, 14 Apr. 1986. Interestingly, Qaddafi's foreign policies were not often cited as a source for his unpopularity with the Libyan public, which was said to be relatively inattentive to foreign affairs (*NYT*, 20 Apr. 1986).

31. *WP*, 13 Apr. 1986, 12 July 1987; El-Khawas, p. 114; Schumacher, p. 342; Lisa Anderson, "Libya's Qaddafi: Still in Command?," *Current History* 86 (Feb. 1987):66; Wright, p. 188; Woodward, pp. 95, 365, 411.

32. One tabulation in November 1985 counted twenty-two attempts to assassinate or overthrow Qaddafi (*WP*, 6 Nov. 1985), and the pattern has since continued.

33. Cooley, pp. 282–83; *WP*, 12 June 1985, 14 Jan., 13 Apr. 1986; Maurizio Cremasco, "Friction for the Future?—Gadaffi's Libya," *NATO's Sixteen Nations* 31 (Dec. 1986-Jan. 1987):26; Schumacher, p. 337; *Middle East Contemporary Survey*, vol. 8:*1983–84*, ed. Haim Shaked and Daniel Dishon (Tel Aviv: Dayan Center for Middle Eastern and African Studies, The Shiloah Institute, Tel Aviv University, 1986), pp. 585–87, 601 (hereafter cited as *MECS* 8); *NYT*, 20 Apr., 14 June 1986; "Instruments of Qaddafi's Repression," p. 9.

34. "The Browning of the Green Book," *Economist*, 5 Apr. 1986, p. 46; "Gaddafi and Terrorism," *World Press Review*, June 1986, p. 22; Schumacher, p. 340; *NYT*, 4

Apr., 14 June, 7 Sept. 1986; "Beyond the Barracks Gates," p. 31; *WP*, 16 Apr. 1986; Blundy, p. 31; El-Khawas, p. 114; "The Libyan Problem," *Department of State Bulletin* 83 (Oct. 1983):71.

35. Daniel Pipes, "No One Likes the Colonel," *American Spectator*, Mar. 1981, pp. 18–19; *Times* (London), 26 Apr. 1986; *WSJ*, 19 Feb. 1981; Pipes, "Arab Influences in South Asia," p. 7.

36. Pipes, *Path of God*, p. 300.

37. Pipes, "No One Likes the Colonel," pp. 19–21.

38. Cooley, pp. 5, 12; Mayer, p. 206; Ramet, p. 105; FBIS-MEA, 2 Jan. 1986, p. D4; *NYT*, 14 June 1986.

39. He has at times made the familiar claim of hating only Israeli usurpers and not Jews in general, but Qaddafi has tended not to make such a distinction in actual practice, and he uses the terms "Israelis" and "the Jews" interchangeably. The slaughter of "scores" of Libyan Jews in 1967 (after which Qaddafi expelled the remainder) was recalled as glorious by the official press (FBIS-MEA, 17 Apr. 1986, p. Q15). In February 1973 a Libyan airliner with a confused crew strayed over the Sinai peninsula and was shot down by Israeli jet fighters. The Israeli government admitted error and offered compensation to survivors of the 108 fatalities (P. Edward Haley, *Qaddafi and the United States since 1969* [New York: Praeger, 1984], p. 47), but Qaddafi would not be mollified. He ordered the commander of an Egyptian submarine on loan to Libya to sink the *Queen Elizabeth II* as it carried American and European Jews on a visit to Israel. President Anwar Sadat of Egypt was horrified and countermanded the order when he heard of it, after which Qaddafi fell into a severe depression (Cooley, pp. 106–8). This episode was publicly admitted by Qaddafi in April 1976 (*Times* [London], 28 Jan. 1986).
   In response to Israel's "Operation Iron Fist" in southern Lebanon in early 1985, Libya broadcast radio appeals to the people of Morocco and Tunisia to massacre their ancient Jewish minorities, which so enraged President Habib Bourguiba of Tunisia that he threw the Libyan foreign minister out of his office after delivering him a tongue-lashing (*NYT*, 11 Apr. 1985). According to Qaddafi, the Jews "believe they are the master race, that they will conquer the world. This is written in their religion. The only way the Zionists will be stopped is by continuous war" (Blundy, p. 30).

40. Wright, pp. 157, 166, 168–69; Pipes, "No One Likes the Colonel," pp. 19, 22; *WSJ*, 19 Feb. 1981; *Washington Times* (hereafter cited as *WT*), 5 Jan. 1989.

41. "Foreign Policy Contradictions," *Arabia: The Islamic World Review*, no. 34 (June 1984), p. 12; Pipes, "No One Likes the Colonel," pp. 21–22; *MECS* 8:61; Cooley, pp. 120, 201, 298; Daniel Pipes, " 'The World Is Political!!': The Islamic Revival of the Seventies," *Orbis* 24 (Spring 1980):31; Pipes, "Oil Wealth and Islamic Resurgence," in Dessouki, pp. 45–51; Pipes, *Path of God*, pp. 297–321.

42. Cooley, pp. 109–13; Wright, pp. 163–64.

43. Bahgat Korany, "Defending the Faith: The Foreign Policy of Saudi Arabia," in Baghat Korany and Ali E. Hillal Dessouki, *The Foreign Policies of Arab States* (Boulder, Colo.: Westview, 1984; Cairo: The American University in Cairo Press, 1984), p. 251. A former chief of Israeli military intelligence was quoted as saying: "For Israel, Qaddafi can be a kind of asset. Who else, in all his frantic efforts to unite the Arabs, is keeping them divided to the extent Qaddafi is? He is a strategic threat, but perhaps a tactical asset; an agent of division of the Arab World" (Cooley, p. 110).

44. *Libya's Foreign Adventures*, Conflict Studies, no. 41 (London: Institute for the Study of Conflict, 1973), p. 10; Pipes, " 'The World Is Political!!,' " p. 30; *WP*, 9 Apr.

1986; Wright, p. 207; Pipes, "No One Likes the Colonel," p. 21; Martin Sicker, *The Making of a Pariah State: The Adventurist Politics of Muammar Qaddafi* (New York: Praeger, 1987), p. 70; Steve Posner, *Israel Undercover: Secret Warfare and Hidden Diplomacy in the Middle East* (Syracuse, N.Y.: Syracuse University Press, 1987), pp. 104–8; Roger Kelly, "Ghaddafi, President and Patron of World Terrorism," *Far Eastern Economic Review*, 6 Jan. 1978, p. 44; Brian Crozier, *The Surrogate Forces of the Soviet Union*, Conflict Studies, no. 92 (London: Institute for the Study of Conflict, 1978), p. 6; Neil Livingstone, *The War against Terrorism* (Lexington, Mass.: Lexington Books, 1982), p. 19.

45. *Libya's Foreign Adventures*, pp. 4–6, 10–11; Kelly, p. 44; U.S. Department of State, *Libya under Qadhafi: A Pattern of Aggression*, Special Report No. 138 (1986), pp. 1–3; Ramet, pp. 102, 104, 108; *NYT*, 28 Feb. 1985; *MECS* 8:417; "The Libyan Problem," pp. 76–77; *MEMB, 1986*, p. 296; Blundy and Lycett, pp. 150–51; Pipes, *Path of God*, pp. 312, 314–15; idem, " 'The World Is Political!!,' " pp. 30–31; *WP*,12 July 1987; Haley, p. 111.

46. John W. Amos II, *Palestinian Resistance: Organization of a Nationalist Movement* (New York: Pergamon, 1980); Cooley, pp. 102, 178.

47. Israel, I.D.F. Spokesman, *Libyan-P.L.O. Relations*, n.d., p. 19; Stefan T. Pussony and L. Francis Bouchey, "Moscow's Support of International Terrorism," *Ukrainian Quarterly* 34 (1978):387.

48. Walter Laqueur, *The Age of Terrorism* (Boston: Little, Brown, 1987), p. 285; Haley, pp. 44, 140. *WT*, 9 Apr. 1986; Alvin H. Bernstein, "Iran's Low-Intensity War against the United States," *Orbis* 30 (Spring 1986) :150; Blundy and Lycett, p. 151; *Libya's Foreign Adventures*, p. 16; Pipes, "No One Likes the Colonel," p. 21; Ramet, p. 104.

49. Kelly, p. 44.

50. *Times* (London), 28 Jan. 1986.

51. Livingstone, *War against Terrorism*, p. 17; Amos, *Palestinian Resistance*, pp. 165, 246; Pipes, "No One Likes the Colonel," p. 21; *San Francisco Chronicle*, 9 Oct. 1978; Haley, pp. 49–54; "The Libyan Problem," p. 77; *WP*, 9 Apr. 1986; M. K. Pilgrim, "Financing International Terrorism," *International Security Review* (Boston, Va.) 7 (Spring 1982):59; Laqueur, *Age of Terrorism*, p. 284; *WT*, 21 Apr. 1986 (UPI); Robert Hotz, "Progress against Hijacking," *Aviation Week & Space Technology* 105 (30 Aug. 1976):9; Edward A. Lynch, "International Terrorism: The Search for a Policy," *Terrorism* (New York) 9 (1987):26; I.D.F. Spokesman, *Libyan-P.L.O. Relations*, pp. 12, 24.; Shlomi Elad and Ariel Merari, *The Soviet Bloc and World Terrorism*, Jaffee Center for Strategic Studies Papers, no. 26 (Tel Aviv: Jaffee Center for Strategic Studies, Tel Aviv University, 1984), p. 40.

52. *NYT*, 28 Apr. 1986; Blundy and Lycett, p. 146, 150; Pipes, *Path of God*, pp. 302, 308; Richard H. Shultz, Jr., "Can Democratic Governments Use Military Force in the War against Terrorism?" *World Affairs* 148 (Spring 1986):208; *WP*, 27 July 1980, 23 May 1986, Amos, "Libya in Chad," p. 10; Jerome B. Weiner, "The Green March in Historical Perspective," *Middle East Journal* 33 (Winter 1979):25; Samuel T. Francis, "Libya's Empire of Terror," *Africa Insight* 12 (1982):6; "The Libyan Problem," p. 76; Cooley, p. 200; Pipes, "No One Likes the Colonel," p. 21; "Polisario Fortunes Slump as Morocco and Libya Sign Treaty," *Arabia: The Islamic World Review* 4 (Oct. 1984):22–23.

53. *Facts on File*, 5 June 1981, p. 370; Posner, p. 1; Charles Holley, "Why Libya

Exports Chaos," *Atlas World Press Review*, Nov. 1976, p. 15; *NYT*, 28 Apr. 1986; Wright, p. 214; *The Middle East*, p. 17; *WP*, 16 Apr. 1986.

54. *WP*, 27 July 1980; Amir Taheri, *Holy Terror: Inside the World of Islamic Terrorism* (Bethesda, Md.: Adler and Adler, 1987), pp. 80–82; Pipes, "The World is Political!!," p. 31; Rt. Hon. Lord Chalfont, "Terrorism and International Security," *Terrorism* (New York) 5 (1982):315; Pipes, "No One Likes the Colonel," p. 21.

55. Haley, pp. 40–41; *Christian Science Monitor* (hereafter cited as *CSM*), 15 Mar. 1977; U.S. Defense Intelligence Agency, "International Terrorism: A Compendium. Volume II—The Middle East (U)" (1979), in *Documents From the US Espionage Den*, ed. Muslim Students Following the Line of the Imam (Tehran: n.p., n.d.) 43:61; "Worldwide Chronology of Terrorism—1981," *Terrorism* (New York) 6 (1982):284; Risks International, "Special Report: Significant Regional Developments, October-December 1984," *Terrorism* (New York) 8 (1985):171.

56. Parker, p. 83; "Master of Mischief," *Time*, 7 Apr. 1986, p. 23; *NYT*, 8 Apr., 14 June 1986; Blundy and Lycett, p. 150; *Focus on Libya*, Jan. 1987; "A Tale of Two Colonels," *Economist*, 17 May 1986, p. 54; Christopher C. Harmon, "Left Meets Right in Terrorism: A Focus on Italy," *Strategic Review* 13 (Winter 1985):43, 46–47; Laqueur, *Age of Terrorism*, pp. 263, 290; Avigdor Haselkorn, "How Qaddafi's Indirect Strategy Is Working," *The World & I* 2 (July 1987):112–15; U.S. Congress, Senate Committee on the Judiciary, Subcommittee on Security and Terrorism, *Terrorism in Italy: An Update Report, 1983–1985*, prepared by Vittorfranco S. Pisano (Washington, D.C.: Government Printing Office, 1985), p. 27. Qaddafi supported the pacifists with the view that "the 'Green' movement and the 'hippies' are factors of exhaustion and fragmentation in the white communities" (FBIS-MEA, 29 Mar. 1985, p. Q4).

57. Pipes, "No One Likes the Colonel," p. 21; Michael Ledeen, "Soviet Sponsorship: The Will to Disbelieve," in *Terrorism: How the West Can Win*, ed. Benjamin Netanyahu (New York: Farrar, Straus & Giroux, 1986), pp. 88, 90; Yonah Alexander, "Libyan Terrorism: Some Strategic Considerations," in U.S. Congress, Senate Committee on the Judiciary, Subcommittee on Security and Terrorism, *Libyan-Sponsored Terrorism: A Dilemma for Policymakers*, 19 Feb. 1986, 99th Cong., 2d sess., p. 107; *WP*, 27 July 1980, 25 Feb. 1985, 9 Apr., 24 May 1986; FBIS-MEA, 29 Mar. 1985, pp. Q3-Q4; *WT*, 6 Nov. 1985; "Washing Libya out of Their Hair," *Time*, 1 June 1987, p. 45.

58. "The Sources of Terror," *U.S. News & World Report*, 28 Apr. 1986, p. 28.

59. Pipes, "Muslims of South East Asia," *8 Days*, 5 July 1980, pp. 26–28; idem, *Path of God*, pp. 317–20; Elad and Merari, p. 24; John Laffin, *War Annual 2: A Guide to Contemporary Wars and Conflicts* (London: Brassey's Defence Publishers, 1987), p. 43; Ariel Merari, et al., *Inter 86: A Review of International Terrorism in 1986* (Boulder, Colo.: Westview, 1987), p. 22; *San Francisco Chronicle*, 9 Oct. 1978; Alexander, "Libyan Terrorism," pp. 91–92, 107; W. Hays Parks, "Crossing the Line," U.S. Naval Institute *Proceedings* 112 (Nov. 1986):41; *WP*, 27 July 1980; Pipes, "Arab Influences in South Asia," p. 8; "The Ways of the Colonel," *Far Eastern Economic Review*, 6 Jan. 1978, p. 43; Dept. of State, *Libya under Qadhafi*, p. 3; *NYT*, 11 May, 7 Sept. 1986.

60. Wright, p. 172; Ramet, p. 104; "Qaddafi and South Africa," *Foreign Report*, 24 Apr. 1986, p. 4; FBIS-MEA, 11 Apr. 1986, p. U1; Haselkorn, p. 115; *MEMB, 1986*, p. 296; Woodward, p. 183; "The Libyan Problem," p. 76; "Washing Libya out of Their Hair," p. 45; Wolfgang Leidhold, "Alien Sharks in the Lagoon?: Libyan Activities in the South Pacific," *TVI Report* 8 (1988):11–20.

61. Ramet, p. 102; Ariel Merari and Shlomi Elad, *The International Dimension of Palestinian Terrorism*, JCSS Study no. 6 (Jerusalem: Jerusalem Post, 1986; Boulder, Colo.: Westview, 1986), p. 75; Pipes, "No One Likes the Colonel," p. 21; Holley, p. 16; *LAT*, 24 Aug. 1975; *WP*, 4 May 1985, 15 Apr., 28 May 1986; Amos, "Libya in Chad," p. 13; Hotz, p. 9; Haley, p. 39; Brian Michael Jenkins, "Libya's Continuing Role in International Terrorism," *TVI Report* 7 (1987):4.

62. I.D.F. spokesman, *Libyan-P.L.O. Relations*, p. 12; *NYT*, 16 July 1976; *Times* (London), 28 Jan. 1986; Parks, p. 41.

63. *Times* (London), 28 Jan. 1986; *WP*, 27 July 1980; I.D.F. spokesman, *Libyan-P.L.O. Relations*, pp. 2, 12, 25; Jenkins, "Libya's Continuing Role," p. 1; Haley, p. 41.

64. *CSM*, 15 Mar. 1977; Parks, p. 41; Pilgrim, p. 51; Kelly, p. 44; Amos, *Palestinian Resistance*, p. 229.

65. Laqueur, *Age of Terrorism*, p. 283; I.D.F. spokesman, *Libyan-P.L.O. Relations*, p. 2; Merari and Elad, pp. 75, 135.

66. Amos, *Palestinian Resistance*, p. 247; *Times* (London), 28 Jan. 1986; Yossi Melman, *The Master Terrorist: The True Story of Abu Nidal* (New York: Adama Books, 1986), p. 147; Christopher Dobson and Ronald Payne, *Counterattack: The West's Battle against the Terrorists* (New York: Facts on File, 1982), p. 102; Arnaud de Borchgrave, "The Soviet Equation," *Newsweek*, 24 Dec. 1979, p. 26; Arnold Beichman, "Qaddafi's Safe Haven for Terrorism," *National Review*, 19 Feb. 1982, p. 187; Ogunbadejo, p. 160; *WP*, 27 July 1980. Some misunderstanding of Libya's direct role in terrorist attacks has been caused by the fact that Qaddafi has preferred to use Libyan gunmen against Libyan dissident targets and to use non-Libyan assailants against other targets. He feels both parts of this dichotomy give him deniability. This is obvious in the case of the attacks against the non-Libyan targets, and in case of attacks against Libyan dissidents abroad, he can claim that such actions are simply the overflowing wrath of the Libyan people against traitors to the revolution, for which he cannot be held personally responsible.

67. Brian M. Jenkins, *Future Trends in International Terrorism*, Rand Paper Series, no. P–7176 (Santa Monica, Calif.: Rand Corporation, 1985), p. 4. For more on the network, see Amos, *Palestinian Resistance*, pp. 231–51. A famous quote illustrating the operation of the international terrorism network was this description of the Lod airport massacre in 1972: "An operation can be planned in Germany by a Palestine Arab, executed in Israel by terrorists recruited in Japan, with weapons acquired in Italy but manufactured in Russia, supplied by an Algerian diplomat financed with Libyan money" (Serge and Adler, "The Ecology of Terrorism," *Survival*, quoted in Amos, *Palestinian Resistance*, p. 234). Not all terrorist groups or states involved in terrorist activities (e.g., South Africa) are in any way associated with the network described here.

68. Having both changed political direction, in the 1980s first Algeria and then Iraq drastically reduced their support for international terrorism. Little or nothing was heard of collusion on their part with other states in supporting terrorism.

69. On Cuban and Nicaraguan support for terrorists as well as guerrillas in Latin America, see R. A. Hudson, "Castro's America Department: Systemizing Insurgencies in Latin America," *Terrorism* (New York) 9 (1987):125–67, and for an audacious example, see *Times* (London), 4 Sept. 1986. On the countries' ties with European and Arab terrorists, see Elad and Merari, pp. 15–16, and Lynch, p. 23.

70. On Soviet and Eastern European support for terrorism, see Elad and Merari; Uri Ra'anan et al., *Hydra of Carnage: The International Linkages of Terrorism and Other Low-Intensity Operations; The Witnesses Speak* (Lexington, Mass.: Lexington Books,

D.C. Heath & Co., 1986); and Roberta Goren, *The Soviet Union and Terrorism*, ed. Jillian Becker, with an introduction by Robert Conquest (London: Allen & Unwin, 1984). Lest anyone should think the Soviets became too pure to support terrorism after Mikhail Gorbachev took power, there is the matter of the KGB-sponsored Afghan Communist onslaught of bombings in Pakistani urban areas that became significant only after his accession (*WP*, 13 March 1988). Those highly sophisticated attacks produced fatalities greatly exceeding those of terrestrial Middle Eastern terrorist bombings.

71. "Worldwide Chronology," p. 285; Paul Wilkinson, "Uncomfortable Truths about International Terrorism," *Across the Board*, Jan. 1982, cited by Elad and Merari, p. 16; *WP*, 3 Feb. 1986; Risks International, "Regional Developments," p. 179; Damian J. Fernandez, *Cuba's Foreign Policy in the Middle East* (Boulder, Colo.: Westview, 1988), p. 111.

72. Pipes, "Arab Influences in South Asia," pp. 9–10; idem, "No One Likes the Colonel," p. 22; Philippe Decraene, "Niger," in *Britannica Book of the Year, 1978* (Chicago: Encyclopedia Britannica, 1978), p. 571; Ogunbadejo, p. 158; Cooley, pp. 115–16, 197, 251; Sicker, p. 56; FBIS-MEA, 12 June 1985, p. Q7; *NYT*, 25 Mar. 1986; Memphis *Commercial Appeal*, 25 Mar. 1986; Parks, p. 42.

73. Haley, pp. 57–60; Dennis Chaplin, "Libya: Military Spearhead against Sadat?," *Military Review* 59 (Nov. 1979): 44; Cooley, pp. 83, 247; Amos, "Libya in Chad," pp. 5–6; "The Libyan Problem," p. 72; Wright, pp. 206–16; Roger F. Pajak, "Arms and Oil: The Soviet-Libyan Arms Supply Relationship," *Middle East Review* 13 (Winter 1980–81):51; Sicker, p. 55.

74. Anderson, "Qaddafi's Islam," p. 144; Ramet, pp. 110–12; Dobson and Payne, p.x; remarks by Yonah Alexander in "Colby College Conference Report," *Terrorism* (New York) 8 (1985):109; Blundy and Lycett, p. 151; Harmon, p. 47; Claire Sterling, "The State of the Art," in Ra'anan et al., pp. 51–52; Posner, pp. 104–8. At the same time that the Cuban-and Soviet-trained Carlos worked for Qaddafi, he maintained his ties with the Cuban DGI and it is believed, the KGB (*CSM*, 15 Mar. 1977; Haley, pp. 40–41, 53).

75. Ramet, pp. 110–11; Parker, p. 151; "The Libyan Problem," p. 72; Chaplin, p. 45; Wright, p. 203; "Libya Was Ready," *Foreign Report* 24 Apr. 1986, p. 3; Pajak, p. 53; John Keegan, *World Armies* (London: Macmillan Press, 1979), p. 446, quoted in I. William Zartman and A. G. Kluge, "Heroic Politics: The Foreign Policy of Libya," in Korany and Dessouki, p. 189; Haley, p. 61; Stephanie G. Neuman, "Third World Military Industries: Capabilities and Constraints in Recent Wars," in *The Lessons of Recent Wars in the Third World*, vol. 2, *Comparative Dimensions*, ed. Stephanie G. Neuman and Robert E. Harkavy (Lexington, Mass.: Lexington Books, 1987), pp. 159, 172.

76. Ramet, pp. 108, 111; "Foreign Policy Contradictions," p. 13; *WP*, 27 July 1980; " 'I Am a Mixture of Washington and Lincoln,' " *U.S. News & World Report*, 10 Nov. 1986, p. 32; Pipes, *Path of God*, p. 307.

77. *Le Monde*, quoted in *WT*, 25 Mar. 1986.

78. *WP*, 27 July, 1980; Haley, pp. 75, 80; "The Shadowy World of America's Mercenaries," *Newsweek*, 3 Nov. 1986, p. 37; Blundy and Lycett, p. 147; Melman, p. 163; *MECS* 8:204; Dept. of State, *Libya under Qadhafi*, p. 3.

79. Chaplin, p. 47; *WSJ*, 19 Feb. 1981; Pipes, *Path of God*, pp. 312, 320; Wright, pp. 166, 204; Haley, p. 36; Cooley, p. 185; Chester A. Crocker, "Libyan Interference in Chad," *Department of State Bulletin* 81 (Oct. 1981):28; Ray S. Cline and Yonah

Alexander, *Terrorism as State-Sponsored Covert Warfare* (Fairfax, Va.: Hero Books, 1986), p. 17; Ogunbadejo, p. 160; Amos, "Libya in Chad," pp. 4–5, 16; "The Libyan Problem," pp. 75–76; "Master of Mischief," p. 23. A Libyan army officer was in charge of negotiations on behalf of the Sudanese insurgents after they seized European hostages in summer 1983 ("The Libyan Problem," p. 75).

80. "The Libyan Problem," pp. 73, 75; Cooley, pp. 196–98, 200, 204, 208; Haley, pp. 204–6; Amos, "Libya in Chad," pp. 2, 4; Francis, p. 9; Ra'anan et al., pp. 567–68. To justify his activities in Africa, Qaddafi cited the need to expel French imperialism, but he provoked African fears, which ironically resulted in a great resurgence of France's influence and military presence in the region ("Foreign Policy Contradictions," pp. 12–13).

81. Ramet, pp. 109–10; "Anti-Libya Scare Grips the Caribbean," *Africa* (London), no. 146 (1983), p. 60; "The Libyan Problem," p. 77; *WP*, 27 July 1980, 11 May 1986, 24 Feb. 1987; Hudson, pp. 138, 147, 151; U.S. Department of State, *Libyan Activities in the Western Hemisphere* (1986), pp. 2–7; Cline and Alexander, pp. 17, 50; *CSM*, 10 Feb. 1987; Blundy and Lycett, p. 150; *NYT*, 18 Aug. 1986; "A Communist Beachhead in Baby Doc's Haiti?," *Business Week*, 18 Apr. 1983, p. 54; *WSJ*, 12 June 1986; *LAT*, 24 Aug. 1975; Woodward, pp. 409–10; Leidhold, pp. 13–14.

82. George P. Shultz, "The Challenge to the Democracies," in Netanyahu, p. 16; Stephanie G. Neuman, *Military Assistance in Recent Wars: The Dominance of the Superpowers*, The Washington Papers, no. 122 (New York: Praeger with the Center for Strategic and International Studies, Georgetown University, 1986), p. 46; *CSM*, 26 Sept. 1985, 28 Nov. 1986.

83. Daniel Pipes, "Syria: The Cuba of the Middle East?" *Commentary*, July 1986, p. 18.

84. *NYT*, 26 Mar. 1986; *WSJ*, 19 June 1985; "Gaddafi: Obsessed by a Ruthless, Messianic Vision," *Time*, 21 Apr. 1986, p. 29; Pipes, "Syria," p. 18.

85. Bernstein, p. 150; Cline and Alexander, pp. 49, 51; Risks International, "Regional Developments," p. 178; Taheri, p. 112; "What Khomeini Will Do Next," *U.S. News & World Report*, 2 May 1988, p. 43; Pipes, "Syria," p. 18; *WP*, 8 Nov. 1985; *WSJ*, 19 June 1985; Yonah Alexander, "The Politics of Terror," *The World & I* 2 (Feb. 1987):24.

86. Viz., the Istanbul synagogue massacre of September 6, 1986 (CBS, "CBS Evening News with Dan Rather," 6 Mar. 1987).

87. *WP*, 20 Aug. 1972, 27 July 1980; Cooley, p. 113; Dept. of State, *Libya under Qaddafi*, pp. 6–8; Laqueur, *The Age of Terrorism*, p. 282; *Times* (London), 14 May 1986; Blundy and Lycett, p. 203; Memphis *Commercial Appeal*, 17 Mar. 1988; Pipes, "Arab Influences in South Asia," pp. 9–10; idem, "No One Likes the Colonel," p. 22. Sadr's disappearance reminded Lebanese Shi'ites of the "hidden" twelfth imam of Shi'ite lore and elevated the Iranian-born holy man to the status of a messianic figure in their sight. Amal, perhaps the only Lebanese Muslim group that refuses Libyan largesse, has mounted numerous anti-Libyan terrorist attacks in memory of Musa Sadr.

88. *Times* (London), 5 Sept. 1986, 24 Mar. 1987; *NYT*, 13 June 1972, 22 Apr. 1986; Haley, pp. 119, 121, 123–34; Congress, *Terrorism in Italy*, p. 28; *WP*, 12 June 1972, 7 Apr. 1985, 27 Apr. 1986; "Libyan Leader of Jama'atut Tabligh Assassinated," *Arabia: The Islamic World Review* 5 (May 1986):45; Zartman and Kluge, p. 186. On one occasion, Libyan hit men are believed to have been loaned to the radical government of Seychelles, resulting in the murder of a Seychelles exile leader (Micah Morrison, "The Seychelles Test," *American Spectator*, May 1987, p. 39).

89. Tareq U. Ismael, *International Relations of the Contemporary Middle East: A Study in World Politics* (Syracuse, N.Y.: Syracuse University Press, 1986), p. 181; *NYT*, 14 June 1986. Israeli officials claimed that fear of Libyan subversion was slowing the progress of their country's campaign in the 1980s to restore diplomatic relations with black African countries (*NYT*, 24 Mar. 1986). Qaddafi issued public calls for the murder of President Mobutu of Zaire, the first African ruler to renew diplomatic ties with Israel; he supported anti-Mobutu guerrilla movements, and according to the State Department was responsible for anti-Zairian bombings in Europe and a thwarted plot to kill the African dictator (*MECS* 8:60–61; Dept. of State, *Libya under Qadhafi*, pp. 2, 6).

90. Pipes, "No One Likes the Colonel," p. 20; *WP*, 25 Apr. 1986; *WSJ*, 19 Feb. 1981.

91. *LAT*, 4, 5 Apr. 1986; *NYT*, 6 Apr. 1986.

92. Arnold, p. 43. In the summer of 1984 Qaddafi's hit squads shot four Libyans in Greece in a six-week period, killing three of them, one having been tortured beforehand. The government of Prime Minister Andreas Papandreou responded with an apparently feeble protest and with the signing of a $1 billion economic agreement when Papandreou visited Tripoli in September (*Facts on File*, 31 Dec. 1984, p. 986; *WP*, 27 Apr. 1986). Papandreou's attitude was undoubtedly influenced by the fact that Libya financially supported the party he headed before and after it came to power in Greece (Nathan M. Adams, "Greece—Sanctuary of International Terrorism," *Reader's Digest*, June 1989, pp. 203, 208).

93. Wright, p. 217.

94. Schumacher, p. 248.

95. Pipes, "No One Likes the Colonel," p. 19.

96. FBIS-MEA, 30 May 1985, p. D3; "Gaddafi: Obsessed," p. 29; *Arab Press Service*, 5 Aug. 1981, quoted in Amos, "Libya in Chad," p. 8; *Times* (London), 4 Sept. 1986.

97. Parker, p. 82.

98. Mayer, pp. 213–14; *NYT*, 11 Jan. 1986.

99. Haley, p. 19; Blundy and Lycett, pp. 22–23; *NYT*, 14 June 1986 (personal testimony of Judith Miller written in third person); Mayer, pp. 198, 199, 201–2, 207–8, 215; Wright, pp. 134, 278; Cooley, p. 275; Anderson, "Qaddafi's Islam," pp. 140, 142; *CSM*, 13 Dec. 1984; "An Anarchic and Naive Ideology," pp. 10–11; Pipes, *Path of God*, pp. 120, 221, 298. Qaddafi's personality cult in Libya even included his followers calling him "prophet" (*WP*, 15 Jan. 1986), an astonishing blasphemy in the Islamic context.

100. Taheri, p. 81; "I Am a Mixture," p. 32; Dept. of State, *Libya under Qadhafi*, p. 2.

101. St John [Nathan Alexander], p. 845; "Gaddafi: Obsessed," pp. 28–29; Haley, p. 233; *WP*, 13 Apr. 1986.

102. Cooley, pp. 83, 136; Memphis *Commercial Appeal*, 13 Jan. 1986; *NYT* 14, 15 June 1986; "Kaddafi's Crusade," *Newsweek*, 7 Apr. 1986, p. 22; Woodward, pp. 328, 347–48.

103. *WP*, 3 Nov. 1985; Blundy and Lycett, p. 24. In proximity to the matters of Qaddafi's relative ignorance and his seeming madness is what might be called the "buffoon factor"; as one commentator noted, "Who but Qaddafi would . . . sign a mutual defense treaty with Guinea? Oftentimes he appears like a character out of opera bouffe or an Evelyn Waugh novel" (Pipes, "No One Likes the Colonel," p. 19). He has periodically made public remarks of an unbelievably silly nature, such as when he rebuked Juan

Antonio Samaranch, president of the International Olympic Committee, for the brutality of Olympics sports including boxing, wrestling, and *bullfighting* ("No Bull," *Sporting News*, 3 Oct. 1988, p. 19). The intriguing suggestion has been made that the Libyan dictator is engaging in the "calculated projection of irrationality" (Amos, "Libya in Chad," p. 12), but no substantial evidence to support that assertion has circulated publicly, and it must be noted that absurd statements and actions have damaged Qaddafi's esteem in the Arab world, a result he never would have wanted. It is true, however, that the buffoon factor has caused many observers to take him far less seriously than he deserves and therefore show reluctance to support appropriate measures against his regime.

2

The United States and Libya, 1969–1983

THE NIXON AND FORD ADMINISTRATIONS

The United States had been closely associated with the Libyan king whom Qaddafi would overthrow. In the 1950s Libya had received more U.S. foreign aid per capita than any other country, including extensive building of infrastructure; in addition, the Wheelus Field air base was Libya's largest source of employment and regular income before the oil boom. U.S. oil companies had obtained most of the concessions in Libya, but in order to operate there had to engage in extensive bribery, which did not endear them to the Libyan public. Furthermore, as in all other Arab countries, but more so in Libya, the image of the United States was much damaged by its support for Israel. This problem was compounded by the presence of the U.S. and British bases, and many Libyans believed Nasser's fabricated claims that aircraft from the bases had helped attack Egypt in the Six-Day War of 1967.[1]

Shortly after Qaddafi's coup, top U.S. policymakers were presented with Defense Department and CIA analyses stating that it would be fairly easy to topple the new regime, but after some debate Washington extended recognition to the RCC on the fifth day after the coup. Given the history of close identification with the Idris regime, there was pessimism in the Nixon administration about the future of relations with Libya; nonetheless, partly on the advice of its new ambassador to Tripoli, Joseph Palmer, the administration made a decision to be conciliatory and tolerant toward the new regime. Palmer expressed hope that U.S. interests would be well served by the young leader's "natural" anti-Soviet and anti-Communist biases. At this point in time the United States did not fear

Islamic revival in the Middle East; in the 1950s the CIA had even attempted to create a "Muslim Billy Graham" to undercut Communism in the Arab world.[2] In 1969 Communism seemed a far greater threat in the region than at present: the Soviets were entrenched in Egypt and a Marxist government had recently been established in South Yemen.

The Nixon administration expressed its concern that the balance of power in the Middle East could be upset by France's huge sale, announced in January 1970, of Mirage fighter bombers to Libya; it was widely regarded as a mere device for selling them to Egypt. The administration later suppressed the prospective sale to Libya by a Los Angeles firm of a nuclear reactor with potential for plutonium production and urged U.S. oil companies not to buy oil from a British Petroleum concession seized by the Libyan government. However, most of Washington's actions toward Libya in Qaddafi's early years in power were amicable. The United States speedily agreed to evacuate Wheelus Field ahead of schedule, sold some of the equipment at the base to Libya, continued to train Libyan pilots, and offered to sell Phantom jet fighters. The CIA is thought to have warned Qaddafi of the first coup plot against him in December 1969. The agency in 1970 abstained from aiding a royalist plot to overthrow the colonel using Chad as a staging ground and urged Mossad to refrain as well. The United States both acted to thwart and warned Qaddafi against a mercenary conspiracy in 1970–71 known as the Hilton assignment. The Nixon administration declined to give strong support to the oil companies when the RCC pressured them for price increases in fall 1970 and responded mildly to the nationalization of oil begun by Libya in 1973. Because of this apparent favor from Washington as well as Qaddafi's anti-Sovietism and his assisting the suppression of the Communist coup in Sudan in 1971, the Libyan dictator was widely viewed in the Arab world as a U.S. agent, and even his seizure of power was interpreted as having been engineered by the United States.[3]

U.S. efforts to maintain good relations with Libya were, however, in vain. Major Jalloud promised Ambassador Palmer Libya's friendship with the United States if it evacuated Wheelus Field, but once the evacuation was completed, he told Palmer that Libya would never have good relations with the United States because of its support for Israel (long Qaddafi's most vehement single complaint against Washington), and senior Libyan officials broke off contacts with the envoy. Qaddafi ungraciously blamed the United States in public for the first two of the above-mentioned coup plots.[4]

In his earlier years of less intensely leftist orientation, Qaddafi's private attitude toward the United States may well have been softer than his public posture: in an April 1972 discussion with Egyptian intellectuals he noted that the prosperity of the United States was self-derived and that it had aided rather than exploited Libya.[5] But the Qaddafi regime seemed to feel it needed an "enemy figure . . . important enough to be accepted as a credible threat but not actually and immediately dangerous,"[6] and the United States was the logical choice. Qaddafi continually boasted of having driven the United States out of its Libyan bases,

Mock up speed

although it had already been scheduled to abandon them before he took power. In the same June 1972 speech in which he bombastically announced his intentions to arm PLO terrorists and Filipino Muslims,[7] the Libyan strongman vowed to make Great Britain and the United States "pay dearly for the wrongs and perfidy they inflicted on us";[8] he would take the fight to their own lands by supporting the IRA in the United Kingdom and blacks, particularly Black Muslims, in the United States. In a December speech he added promises of support to violent Latin American organizations hostile to the United States. He had already given $300,000 to the Black Panthers but had stopped his support once he discovered they were still using alcohol and marijuana.[9]

As the year 1973 saw significant deterioration of Libyan-U.S. relations, the United States shifted from a policy of conciliation toward Libya to a policy of low-key, low-priority opposition. In fall 1972, frustrated at the continuing refusal of consequential Libyan officials to deal with him, Ambassador Palmer had obtained his recall from the Tripoli post, and in early 1973 the decision was made in Washington not to replace him, reducing U.S. representation in Libya to the chargé d'affaires level. In early March the government of Sudan revealed the Libyan role in the PLO embassy seizure in Khartoum in which two U.S. diplomats were murdered, and later in the month, before Qaddafi's public claims to the Gulf of Sidra, two Libyan Mirage fighters fired at U.S. naval aircraft over the high seas. Toward the end of the year Qaddafi would seek the assassination of Secretary of State Henry Kissinger in order to scuttle Middle East peace negotiations. Citing Libyan involvement in terrorism and subversion, the State Department forbade transfer to Libya of equipment that could enhance that country's military capability, an action that blocked the delivery of eight C–130 transport aircraft already paid for by Libya. Washington soon began to pressure its allies also not to supply weapons. The arms embargo was, of course, heatedly denounced by the Qaddafi regime, which nonetheless saw fit to continue to separate business and politics in dealing with the United States. Although Qaddafi had publicly called for terrorists to launch an intensive campaign against U.S. interests, he imprisoned a Black September squad that had the lack of discretion to respond by attacking an American-owned oil depot in Libya itself. Qaddafi valued the expertise of the U.S. oil companies, and though he would repeatedly in the 1970s threaten to turn the "oil weapon" against the United States, Libya clandestinely violated the 1973–74 Arab oil boycott against America, while refusing formally to end the boycott until long after other Arab states had.[10]

Americans continued to die in Libyan-sponsored terrorist attacks, and the Ford administration became so disenchanted with Colonel Qaddafi that, when solicited by Sadat in 1976, it gave Egypt a commitment to deter Soviet intervention should Egypt launch a military assault on Libya. Qaddafi responded in anger to Israel's July rescue of the Entebbe hostages (which foiled a Libyan-supported operation) by seeking unsuccessfully to instigate terrorist attacks at the 1976 Democratic and Republican conventions. A U.S. intelligence report claimed that he had issued orders for his jet fighters to shoot down a plane carrying Kissinger. The annual Defense Department report of January 1977 contained a reference to Libya that Qaddafi interpreted as designating his country the fourth-leading enemy of the United States, and he repeatedly celebrated his presumed status.[11]

THE CARTER ADMINISTRATION

Upon taking office in 1977, the administration of President Jimmy Carter immediately revoked the U.S. commitment to deter the Soviets if Sadat went to war with Libya, but the Egyptian leader did so anyway; it has also been reported that overtures from Sadat concerning efforts to overthrow Qaddafi were rejected in the Carter years. Nonetheless, the administration continued the policy of mild, low-key punishment of Libya while leaving open the door to possible improvement in relations. Qaddafi's anti-Americanism, accompanied by extreme verbal abuse, seemed to grow considerably in the Carter years; obviously the major reason for this was Washington's sponsorship of the Middle East peace process. Qaddafi faced his nightmare of nightmares: an Arab state making peace with Israel, a frontline Arab state abandoning its responsibility to seek the destruction of the Zionist entity. Part of his wrath was directed at Hermann Eilts, the U.S. ambassador to Egypt; Carter was forced to send two handwritten personal letters in 1977 warning Qaddafi to abandon the intricate plot he had hatched to assassinate Eilts.[12]

Despite this hostility and his refusal to oblige the U.S. chargé in Tripoli in his desire for a meeting, the Libyan leader frequently put out the word that he wanted to improve relations with the United States. Washington's "attempts to follow up led nowhere or to the dead end of the C–130 issue,"[13] which became quite an obsession for the Qaddafi regime; U.S. offers to return the payments for the planes were rejected. The Libyan government began a "people-to-people" campaign to reach the American people directly in order to create pressure for Libyan–U.S. rapprochement on Qaddafi's terms, including the release of the C–130s. (Qaddafi has always failed to grasp that his totalitarian socialism, export of terrorism, foreign aggression, and maniacal anti-Zionism are as repulsive to the U.S. public as to the U.S. government.) The campaign included goodwill tours, efforts to create friendship societies, granting endowments to universities in hopes of influencing U.S. academia, contacts with Black leader Jesse Jackson, and assistance to his Operation PUSH and to organizations representing Black Muslims, Arab-Americans, and American Indians. The outreach to minority organizations was partly intended to cultivate potential channels for support of terrorism and subversion in the United States.[14] The most famous aspect of the people-to-people campaign was the cultivation of the president's alcoholic brother Billy as an agent for Libyan interests, which resulted in the "Billygate" scandal that hampered Carter in the 1980 election year.

In early 1978 the State Department blocked additional items for export to Libya on the grounds of its continuing support of terrorism, but a temporary reversal of policy took place later in the year. With an eye to exploring possibilities for dialogue, sales of heavy trucks, Boeing 727s, and Boeing 747s were approved in September and October 1978 and January 1979, respectively. A series of secret negotiations between Libyan and U.S. officials, including Secretary of State Cyrus Vance, took place in 1978–79, but no breakthroughs were achieved. One major stumbling block for the diplomacy was Libya's intervention in Uganda on behalf of Idi Amin, in which older C–130s and 727s were employed. Congress was appalled, and in May 1979 the State Department blocked the export of the 747s.[15]

Negotiations continued, but the Jamahiriyah's public support for the Iranian hostage seizure (carried out largely by Libyan-trained militants) provided yet another stumbling block. President Carter nonetheless in his desperation turned to Billy and sought Libyan help to obtain the release of the hostages. Qaddafi played along with the suggestion, knowing full well that Khomeini was not on speaking terms with him because of Musa Sadr. Shortly after the Libyan dictator told a U.S. journalist of his desire for improved relations with the United States, a mob of two thousand persons on December 2 sacked and burned the U.S. embassy in Tripoli, as personnel inside fled for their lives. Government officials provided wrecking bars and axes for the assault (which was thought to have been intended to warn the Carter administration against strong anti-Iranian action), and embassy files were carried off in Libyan army trucks.[16]

Relations with Libya were further damaged when on January 27, 1980, three hundred Tunisian guerillas from Libyan camps attacked the Tunisian town of Gafsa in an effort to set up a "revolutionary government," which would swiftly call for direct Libyan intervention against the regime of Habib Bourguiba. Paris and Washington quickly came to the aid of their long-standing small ally: France flew Tunisian troops to Gafsa in its military transports; the United States rushed ten armored personnel carriers, one C–131 transport, and ammunition to Tunisia; and both powers sent naval vessels to cruise off the Tunisian coast. The rebels were defeated in several days' fighting. Qaddafi denied responsibility for the attack but openly voiced his determination to see Bourguiba's downfall, and, predictably, the French and Tunisian embassies in Tripoli and the French consulate in Benghazi were sacked and burned. The Bourguiba regime was deeply alarmed over the Libyan destabilization effort and sought to move closer to its Western allies. The episode caused rising pressure on the Carter administration to take a strong stance against Qaddafi and provided a new stimulus for policies of arming and supporting friendly governments in the region.[17]

As the Qaddafi regime set in motion its campaign of terrorism against exiles, the Carter administration in April unceremoniously expelled two Libyan diplomats for intimidation of Libyans in the United States and for distribution of leaflets calling for assassinations. The intended message to Tripoli did not seem to take hold, so on May 2 the State Department announced the expulsion of four of the five remaining Libyan diplomats in Washington due to continuing threats. Simultaneously, in view of the evident dangers and Qaddafi's unwillingness to receive the American chargé, the United States withdrew its remaining representatives in Tripoli and closed its embassy there, while formally maintaining diplomatic relations with the Jamahiriyah. Qaddafi responded by threatening to withdraw assets from and cut off oil supplies to the United States and by suddenly discovering "espionage" among American oil workers, expelling twenty-five of them and detaining two.[18]

Regional problems further exacerbated the decline in U.S.-Libyan relations. Implementation of the Carter Doctrine, involving naval buildup and negotiating access rights to bases in the region that national security adviser Zbigniew Brzezinski termed the "arc of crisis," drew great hostility from Qaddafi. He sharply increased support of the Marxist rebels opposing the Sultan of Oman in order to punish him for cooperation with Washington. In October he urged Arabs to attack U.S. "bases," and in a message to the two presidential candidates, reproduced in an advertisement in the *Washington Post*, he threatened war against the United States unless it withdrew from Egypt, Somalia, Oman, and Saudi Arabia and stopped reconnaissance flights over the Gulf of Sidra. In black Africa, Libya was having its busiest year yet for subversion, and the autumn occupation of Chad formed a fitting climax for its activities there. At first, the Carter administration had responded nonchalantly to the Chad intervention, but eventually it grew alarmed and showed satellite photographs of Libyan troop concentrations to African heads of state.[19] President Carter had aptly stated in August: "There are few governments in the world with which we have more sharp and frequent policy differences than Libya."[20]

THE REAGAN ADMINISTRATION

On November 29, 1980, Colonel Qaddafi had welcomed the election of Ronald Reagan as president of the United States on the grounds that the Republicans had been more favorable to the Arab cause than had the Democrats;[21] he would apparently be quite startled at the changes in U.S.-Libyan relations that ensued. Reagan had campaigned against what he considered a foreign policy of weakness by Jimmy Carter, and he and his advisers were determined to implement assertive, forceful policies to reverse the decline in America's position in the world. The American people, deeply angered by the Iranian hostage crisis and the Soviet invasion of Afghanistan, were also in a mood to exchange the self-depreciation of the Vietnam era for a return to unabashed nationalism. According to pollsters at that time:

The actions encouraged by the new public mood include: a tougher stance in dealing with the Soviet Union; adding muscle to our defense capabilities; showing a willingness to aid our allies, with military force, if necessary, in the event of Soviet aggression; brushing aside the moral squeamishness that diminished the usefulness of the CIA; employing trade as a legitimate weapon in support of our national interests; and in general acting more forcefully against enemies and on behalf of our friends.[22]

At this juncture in time the new administration's hostile attention toward Libya was provoked by two factors: first, Qaddafi's regional activities, especially the shocking announcement of the Libya-Chad merger/annexation, which Reagan and his new secretary of state Gen. Alexander M. Haig, Jr., harshly denounced. Soviet military advisers had accompanied the Libyan army into Chad and reportedly masterminded the military operations; the Kremlin gave its public blessing to the endeavor. At the same time reports of accelerated Libyan efforts to recruit and train subversive Tunisian elements were reaching Washington; the president and his top advisers saw the Chad adventure and Qaddafi's foreign policy in general as a form of the surrogate Soviet expansionism they had pledged to halt. The second key factor at this juncture was heightened concern over terrorism stimulated by the traumatic hostage crisis. Haig, himself the survivor of a terrorist assassination attempt, soon declared that the United States would never again negotiate with terrorists and that the Carter administration's theme of human rights would be applied to terrorism as the greatest of all human rights violations.[23] Qaddafi's role as the most generous and brazen state supporter of terrorists logically drew the administration's fire.

On the day after his inauguration Ronald Reagan presided over a National Security Council meeting in which Libya was a major topic. Secretary Haig later flatly rejected recommendations from the State Department for a mild approach to the Libyan problem.[24] U.S. policy toward Libya shifted from one of administering the country a few slaps on the wrist but mostly ignoring it to a policy of determined opposition. Two major considerations drove the new policy: limiting the colonel's ability to do harm and preparing the way for his eventual downfall, mindful of increasing anti-Qaddafi dissidence. The openly professed goal was to bring about a change in Qaddafi's behavior, but privately the administration considered him to be utterly incorrigible. The new approach to Libya, termed by one writer "containment, rollback, and bleeding all at the same time,"[25] was a revolutionary development in dealings with the phenomenon of the Middle Eastern outlaw regimes, which had long played such a crucial role in the international terrorist network, waging proxy warfare against the West thereby and yet enjoying business as usual or even pampering rather than reaping penalties.[26] Contrary to assertions of its critics, the Reagan administration recognized that Libya was not the entire problem but felt that it was the most appropriate place to begin drawing the line.

The first step in the new Libya policy was instituting a campaign of verbal exposure and sharp denunciation of Qaddafi's policies for the purposes of making Libya the pariah in the international community that the Reagan administration felt it ought to be and of preparing the U.S. Congress and public to support whatever action the administration might see fit to take against Libya. In sharp contrast to its other endeavors in foreign policy, the administration found the demographically liberal Democratic news media to some extent helpful in the case of Libya, for several apparent reasons. First, since Qaddafi was not a Marxist, the prejudice that has been dubbed "anti-anti-Communism" did not come into play; additionally, his reputation in the West as a "religious fanatic" did not endear him with journalists in the wake of the emergence of the Ayatollah Khomeini. Further, Qaddafi as villain ideally suited the needs of the press: a romantic antihero, bizarre, crafty, conspiratorial, and astonishingly unscrupulous. The American public was responsive to the administration's verbal campaign against the Libyan dictator, having been especially well prepared for it by the publicity that had been generated by "Billygate,"[27] the Chad intervention, and revelations about the former CIA agents Frank Terpil and Edwin Wilson, formidable antiheroes themselves.

A $100 million Libyan loan to Nicaragua was noted in Washington, and Reagan condemned the Jamahiriyah along with other states in April 1981 for supporting the El Salvadoran guerrillas; the administration well understood that Qaddafi's support for Marxism in the Western Hemisphere was intended to harm the United States. On May 6 the United States announced the expulsion of the Libyan diplomats in Washington and the closure of their "people's bureau" (the new term for a Libyan embassy), citing a "wide range of Libyan provocations and misconduct," including Tripoli's support for international terrorism and subversion, its expansionism in Africa, its military relationship with the USSR, and its hit squad campaign, including the shooting of a Libyan in Colorado whose assailant had recently been arrested; Libya had publicly claimed responsibility for the shooting. United States policies, it was also stated, would not be affected by the "oil relationship" that accounted for 40 percent of Libya's total exports and 10 percent of United States oil imports. The next day the administration declared that it considered travel by Americans to Libya to be hazardous and urged U.S. oil companies operating in Libya to begin an orderly withdrawal of American employees and to eliminate nonessential operations. The administration wanted to remove the potential for a new hostage crisis, but the oil companies did not heed its warnings. Qaddafi sent his personal envoy Ahmed al-Shahati to Washington for discussions at the State Department in June, but the talks were fruitless.[28]

The administration made diplomatic isolation a major part of its effort to coordinate containment of Qaddafi with foreign governments; predictably, governments did or did not cooperate with the campaign to isolate Libya on the basis of their own perceived short-term interests. In addition, Assistant Secretary of State for African Affairs Chester A. Crocker announced in summer 1981 that the United States would increase its aid to regional states wishing to resist Libyan interventionism, and Secretary Haig's "strategic consensus" policy was explicitly aimed at thwarting Libyan as well as Soviet designs. U.S. military aid to Tunisia, Morocco, and Sudan was drastically increased, and the anti-Libyan theme blended well with efforts to secure access rights for the Rapid Deployment Force.[29]

Qaddafi was an especially strong nemesis to new CIA director William J. Casey, and the administration increased intelligence collection assets directed at Libya. Rough contingency plans for a strike against Libya would be carried by every U.S. battle group in the Mediterranean, but President Reagan rejected military action against Libya unless it was tied to a specific Libyan action. The idea of assassinating Qaddafi was out of the question. Reagan reissued in his own name the executive order forbidding assassinations, and when the administration of French president Valéry Giscard d'Estaing approached Washington for help in a Franco-Egyptian plan to kill Qaddafi in 1981 it was refused.[30]

There were other approaches available, however. Early in the administration Reagan signed an intelligence finding that authorized the CIA to support Habré's insurgency against Libya and Goukouni with money, arms, and technical assistance. Preceding Washington's direct support for the Nicaraguan *contras* as it did, this covert action might be considered the beginning of the "Reagan Doctrine." The motivation was twofold: the governments of Egypt and Sudan were beckoning the United States to take a strong role against Libya in Africa, and the aid was coordinated with them; additionally, it was hoped that a prolonged, unsuccessful military involvement on Libya's part would help undermine Qaddafi's position at home.[31]

On June 18 Reagan signed another finding, which authorized clandestine political work with Libyan exiles in order to form a legitimate opposition to Qaddafi, with "non-lethal" support and training from the CIA. The United States became only one of the assortment of countries supporting the Libyan exiles rather than assuming a dominant role. The exile organizations suffered from penetration by Qaddafi's secret agents, and none of them was able to develop genuine military or paramilitary capabilities in the period under review. Their essential "forte," as a State Department official admitted, was broadcasting into Libya news (as well as propaganda) that Qaddafi did not want Libyans to hear. In the short term, however, a sensational Congressional leak appeared in *Newsweek* in late July portraying the administration's modest program as a projected massive sabotage campaign inside Libya, including the possible assassination of Qaddafi. Though erroneous, the leak increased tensions with Libya.[32]

The Intellectual Debate over Policy toward Libya and Terrorism

As the Reagan administration embarked on a new activist approach toward Muammar Qaddafi's Libya and toward terrorism, numerous objections arose from like-minded Arabist professors and policy analysts in think tanks who formed the mainstream of Middle East experts and will be referred to in this book as the Middle East experts. These scholars generally devoted very little study to the phenomenon of terrorism per se, and their contribution to the literature on Middle Eastern terrorism was almost nil, but they were extensively interviewed and quoted by the news media in times of terrorism crisis. Their distinctive opinions, which framed much of the debate over the conflict between Libya and the United States until and after the 1986 bombing raids, were prevalent among Western journalists and diplomats assigned to the Middle East (including

American ones) and were also fairly popular in Western European cabinets; such views provided a rationale for the policies the Europeans were already pursuing, for the most part because of their economic interests. The mainstream Middle East experts tended to be characterized by a warm sympathy for the Palestinian fedayeen and a defensiveness about the Islamic religion (although the overwhelming majority of them did not adhere to it). Typical among them also was the attitude that paramilitary violence in the Middle East was essentially the consequences of Israel, a view that was not characteristic of a different category of scholars termed here as the heterodox school of Middle East specialists. A more critical view of the PLO and of Islam was taken by the heterodox school, which included (but did not entirely consist of) sympathizers of Israel and, in contrast to the mainstream school, produced a respectable amount of research on Middle Eastern terrorism. The heterodox scholars, however, were much less numerous than the mainstream scholars and were not quoted with great frequency by the news media.

According to the mainstream Middle East experts, forthright opposition to Qaddafi was counterproductive, because it would give him the world attention he so greatly relished, would only increase his stature in Libya and the Arab world (an argument with obvious precedent in the boost that Nasser had received, even in military defeat, from the Suez crisis in 1956), would force his opponents underground lest they appear to be imperialist lackeys, and would force moderate Arab leaders who loathed him to rally around him publicly, leading to the passage by regional organizations of anti-American resolutions, to which many Middle East experts responded as though they were truly staggering blows delivered to the United States. In an argument with echoes of the now-discredited notion that Washington drove Fidel Castro into Communism and the Soviet orbit, it was asserted that pressure from the United States would only drive Libya into the arms of Moscow, make it a Soviet client state, and perhaps even lead to the granting of military bases to the USSR, fears that Qaddafi openly and deliberately cultivated. The Middle East experts repeatedly indicated their belief that the United States should not become exercised over Qaddafi terrorizing Libyans on U.S. and other foreign soil. Libya, in their view, was only a small country and therefore incapable of doing much harm, a nuisance at the most. Worst of all, fixation on Qaddafi, they claimed, resulted in the neglect of the more important task of pursuing Arab-Israeli peace.

In reality, Qaddafi had shown superb skill at keeping his name in the headlines for years regardless of how the United States had responded to him. The Suez intervention had boosted the standing of a leader who was already popular in his country and the Arab world, but whether U.S. opposition would rescue the declining domestic popularity of a leader who was bringing tyranny and economic chaos to his land was another question. Furthermore, since nobody believed that Qaddafi would ever hold a genuine plebiscite on his rule, as General Pinochet of Chile did in 1988, one might ask how Qaddafi's hypothetical approval rating in Libya at any given moment would be relevant to U.S. interests. It could only be so if some U.S. action resulted in a fatal delay in the timing of a coup attempt against Qaddafi. No evidence of such occurrences emerged, and in fact several coup attempts against Qaddafi in the 1980s took place in the wake of confrontations with Western powers. The NFSL as early as 1981 had advocated a Western boycott of Libyan oil, and one heterodox Middle East specialist claimed that the failure of the West to isolate Qaddafi had made the Libyan opposition's task much more difficult.[33] Year after year during the decade, real evidence of a rise of Qaddafi's stature in the broader Arab world would seem to elude revelation. Reagan administration officials shrugged off the occasional anti-American resolutions stimulated by the conflict with Libya as examples of the hollow "verbalism" that Arabs privately admit characterizes their political life, and the officials claimed to be receiving different signals in private from Arab governments.

Assistant Secretary of State Richard W. Murphy and other State Department officials were in actuality very active in Arab-Israeli diplomacy during the Reagan years. The Middle East experts, however, saw fit to focus only upon the long absence of new high-profile initiatives after the regional parties rejected the Reagan peace plan of 1982 and upon the withdrawal of George P. Shultz, secretary of state from mid–1982, from personal participation in the peace process after the collapse of his Lebanon-Israel peace treaty. Those situations were caused not by the administration's attention to Libya or terrorism but by Shultz's wariness concerning the readiness for peace of the parties in the Arab-Israeli dispute.[34] One must also note the irony of scholars who prided themselves on their knowledge of the region's complexities and dilemmas continually speaking as though lack of political will in Washington were instead the major obstacle to peace.

The consideration of how U.S. policy would affect Libyan-Soviet relations was certainly a weighty one; it could be argued, however, that the United States cannot always allow itself to be blackmailed by a threat to move closer to the Soviet Union, which can be employed by almost any country. On the basis of the evidence, it was hard to conclude that Libya was not already a Soviet client state, although Qaddafi apparently still denied the Soviets control of bases in Libya. However, Tripoli had reportedly made an agreement in 1974 to permit limited use of Libyan bases by Soviet forces. From the mid–1970s on, Soviet planes had been flying reconnaissance missions from Libyan bases, and the Soviet navy had enjoyed the use of harbor facilities along the Libyan coast, establishing a routine presence there.[35] According to one expert, the Soviet Union had been "constructing a huge military infrastructure in Libya, intended first and foremost for Soviet use."[36] Even before the administration had unfolded its anti-Qaddafi campaign, military analysts had become convinced that the Soviet Union would have free use of Libya in the event of an outbreak of East-West warfare. In connection with the possibility of the Soviets being granted permanent bases in Libya, it should be noted that Qaddafi had based his claim to legitimacy upon ending "foreign occupation" of Libya and had explicitly promised never to give another foreign country bases.[37] Therefore, in order for him to grant bases to the Soviets, they would have had to put forward a truly significant quid pro quo: probably only a commitment to defend Libya would suffice. In the long run the Soviets would prove unwilling to make that commitment, and the Reagan administration's antagonism toward the Qaddafi regime and its insistence on ending the international silence about Libyan enormities quite likely influenced them.

Also central in the debate over dealing with Qaddafi was the idea that the very enterprise of fighting terrorism per se was foolish and even morally illegitimate because, according to some Middle East experts, the problems of terrorism and of Qaddafi simply boiled down to the grievances of the Palestinians, and the reason that Qaddafi pursued his nefarious ways and that terrorists planted bombs or hijacked airplanes was that they were provoked about the United States supporting Israel. Such utterances seemed to ignore the fact that terrorist groups have emerged in all parts of the world and not just the Arab world, as well as the fact that much Arab terrorism is carried out by non-Palestinians. It is also noteworthy that although Arabs tend to pay close attention to differences among Western countries in Middle East policy, Qaddafi long supported terrorism against Spain, which did not even recognize Israel until 1986, and against France, a country that has long tilted away from Israel and toward the Arabs but has nonetheless suffered Middle Eastern terrorism in the 1980s on a scale similar to the United States.[38] Many commentators, including heterodox Middle East specialists, noted that terrorism seemed to be embedded in the political culture of the Middle East quite independent of the Arab-Israeli conflict: the medieval sect of the Assassins and the Barbary pirates, practitioners of *jihad* (holy war), were cited, as well as the pervasiveness in the region in recent decades of terrorism, most varieties of which have had little or nothing to do with the matter of Israel.[39] Although the rise of Palestinian global terrorism in 1967–68 had provided inspiration for the emergence of more terrorism all across the world, it was far from true that the Palestinian problem was the root cause whose resolution would lead to the subsiding of world terrorism. It is interesting to note also that in their preoccupation with their Palestinian grievances agenda, the Middle East experts overlooked the fact that although the Palestinian problem may be the leading focus of anti-Americanism in the Middle East, it is probably no longer as important a factor in international terrorism as the unsolved Lebanon problem. Not only does the citizenry of Lebanon provide a recruiting pool for terrorists comparable to that of the Palestinians, but the anarchic condition of the country also makes it the perfect refuge for terrorists, whom governments are able to maintain there with assured deniability.

Many of the Middle East experts knew better than to assert that the problem of terrorism simply boiled down to the Palestinian issue; their more sophisticated notion was that terrorism arises deterministically from misery and injustice and the legitimate grievances of disaffected groups. The Middle East experts' statements often remarkably paralleled the terrorists' own propaganda, in which the latter portrayed themselves as desperate people with nowhere to turn and hardly able to prevent themselves from performing violent acts out of a kind of anomic animal fury. Middle East experts downplayed the evidence about state sponsorship or asserted that it was of trivial importance. In their view, the appropriate response for the West was to ''understand'' Qaddafi and terrorists. Some pundits furthermore reckoned that since (in their view) human beings were basically good and reasonable, and conflict resulted only from faulty communication and perception, terrorists were therefore reasonable at heart, and if one would simply sit down and negotiate with them, wonderful results would surely ensue.[40]

Many commentators in turn reproached the arguments of the Middle East experts as virtual apologies for terrorism and for promoting paralysis in the face of it. It has been pointed out there are probably fewer groups with grievances spawning terrorists than there are groups with grievances not spawning terrorists. It was also noteworthy that with only rare exceptions terrorists do not enjoy the moral support of the greater part of the constituencies they claim to represent, and the resort to terrorism was widely noted to be a symptom of an organization's political weakness. Extensive empirical research failed to demonstrate any connection between terrorism and poverty, scarcity, or any other socioeconomic indicators. Terrorism certainly does not arise deterministically from conditions of deprivation; other factors likely to play crucial roles are cultural traditions of violence or nonviolence, foreign support, the influence of external propaganda, individual leadership, and contacts of such potential leaders with evangelistic Marxists on university campuses (about 80 percent of terrorist groups are Marxist-Leninist, and Marxists have actively sought to encourage even confirmed Muslims to turn to violence). Moreover, as Walter Laqueur has pointed out, it is not actually grievances but the *perception* of grievances that matters in terrorism.[41] Political extremism is a prerequisite for terrorism, and the error of assuming that the development of such passions is rational is illustrated in the violent white supremacist groups in the United States, whose perceived grievance is that America is being ruled by a Jewish/Negro cabal that is leaving ''white people'' out in the cold.

Furthermore, the portrayal of terrorists as killing out of desperate fury was absurd: terrorist incidents are coolly, carefully planned, usually well in advance, by terrorist leaders (and sometimes government intelligence officers) who prefer not to use individuals of poor self-control.[42] As terrorism expert Neil C. Livingstone has noted, ''Most terrorist leaders, and a large percentage of the rank-and-file in many cases, come from privileged backgrounds. . . . Nearly all terrorists have other options available to them; few become terrorists out of personal desperation.''[43] For example, Rasmi Awad, one of the Abu Nidal group's leading operatives in Europe, was a prosperous Madrid physician.[44]

The unfortunate fate of the Anglican hostage negotiator Terry Waite would mock the notion that negotiation was a panacea for terrorism.[45] Few disputed that efforts to redress legitimate grievances were desirable; however, it was a matter of historical record that governments had many times responded to terrorism with sincere efforts to redress grievances, but terrorists had rarely been placated by such efforts and were indeed often hostile to them. Most observers would agree on the perniciousness of promoting a formula for viewing terrorism that automatically shifts the blame from the terrorists to their victims. Terrorists are usually maximalists who do not seek political compromise and instead work assiduously to destroy the middle ground in conflicts. This is notably true in the Middle East, where outbreaks of increased terrorism have typically arisen in response to increased peace efforts. In the 1980s most Palestinian terrorism was performed by groups sworn to oppose any prospect of a peace settlement, and the predominant strain of Shi'ite terrorism was that of Hezbollah, which, rather than merely seeking increased Shi'ite representation in the government that does not govern Lebanon, has sought to create an Islamic republic in a land in which about half the population is Christian or Druze. As for Qaddafi, both ignoring him and showing him understanding had been abundantly essayed by the West, but he had only exploited and demonstrated his contempt for these approaches.

With its fueling of extremism around the world, its support for terrorist groups and often specific incidents and its pursuit of weapons of mass destruction, Libya should be seen as an example of why the notion that a small country cannot do much harm is obsolete. There were those who argued the callous view that terrorism should be seen as unimportant because the casualties it produces are far less than those of conventional war; but the harm inflicted by terrorism is extensive and cannot be measured by body counts alone. The State Department's response in 1983 to arguments that Libya should be seen as irrelevant went as follows:

Qadhafi has altered the power balance in northeastern Africa and created a permanent state of anxiety on the part of his weaker neighbors, distracting them from economic development. His machinations throughout Africa have contributed to instability and encouraged anti-American elements. Money and arms have been dispersed throughout the continent, available to virtually any bidder willing to do obeisance to him. In the Middle East . . . the ever-present lure of his money and his Soviet arms has been a constant fixture, tilting the balance away from moderation and compromise. Those bent on violence and terror have found encouragement, and those inclined to compromise and constructive resolutions to complex problems have often been bullied into silence. They have had to cope with the very real threat of Qadhafi-supported terrorism. Qadhafi's accomplishment has been to increase markedly the level of fear among the weak or the humane, to set back the momentum of accommodation and peace in the Middle East, and to sow instability among the poverty-stricken fledgling states of Africa.[46]

Furthermore, a passive response to Libya could be seen as carrying potential dangers of its own. The flagrant defiance of international law and norms on a daily basis by the leader of a country as small as Libya posed a potential threat to those norms. Acquiescence in the aggression of state-supported terrorism could only encourage other states to employ it themselves; as G. Henry M. Schuler noted, ''Libya's goals are also achieved when other nations, groups, or individuals emulate its tactics.''[47] When the Khomeini regime made its decision to pursue a policy of terrorism against the West, it had to be consciously or unconsciously influenced by the example of Qaddafi suffering no punishment for such policies. Experts on terrorism were generally agreed that, despite the dismissals of the Middle East experts, the valuable aid provided by state sponsors made terrorism a far worse problem in the world than it would have been otherwise. In particular, the resources and technology being provided by governments were promoting the trend toward increasing lethality in terrorist attacks in the 1980s, and additionally, state sponsorship made terrorist groups' degree of popular support largely irrelevant. Although Palestinians overwhelmingly supported Fatah, Fatah's irreconcilable enemies in the Palestinian resistance were a powerful force because of the support they received from Libya and Syria; with massive Iranian aid, the extremist Hezbollah became one of the most powerful actors in Lebanon despite its base of popular support being limited to a minority of the Shi'ite minority.[48] Greater enormities yet might be expected to follow unchallenged sponsorship of kidnappings, hijackings, and bombings. It was probably beyond the capability of the West to keep Middle Eastern regimes from inflicting terrorism upon one another, but Western governments had a definite interest in making clear that they would not tolerate such activities against themselves, lest those acts widen in scope or intensify when technological advances brought more dangerous weapons into the hands of smaller states and perhaps terrorists as well.[49]

Intensified Estrangement

In August 1981 the United States' Sixth Fleet carried out well-publicized maneuvers in the Mediterranean Sea, including the Gulf of Sidra, for the stated purposes of training in the use of naval missiles and challenging the validity of Libya's nautical claims, which the United States had often defied and which, if upheld, would have indeed significantly hampered the fleet's routine air activities. Privately, however, the administration's main objective was believed to be teaching Qaddafi a lesson. Aware of Libyan jets having fired on U.S. aircraft over the high seas in 1973 and having made two apparent efforts to down U.S. aircraft in autumn 1980, officials made preparations in expectation that the Libyans would fire again. After the Libyans had flown over one hundred sorties without firing (in a seeming effort to lull U.S. pilots into relaxing their guard), Libyans SU–22s suddenly opened fire on a pair of American F–14s thirty miles from the Libyan coast on August 19. The SU–22s missed and were themselves rapidly shot down. Qaddafi responded angrily, issuing a call for Arab "active forces" to strike at the United States and threatening to attack NATO nuclear depots should the United States enter the gulf again. At the time of the incident, he had been in Aden negotiating a military pact with South Yemen and Ethiopia under the guidance of a senior Soviet official, but the Soviet Union kept aloof from the Gulf of Sidra.[50]

At the beginning of October 1981, Egyptian Vice President Hosni Mubarak revealed to U.S. officials in Washington a plan for Egypt and Sudan to attack Libyan forces in Chad; the Reagan administration gave a new promise to deter the Soviets in case of a war between Egypt and Libya. On October 6, however, President Sadat was assassinated. His assassins belonged to a fanatical Muslim underground group that was known to enjoy Libyan support. U.S. officials were unable to connect Libya directly to the conspiracy; by one account, Israeli intelligence did draw such a link. Reagan administration anger toward Qaddafi was heightened by his open gloating and his calls for the same fate to befall President Nimiery of Sudan, even as Libyan planes were bombing Sudanese border villages. The pressure upon Qaddafi was turned up by several weeks of intense prior publicity about a huge set of military maneuvers in November by the United States and its regional allies under the name Operation Bright Star, complete with two AWACS radar aircraft patrolling Egypt's border with Libya.[51]

Meanwhile the Libyans engaged in a new round of terrorist plots. Already in July a Libyan student who had refused to return to the Jamahiriyah had been murdered in Utah. In September Italian authorities seemed to have scotched an assassination plot against Maxwell Rabb, the Jewish U.S. ambassador to Rome, with the expulsion of a number of Libyans, but the dispatch of a new Libyan hit team to Italy prompted U.S. officials to hustle Rabb out of the country without even a change of clothes in late October. In October the Qaddafi regime also sent Egypt a present in the form of suitcase bombs a week after the killing of Sadat[52] and dispatched hit men to Sudan to attempt to kill Hissen Habré as he visited.[53] In November Kenyan officials foiled a Libyan plot involving explosives planted in stereo speakers being flown to Khartoum for detonation at a Saturday night dance at the American Embassy Club where hundreds would be in attendance. Speculation had it that the plots against Americans were efforts to obtain revenge for Libya's defeat in the Gulf of Sidra.[54]

Three days after the Gulf of Sidra dogfight, Qaddafi had told Mengistu in the presence of a CIA mole in the Ethiopian government that he was going to have Reagan killed; he had soon afterwards repeated the assertion in a phone conversation intercepted by the National Security Agency (NSA). Over the next three months reports of Libyan plotting against Reagan and high U.S. officials reached Washington from a number of independent sources, including a Lebanese defector who claimed to have participated in preparing the hit team and passed several lie detector tests. Many officials such as Lillian Craig Harris, an Arabist for State Department intelligence, were skeptical of the reports.[55] However, deputy CIA director Bobby Inman, who was well respected in Washington for not being a ''Reagan administration ideologue'' and had better access to the intelligence traffic than Harris and others, said there was ''hard and convincing evidence. . . . We had information about the planning of the attempt. The Libyans intended to hit a presidential convoy in the United States.''[56] A flood of news leaks ensued, and rumors about Libyan hit squads entering the United States became one of the major news stories of 1981. Extraordinary security measures were taken, including stationing of antisniper patrols on the White House roof; security was also tightened at U.S. embassies in Turkey and Greece, where Libyans were reported to be staking out U.S. officials. The Libyan community in the United States was put under permanent surveillance. The administration prepared plans for a naval blockade or air raids against Libya in the event of further Libyan attempts on U.S. officials or facilities, and stern warnings were sent to Tripoli. Qaddafi apparently felt obliged to back down, but Reagan's revulsion toward him had further grown, and the episode had prepared the way for further steps against Libya under contemplation within the administration.[57]

On December 10, at the height of the tension over the hit squad stories, President Reagan issued a call for all Americans to leave Libya and U.S. passports were declared invalid for travel to the Jamahiriyah, with only journalists exempted. Most of the Americans did reluctantly leave, and the U.S. oil companies replaced them with nationals of other countries, while some Americans remained in management and consulting roles even in Libya's state oil company. Meanwhile liberals and conservatives alike in Congress were calling for a halt to Libyan oil imports, whose levels had for years shown an inverse relation to the downward trend in U.S. Libyan political relations. After a delay to give U.S. citizens time to depart from Libya and to allow for consultations with allies and regional friends, the administration on March 10, 1982, announced a boycott on importation of Libyan oil, the requiring of licenses for all exports to Libya except food and medical supplies, and the barring of export of oil and gas technology, high technology equipment, and equipment of potential military usage. The other NATO countries refused to join the sanctions and purchased much of the oil made available by the embargo. The sanctions did hamper Libya economically, and even three years later their effects were still being felt there, but the allies' refusal to join greatly weakened their impact.[58]

In 1982 and 1983 the administration's focus on Libya would primarily concern regional containment rather than terrorism. In April 1982 Libya-backed commandos entered Niger (to sabotage uranium mines and take French technicians hostage) and Tunisia, despite both countries' having undertaken rapprochement with Tripoli in the preceding two months. Clandestine terrorist activities by Libya continued during the year, but by the standards of the Qaddafi era, Libya was on its best behavior in 1982; the State Department did not attribute any terrorist incidents to direct Libyan responsibility. The relative moderation of Qaddafi's behavior and his unexpected withdrawal from most of Chad in November 1981 were attributed to his desire to obtain the chairmanship of the OAU (which would come about if a quorum of nations attended the OAU conference in Tripoli) and to the military pressure of the United States. In June, Hissen Habré's forces defeated the government of Goukouni Oueddei in Chad, bringing a major victory for U.S. policy. Two boycotts of attempted OAU summits in Tripoli ensued, with the admission of Polisario and the question of whether Habré's regime or Goukouni's government-in-exile should be seated as the ostensible causes, although antagonism toward Qaddafi on the part of African regimes actually played a major role. Therefore, Qaddafi's bid for the OAU chairmanship was foiled, to Washington's glee.[59]

In early 1983 Qaddafi perceived that the Israeli invasion of Lebanon and the controversial Western troop deployment in Beirut had created an atmosphere ripe for his taking the offensive again. Even as accurate rumors of an impending invasion of Chad circulated, Qaddafi moved a large part of his air force to the air base at Kufra in southeastern Libya, preparing to attack Khartoum in coordination with pro-Libyan revolutionary cells in the city, with intent to bring down Nimeiry. The *Washington Post* would report in 1987 that what Qaddafi did not know was that the revolutionary cells were Sudanese secret agents carrying out a scheme conceived by the Nimeiry regime and later joined by the governments of Egypt and the United States when they saw that Tripoli had been lured. In the late form of the plan, when Qaddafi launched his attack, the Egyptian air force would launch a devastating counterattack against the Libyan air force, aided by U.S. AWACS surveillance planes and, if necessary, KC–10 and KC–135 refueling tankers. The three allies hoped to teach Qaddafi a lesson that would deter him from further destabilization of his neighbors. An ABC News leak on February 16 about movement of the AWACS and the aircraft carrier *Nimitz* scuttled both Qaddafi's attack and the planned counterattack. The Reagan administration publicly claimed success in deterring Qaddafi from moving against Sudan[60] (which *was* ironically the case), and Shultz uttered his memorable line: "Qaddafi is back in his box where he belongs."[61]

Nonetheless, in May the forces of GUNT (Transitional Government of National Unity) advanced southward in Chad, with their leader Goukouni reluctantly playing the role of a Libyan puppet; the Jamahiriyah's Islamic Legion, regular ground forces, and air force made victories over Habré's forces possible. Within the constraints it faced, the Reagan administration responded vigorously: it persuaded President Mobutu of Zaire to send troops to shore up Habré, sent $25 million in military aid to Chad, sent the aircraft carriers *Eisenhower* and *Coral Sea* to take up positions off the Libyan coast, dispatched two AWACS to Egypt, and quite importantly, pressured France to intervene in its traditional role as protector of the central government in Chad. President François Mitterrand, who had criticized his predecessor Giscard d'Estaing for interventions in Africa, rejected Habré's initial request for French troops. On August 6, as Habré fared poorly, the United States sent eight F–15s and two AWACS to Sudan, stating that the AWACS were to assist French troops deployed on behalf of Habré, although the French had not yet decided to deploy troops.[62]

Finally, spurred on by a Libyan-sponsored radical coup in Upper Volta and additional pressure from the francophone states in Africa but openly resentful of U.S. nagging, Mitterrand sent troops to Chad, and the Libyans eventually halted their advance. Qaddafi resumed calls for unity between Libya and Chad, and the French drew a line across the map of Chad, creating a tacit partition of the country into a Libyan-occupied northern half and a southern half protected by France and administered by Habré, but with some degree of armed dissidence. The Reagan administration was disappointed that the French, apparently preferring to preserve their oil and arms trade with Tripoli, refused to strike at Libyan troops and secure their retreat.[63] However, Washington could be pleased with the preservation of President Habré's regime, which would see better days. As a stalemate developed in Chad, the Reagan administration's attention was drawn to troubles farther east that would have a significant impact upon its actions toward Libya.

NOTES

1. John Wright, *Libya: A Modern History* (Baltimore, Md.: Johns Hopkins University Press, 1982), pp. 84, 116; Lorna Hahn with Maureen Muirragui, *Historical Dictionary of Libya*, African Historical Dictionaries, no. 33 (Metuchen, N.J.: Scarecrow Press, 1981), p. 81; John K. Cooley, *Libyan Sandstorm* (New York: Holt, Rinehart & Winston, 1982), p. 57; Richard B. Parker, *North Africa: Regional Tensions and Strategic Concerns* (New York: Praeger, 1984), p. 67; Gideon Gera, "Libya and the United States—A Relationship of Self-fulfilling Expectations?," in *The Middle East and the United States: Perceptions and Policies*, ed. Haim Shaked and Itmar Rabinovich, Collected Paper Series of the Shiloah Center for Middle-Eastern and African Studies (New Brunswick, N.J.: Transaction Books, 1980), p. 198. Qaddafi and his followers joined an abortive plot to sabotage the foreign bases after the 1967 war (ibid.).

2. *Washington Post* (hereafter cited as *WP*), 22 Apr. 1986; P. Edward Haley, *Qaddafi and the United States since 1969* (New York: Praeger, 1984), pp. 5, 22–24; Parker, p. 68; Miles Copeland, quoted in Martin Kramer, *Political Islam*, The Washington Papers, vol. 8, no. 73 (Beverly Hills, Calif.: Sage Publications for the Center for Strategic and International Studies, Georgetown University, 1980), p. 87.

3. Wright, pp. 144–45; Cooley, pp. 64, 71–72, 93, 96–100, 160, 230–31; *Washington Times* (hereafter cited as *WT*), 1 Sept. 1986; Hahn with Muirragui, p. 81; David Blundy and Andrew Lycett, *Qaddafi and the Libyan Revolution* (Boston: Little, Brown, 1987), p. 70; Haley, pp. 20, 23, 171; Parker, p. 71. Wheelus Field, renamed Uqba bin Nafi by the Libyans, ironically became among other things, a site for training of terrorists and a stopover point for Soviet aircraft supplying Moscow's client regimes in Africa (John W. Amos II, *Palestinian Resistance: Organization of a Nationalist Movement* [New York: Pergamon, 1980], p. 246; *WT*, 1 Sept. 1986).

4. Haley, pp. 5, 24; *Facts on File*, 18–24 Dec. 1969, p. 824; Wright, p. 138; Cooley, p. 100.

5. Ruth First, *Libya: The Elusive Revolution* (New York: Africana, 1975), p. 242.

6. Gera, p. 199.

7. Ibid., p. 200; *WP*, 12 June 1972.

8. *New York Times* (hereafter cited as *NYT*), 12 June 1972.

9. Ibid.; Gera, pp. 200–201; *WT*, 1 Sept. 1986; Roger Kelly, "Ghaddafi, President and Patron of World Terrorism," *Far Eastern Economic Review*, 6 Jan. 1978, p. 43.

10. Haley, pp. 24, 170, 171, 227; U.S. Department of State, *U.S.-Libyan Relations since 1969*, prepared by David D. Newsom, Current Policy No. 216 (Washington, D.C.: Government Printing Office, 1980), p. 3; Gera, pp. 201–2; Cooley, pp. 249, 251; *Libya's Foreign Adventures*, Conflict Studies, no. 41 (London: Institute for the Study of Conflict,

1973), p. 7; Hahn with Muirragui, p. 80; *The Middle East*, 6th ed. (Washington, D.C.: Congressional Quarterly, 1986), pp. 112–13.

11. Haley, p. 282; Martin Sicker, *The Making of a Pariah State: The Adventurist Politics of Muammar Qaddafi* (New York: Praeger, 1987), p. 114; *Times* (London), 28 Jan. 1986; Gera, pp. 202, 205.

12. Haley, p. 5; Steve Posner, *Israel Undercover: Secret Warfare and Hidden Diplomacy in the Middle East* (Syracuse, N.Y.: Syracuse University Press, 1987), p. 111; *Wall Street Journal* (hereafter cited as *WSJ*), 19 Feb. 1981; Anthony Lake, "Third World Radical Regimes: U.S. Policy under Carter and Reagan," *Headline Series*, no. 272 (1985), p. 22; Cooley, pp. 80–81; Blundy and Lycett, pp. 152–53. Carter ordered that the episode be kept secret (*WP*, 20 Apr. 1986).

13. Parker, p. 68.

14. Haley, pp. 149, 176–77; Hahn with Muirragui, pp. 78–79; Cooley, pp. 252–53; Sicker, pp. 114–15, 120–21.

15. Haley, pp. 79, 171–75; Dept. of State, *U.S.-Libyan Relations*, pp. 3–4.

16. Haley, pp. 175, 228; Yossef Bodansky, "Soviet Military Presence in Libya," *Armed Forces Journal International* 118 (Nov. 1980):89; Cooley, p. 261; Vincent S. Kearney, "The Greening of Libya," *America*, 19 Jan. 1980, p. 39; *WP*, 27 July 1980.

17. Haley, pp. 111–18; "Why the U.S. Must Take a Stand on Qaddafi," *Business Week*, 3 Mar. 1980, p. 41; U.S. Department of State, *Libya under Qadhafi: A Pattern of Aggression*, Special Report No. 138 (1986), p. 7.

18. Haley, pp. 124, 127, 227–28; Hahn with Muirragui, pp. 79–80; Dept. of State, *U.S.-Libyan Relations*, pp. 4–5.

19. Abdul Kasim Mansur (pseud.), "Oman: Some Competence, and Some Corruption," *Armed Forces Journal International* 118 (Nov. 1980):68; I. William Zartman and A. G. Kluge, "Heroic Politics: The Foreign Policy of Libya," in Baghat Korany and Ali E. Hillal Dessouki, *The Foreign Policies of Arab States* (Boulder, Colo.: Westview, 1984; Cairo: The American University in Cairo Press, 1984), p. 189; Haley, pp. 224–25; Oye Ogunbadejo, "Qaddafi's North African Design," *International Security* 8 (Summer 1983):164; Cooley, pp. 200–201.

20. Cooley, p. 82.

21. Hahn with Muirragui, p. 80.

22. Daniel Yankelovich and Larry Kaagan, "Assertive America," *Foreign Affairs* 59 (1981):705.

23. Ogunbadejo, p. 164; Lisa Anderson, "Qadhdhafi and the Kremlin," *Problems of Communism* 34 (Sept.-Oct. 1985):38; Brian Crozier, "Moscow's Libyan Tool," *National Review*, 6 June 1986, p. 26; Haley, pp. 250, 254; Bob Woodward, *VEIL: The Secret Wars of the CIA, 1981–1987* (New York: Simon & Schuster, 1987), p. 85; Cooley, p. 82.

24. *WP*, 14 Jan. 1986; Haley, p. 274.

25. Lake, p. 32.

26. To its credit, the Carter administration, in contrast to its NATO allies, had firmly insisted to Qaddafi that improved relations with the United States could only come if Libya abandoned its support of terrorism (Haley, p. 174) and had formally branded Libya (as well as several other countries) as a terrorism sponsor starting in 1979. Only in 1981, however, did Qaddafi truly begin to feel pressure for his terrorist activities.

27. Haley, p. 197.

28. Cooley, pp. 227, 271, 273; Haley, pp. 255–58, 275; Sicker, pp. 119–21; David

C. Martin and John Walcott, *Best Laid Plans: The Inside Story of America's War against Terrorism* (New York: Harper & Row, 1988), p. 74; *NYT*, 7 June 1981; Lake, p. 32.

29. Haley, pp. 292–97; *NYT*, 25 Apr. 1982.

30. *WP*, 26 Mar., 20 Apr. 1986; *NYT*, 5, 8 Jan., 17 Apr. 1986.

31. Woodward, pp. 96, 97, 157; Jennifer Seymour Whitaker, "Africa Beset," *Foreign Affairs* 62 (1984): 757; *Focus on Libya*, Aug.-Sept. 1987.

32. "Is Covert Action Necessary?," *Newsweek*, 8 Nov. 1982, p. 55; Martin and Walcott, pp. 79, 262; *Focus on Libya*, Aug.-Sept. 1987, June 1988; *WP*, 30 Nov. 1986; State Department Background Briefing: Situation Report on Libya, 9 Apr. 1987, LEGISLATE, 220166; "A Plan to Overthrow Kaddafi," *Newsweek*, 3 Aug. 1981; Woodward, pp. 158–60.

33. Cooley, pp. 284–85; *Focus on Libya*, Sept. 1985.

34. *NYT*, 22 May, 2 Sept. 1986.

35. *Focus on Libya*, Dec. 1985; Bodansky, pp. 89–90, 92; "Libya Was Ready," *Foreign Report*, 24 Apr. 1986, p. 3; Gordon H. McCormick, *The Soviet Presence in the Mediterranean*, Rand Paper Series, no. P–7388 (Santa Monica, Calif.: Rand Corporation, 1987), pp. 14, 20.

36. Bodansky, p. 89. For example, some Libyan runways were lengthened far beyond the needs of Libyan aircraft but appropriately for Soviet Backfire bombers, such as the one that visited Libya in July 1981 (Cooley, p. 240).

37. *NYT*, 1 Mar. 1981; Wright, p. 142.

38. Jean-Francois Revel, "The Terrorist Strategy," *Encounter*, June 1986, p. 37; Sicker, p. 32. One terrorism expert's tabulation of attacks by a selection of highly active Middle Eastern groups in the 1968–1986 period counted twice as many attacks directed against France as attacks directed against the United States (Xavier Raufer, *La Nébuleuse: Le Terrorisme du Moyen-Orient* [Paris: Fayard, 1987, p. 372]).

39. Terrorism was prominent in anticolonial struggles in Morocco, Algeria, and South Yemen, and the Muslim Brotherhood waged notable terrorist campaigns against the regimes of Nasser in Egypt and Assad in Syria. Terrorism was a great problem inside Iran, both before and after the fall of the shah, and, of course, since 1975 terrorism has become everyday political intercourse within Lebanon. In the 1970s, Turkey was devastated by terrorism, fomented to a significant extent by the Soviet bloc. The Polisario guerrillas waged terrorism against foreign fishing boats off the coast of Western Sahara. Terrorist attacks against exiles on a smaller scale than those of Qaddafi were undertaken by Iran, Syria, and Libya's neighbors in the Maghreb (Parker, p. 84). Perhaps most importantly, terrorism has been employed as a "tool of statecraft" by Middle Eastern regimes against one another, providing deniability in most cases and proving far less costly than overt warfare (*WP*, 23 Apr. 1986). Thus the president of North Yemen was assassinated in 1978 via a letter bomb from the government of South Yemen, and the governments of Iran and Iraq engaged in a harsh terrorist war against one another for several months in 1980 before the outbreak of conventional war. The seizure of the Iranian embassy in London was a part of this terrorist war (Dennis Pluchinsky, "Political Terrorism in Western Europe: Some Themes and Variations," in *Terrorism in Europe*, ed. Yonah Alexander and Kenneth A. Myers [New York: St. Martin's Press, 1982], p. 65; Yossi Melman, *The Master Terrorist: The True Story of Abu Nidal* [New York: Adama Books, 1986], p. 133).

40. The debate in the West over terrorism was in some ways parallel to the debate

over criminal justice: should criminals be dealt with sternly or looked upon as "victims of society" not fully accountable for their actions? An apt passage from Nietzsche quoted in a letter to the *New York Times* published after the April 1986 attack on Libya reads, "There is a point in the history of a society when it becomes so pathologically soft and tender that among other things it sides even with those who harm it, criminals, and does this quite seriously and honestly. Punishment somehow seems unfair to it" (*NYT*, 1 May 1986).

41. Charles Krauthammer, "Terror and Peace: The 'Root Cause' Fallacy," *Time*, 22 Sept. 1986, pp. 97–98; Brian M. Jenkins, *Future Trends in International Terrorism*, Rand Paper Series, no. P–7176 (Santa Monica, Calif.: Rand Corporation, 1985), p. 6; *Christian Science Monitor*, 12 Sept. 1985; Charles Russell and Bowman Miller, *Portrait of a Terrorist*, cited by Stephen Segaller, *Invisible Armies: Terrorism into the 1990s* (San Diego: Harcourt Brace Jovanovich, 1987), p. 291; Walter Laqueur, "Terrorism—A Balance Sheet," in *The Terrorism Reader: A Historical Anthology*, ed. Walter Laqueur (New York: New American Library, 1978), p. 255.

42. *NYT*, 2 Sept. 1986.

43. Neil Livingstone, *The War against Terrorism* (Lexington, Mass.: Lexington Books, 1982), p. 38. According to the profile of Risks International, the average terrorist is from a middle- or upper-class family and has 2.5 years of college education ("The Rise of World Terrorism," *U.S. News & World Report*, 8 July 1985, p. 27).

44. *WSJ*, 15 Oct. 1987. Most commentators would probably agree that the Palestinian *intifadah* begun in 1987 has done far more for the Palestinian cause than many years of terrorism. This creates a problem for Middle East experts who for years explained Palestinian terrorism by saying that the Palestinian people had no other way to dramatize their grievances.

45. Memphis *Commercial Appeal*, 4 Feb. 1987.

46. "The Libyan Problem," *Department of State Bulletin* 83 (Oct. 1983): 78. Were Qaddafi to succeed in bringing down the Bourguiba regime in Tunisia, a significant blow would have been inflicted upon the West, and it could have been anticipated that the country would become the newest lair of international terrorists.

47. *WP*, 27 July 1980.

48. Jenkins, *Future Trends*, pp. 5, 14; Edward A. Lynch, "International Terrorism: The Search for a Policy," *Terrorism* (New York) 9 (1987):47; Ray S. Cline and Yonah Alexander, *Terrorism as State-Sponsored Covert Warfare* (Fairfax, Va.: Hero Books, 1986), p. 53.

49. "Appointment in Tripoli," *Economist*, 19 Apr. 1986, p. 11.

50. Parker, p. 69; Haley, pp. 226–27, 274–77; Cooley, pp. 266–69; Gera, p. 201; W. Hays Parks, "Crossing the Line," U.S. Naval Institute *Proceedings* 112 (Nov. 1986): 41–43; *NYT*, 20 Apr. 1986; Crozier, "Moscow's Libyan Tool," p. 26.

51. Haley, pp. 260, 282–87; *WP*, 27 July 1980; Martin and Walcott, p. 78; Posner, pp. 122–25.

52. Haley, pp. 134, 262; Woodward, pp. 181–82; *NYT*, 22 Apr. 1986; *Times* (London), 28 Jan. 1986; "Worldwide Chronology of Terrorism—1981," *Terrorism* (New York) 6 (1982): 285.

53. Larry Pressler, "Libya," *Department of State Bulletin* 87 (Jan. 1987):88.

54. *Facts on File*, 12 Mar. 1982, p. 178; Haley, p. 290; Martin and Walcott, p. 372.

55. Woodward, pp. 167, 181–82; Martin and Walcott, pp. 72–73; Haley, pp. 263–64.

56. Blundy and Lycett, p. 6.

57. Woodward, p. 184; Blundy and Lycett, p. 6; Haley, pp. 261–70; Cooley, p. 269; "Searching for Hit Teams," *Time*, 21 Dec. 1981, p. 18; *WP*, 26 Mar. 1986; "Hitting the Source," *Time*, 28 Apr. 1986, p. 23.

As the Iran-Contra scandal raged in 1987, information emerged about how Iranian businessman Manucher Ghorbanifar's bad reputation with the CIA had developed partly because the latter adjudged the information on the Libyan hit squads that he provided as fabricated. This was soon embellished in press reports into a story that Ghorbanifar was the original and/or primary source of the information on plotting to assassinate Reagan, which was not the case.

58. Parker, p. 70; Haley, pp. 288, 290; *WP*, 12 Apr. 1985, 14, 30 Jan. 1986; Zartman and Kluge, p. 185; "Barter Deals Push Libyan Oil Output Up," *Arabia: The Islamic World Review*, no. 20 (Apr. 1983), p. 53; *WSJ*, 10 Apr. 1985.

59. Parker, p. 60; Zartman and Kluge, p. 190; Philippe Decraene, "Tunisia," in *Britannica Book of the Year, 1983* (Chicago: Encyclopaedia Britannica, 1983), p. 676; idem, "Niger," in *Britannica Book of the Year, 1983* (Chicago: Encyclopaedia Britannica, 1983), p. 554; Roger Wall, "Politics and Poverty in the Sahel," *Africa Report* 28 (May-June 1983):63; *WP* 9 Apr. 1986; Dept. of State, *Libya under Qadhafi*, p. 7; Haley, p. 274; Mary-Jane Deeb, "Qaddafi's Calculated Risks," *SAIS Review* 6 (Summer-Fall 1986):159; John de St. Jorre, "Africa: Crisis of Confidence," *Foreign Affairs* 61 (1983):678–80.

60. Haley, pp. 301, 308–9; *WP*, 12 July 1987.

61. Haley, p. 309.

62. Ibid., pp. 317–19; *Middle East Contemporary Survey*, vol. 8: *1983–84*, ed. Haim Shaked and Daniel Dishon (Tel Aviv: Dayan Center for Middle Eastern and African Studies, The Shiloah Institute, Tel Aviv University, 1986), p. 589; Ellen Laipson, "U.S. Policy in Northern Africa," *American-Arab Affairs* 7 (Fall 1983):53; J. A. Allan, "Libya," in *Britannica Book of the Year, 1984* (Chicago: Encyclopaedia Britannica, 1984), p. 486.

63. Parker, pp. 72, 73; Mireille Duteil, "France and Africa," *France Magazine*, no. 8 (1987), p. 24; Haley, p. 320; Laipson, p. 54; Allan, "Libya," in *Britannica Book of the Year, 1984*, p. 486.

3

The United States and Libya on a Collision Course

Seven days after his inauguration, in a brief but widely reported passage in a speech welcoming the American hostages home from Iran, President Ronald Reagan had declared:

Let terrorists be aware that when the rules of international behavior are violated, our policy will be one of swift and effective retribution. We hear it said that we live in an era of a limit to our powers. Well, let it also be understood, there are limits to our patience.[1]

It was a vow that the president would find difficult to keep. The inspiration for the promise of "swift and effective retribution" was obviously the military reprisal policy of Israel. Israel, however, a small country with few friends and little to lose, has a strong national consensus on the use of military force, a press subject to censorship in military matters, a geographical location close to the bases of its terrorist enemies, an overseas presence not so ubiquitous as to give terrorists targets to attack literally anywhere in the world, and a significant degree of endurance in its national character. In every one of these aspects Israel was antithetical to the United States. Reagan's promise of retaliation against terrorism nonetheless took on a significance of its own.

THE REAGAN ADMINISTRATION BESET BY TERRORISM

When the Reagan administration deployed Marines in West Beirut in 1982 it had not realized that it had fallen into a trap that would bring great humiliation to the United States. The Marine presence in Beirut stimulated not only shelling from the hills but, more importantly, an anti-Western "Islamic Jihad" terrorist campaign, as well. The campaign was carried out by Iran with Syria's blessing through the Hezbollah (Party of God), a Lebanese Shi'ite organization created by Tehran, possessing family ties to the Iranian leadership, intimately entwined with the Iranian Revolutionary Guards in Lebanon, and openly professing obedience to the Ayatollah Khomeini.

On April 18, 1983, the U. S. embassy in West Beirut was devastated by a car bomb that killed 63 persons, including 17 Americans; the CIA bureau in Lebanon was reportedly wiped out. In an attack actively aided by Syria and, reportedly, radical PLO operatives, one of the most powerful conventional bombs ever built killed or mortally wounded 241 Marines on October 23. Hezbollah's bombing of the American embassy annex in East Beirut on September 20, 1984, killed 24 persons, including 2 Americans, and wounded the U. S. ambassador to Lebanon. Islamic Jihad bombings whose consequences are still being felt today were carried out on December 12, 1983, against the American and French embassies and several other targets in Kuwait by Hezbollah and Tehran's Iraqi terrorist vassal al-Dawa, killing 4 persons and injuring 63.[2]

The impact of the Islamic Jihad campaign upon U. S. policymakers was enormous. Secretary of State George Shultz, a former Marine, was most deeply affected: he (and outside observers as well) blamed the terrorist campaign for the withdrawal of the Marine contingent, which he felt to be an essential support for American diplomatic objectives in Lebanon, and for the collapse of his beloved project, the Israel-Lebanon peace treaty. The previously strong influence of the State Department's Arabists over Shultz evaporated, and he became personally obsessed with military punishment of terrorism. The Reagan White House meanwhile became haunted with the specter of terrorism becoming the sort of deadly domestic political liability that it had been for Jimmy Carter in the Iranian hostage crisis.[3]

THE ISSUE OF RETALIATION AGAINST TERRORISM

The issue of transnational military retaliation against terrorism, which became a subject of heated debate both inside and outside the administration, was a qualitatively different issue from the issue of military retaliation by a government against terrorists in areas under its own sovereignty (not likely to arise for the United States), the issue of returning the conventional fire of the militias and the Syrians in Lebanon, the issue of military hostage rescue operations, and the issue of violent covert action against terrorists. Only a few nations had ever undertaken transnational military retaliation against terrorism, and the United States was not among them. In the public debate over the issue, from 1983 through the U. S. air raids on Libya in 1986, former Secretary of State Haig was the most dedicated advocate outside government for retaliation, and the Middle East experts led in opposing it.

In this debate the Middle East experts naturally brought out all of their above-mentioned arguments against the very concept of confronting terrorism, such as its not addressing what they saw as root causes and so forth. Additionally, they argued that retaliatory attacks served to scuttle the the Middle East peace process and that the United States should not undertake them because they would stimulate hostility in the Arab world; being generally unfavorable to punishing terrorism with nonmilitary sanctions as well, the Middle East experts seemed to believe that counterterrorist policy should be limited to silent defensive measures such as tightening airport security and police and intelligence work. Retaliatory strikes, they maintained, would only legitimize violence in the eyes of Middle Eastern youth, breed more terrorists, and create a cycle of violence. A number of Middle East experts would confidently assert in 1986 that the Israeli air raid on PLO headquarters in Tunis on October 1, 1985, was the cause of the *Achille Lauro* hijacking six days later and of the Rome and Vienna massacres of December.

Furthermore, the Middle East experts made the argument that military force can avail for nothing against terrorism. This was in part a component of the notion that military force has lost its utility in the complex modern world, held by the Carter administration and a vast body of Europeans. Also involved was the image fostered by the Middle East experts of terrorists as an invincible variety of fighters, not susceptible to being deterred, dissuaded, disheartened, or even discouraged in any way; attacking them would only satisfy their craving for martyrdom. The suicide bombing attacks in Lebanon greatly enhanced this image. Israel's policy of retaliation was adjudged a complete failure by the Middle East experts: after all, they reasoned, terrorist attacks against Israel still take place. Finally, there was the assertion, repeated by many in addition to the Middle East experts, that violent retaliation constituted fighting terrorism with terrorism and that the government that carried it out lowered itself to the same moral level as the terrorists; often, though not always, this idea was premised upon the killing of innocent civilians along with the targeted military or terrorist personnel.

The latter viewpoint naturally aroused strenuous objections. To posit a moral equivalency between terrorists targeting and killing noncombatants on the one hand and governmental forces unintentionally killing noncombatants in military attacks upon military or terrorist targets on the other hand, amounted to utter pacifism, eliminating any distinction between normal warfare and terrorism or between war and war crimes. As one commentator pointed out, "An inflexible rule against civilian casualties would make any military action virtually impossible" and an "absolute prohibition on civilian casualties provides the terrorist [or any kind of aggressor] with an invincible shield."[4]

The Middle East experts always desired to see the United States pursue the policy that would play well in the Muslim Middle East, which is unsurprising for regional specialists. Washington policymakers would be unwise not to contemplate the effect of their decisions upon opinion in the region, but it was far from clear to many observers that America's overall best interests were always served by pursuing the policy that would be popular in the Muslim Middle East,[5] particularly when such a stance entailed passivity in the face of terrorism. A number of heterodox Middle East specialists emphasized the cliché that "the Arabs respect power." As for the Middle East peace process, the historical record showed that when Arab regimes were truly interested in such diplomacy, they did not allow themselves to be dissuaded for long by military strikes against terrorism.

That the task of overcoming terrorism is an extremely formidable one is beyond denial, but terrorists are not in fact properly viewed as oblivious to comparisons of benefits with risks. A number of terrorism experts pointed out that, contrary to popular impression, terrorists preferred low-risk actions, and that suicide terrorists were not typical. According to some researchers, the suicide car bombers were typically *not* occupational terrorists, but individuals of vulnerable personal circumstances coerced into single operations; a number of them are believed to have been tricked into thinking they would have a chance to escape before the explosion killed them. Terrorists taking hostages inside Israel or seizing embassies in various part of the world eventually became rare because of the application of military force in such situations.[6] Against the argument for refraining from military reprisals lest new terrorists be created was the stark reality that there was already a more than adequate supply of willing young men for terrorist recruiters in the Middle East, because of the Arab-Israeli conflict, regional traditions, and a complex set of domestic political, social, economic, and religious tensions[7] over which the United States had scant influence.

It must be stated that the Middle East experts certainly exaggerated the extent to which terrorism was the result of reprisals against terrorism. The *Achille Lauro* hijacking was revealed to have been planned months before the Tunis air raid; the revelation doubtless came as no surprise to students of terrorism. There is evidence as well that points to the likelihood that Abu Nidal was planning airport massacres, including the Rome and Vienna attacks, before the Tunis air raid.

While acknowledging that reprisals could provide stimulus for more terrorism, proponents of retaliation against terrorism asserted that more terrorist attacks were coming anyway and that simply allowing terrorists to attack with impunity was providing powerful incentives for more terrorism. They contended that defensive measures alone against terrorism could not suffice and that retaliation against terrorists by the United States would produce a deterrent effect; retaliation for the sake of retaliation was not what they advocated and was rejected by President Reagan from the start.[8] Proponents of retaliation usually believed that more than one reprisal would be necessary to produce the deterrent effect, but this raised a number of questions, including: were the American people sufficiently rid of the "Vietnam syndrome" to be willing to endure a protracted struggle? Haig seemed to go even further in spring 1986 when he advocated "the punishment necessary to defeat the terrorists, not a 'tit for tat' which leaves to them the choice of escalation."[9] His proposal sounded as though it would require an invasion, something the Israelis had tried without lasting success in 1982.

An ancillary aspect of the debate over punishing terrorism involved the possibility of clandestinely tracking down and killing terrorists, a policy for which Israel was most famous and that Jordan and America's NATO allies Spain and Turkey had also pursued at times. American terrorism experts were apparently more likely to favor this option than that of overt military retaliation; the prospect of greater precision was seen as one of its major advantages. However, until terrorism became drastically worse, the political costs of such a policy seemed to most serious observers, particularly those in the government, to outweigh the benefits.

As noted above, there were a number of differences between the United States and Israel that greatly weakened the analogy between the two countries as military punishers of terrorism, but there could possibly have been lessons in Israel's experiences for U. S. policymakers if those limitations were kept in mind. Although Israel indeed continued to suffer terrorism, it should be clear to the thoughtful observer that the country's terrorism problem could quite conceivably have been far worse than it was. Israeli military retaliation influenced Egypt and Jordan to lose interest in supporting terrorism and led to those two countries and Syria becoming unwilling to allow their territory to be used as springboards for terrorist attacks; it did, however, take the Israelis a long time to achieve those results.[10] Only the absence of a strong central government (even before 1975) prevented the same results from being achieved in Lebanon. The Israelis could not by a policy of air strikes over Lebanon persuade the PLO fedayeen to give up terrorism, but there was a logic for Jerusalem in maintaining at least some level of military retaliation. Had the Israelis allowed the PLO to strike at them with impunity, the Israeli public would have become demoralized, and the Palestinians would have experienced a sense of triumph that would doubtless have spurred them to more and more terrorist attacks.

A second case study on transnational military retaliation against terrorism available to Reagan administration officials (although it is not known whether they considered it) involved France and the Polisario guerrillas in 1977, when the latter were fighting against Mauritania as well as Morocco. Polisario in 1977 had launched a terrorist campaign aimed at driving French citizens out of Mauritania and thereby dealing the latter country a crippling economic blow. In May and October, the guerrillas had murdered two French civilians and kidnapped a total of eight more. Paris had no way of locating the hostages in the desert expanses, so it resolved to respond to Polisario's terrorism with air strikes. French Jaguars began attacking Polisario in early December 1977, and the guerrillas quickly decided to release the French hostages. France's military pressure sufficed to persuade Polisario to cease attacking French citizens and to concentrate fully on its ongoing guerrilla war against Morocco and Mauritania.[11] Therefore, the limited historical experience with transnational military retaliation against terrorism did not offer hope that it would persuade terrorist groups to shut down operations altogether, but did suggest that it might persuade states to stop supporting or harboring terrorists and that it might persuade the latter to abandon attacks on a country that was a secondary target for them. In spite of the high number of anti-American terrorist attacks in the world, the United States was not typically the primary target of a particular group.

THE ADMINISTRATION GRAPPLES WITH RETALIATION

As one former U. S. official has stated, "American foreign policy is made less by design than by struggle."[12] Arguments of both the Middle East experts and of advocates of retaliation against terrorism were represented within the Reagan administration, and the issue of responding to terrorism added turmoil to a conflict-ridden foreign policy apparatus. Secretary of State Shultz and Secretary of Defense Caspar W. Weinberger disagreed on most serious policy issues, compounding their long-standing personal antipathy, and top officials (including Shultz) sometimes concealed diplomatic maneuvers from other top officials. The most fundamental problem was the passivity of a president whose interest in foreign affairs was known to be weak, his failure to referee among factions and impose decisions upon them.[13]

There was great divergence of outlook within the government upon the use of military force in general. The CIA and the Pentagon, uninformed stereotypes notwithstanding, were strong proponents of caution; it was believed that this was caused by the agencies' respective traumas: for the Pentagon, the experience of Vietnam, especially having to fight without popular support, and for the CIA, the pillorying it received in the scandals of the mid–1970s. Robert C. "Bud" McFarlane, like Shultz, was a former Marine and was deeply affected by the October 1983 bombing, which took place a week after he assumed the post of national security adviser; he was favorable to using force,[14] and in a deliberate effort to counterbalance the perceived timidity of the large bureaucracies, he assembled on the National Security Council (NSC) staff activists whose motto was "There are no problems, only opportunities."[15] Secretary Weinberger was the administration's leading proponent of military procurement and its leading opponent of military action, a juxtaposition not really illogical in the bureaucratic context. He was not only sensitive to the things that could go wrong in military operations, but also, surprisingly, seemed more worried than did the secretary of state about the overseas ramifications of American use of force. President Reagan himself was said to be more cautious about using force than many of the people around him and was particularly susceptible to being swayed against it by Weinberger. The Grenada mission was reported to have been made possible by the presence of Shultz and McFarlane, but not Weinberger, with the president on his golfing weekend in Georgia.[16]

Although no officials would openly differ with the president on his endorsement of the principle of reprisals against terrorism, there was in effect a division into "dove" and "hawk" factions on the issue in the administration. The reported members of the dove faction were Weinberger, the Joint Chiefs of Staff and the Defense Department as a whole, Vice-President George Bush, the CIA as an agency, and the State Department regional bureaus. The reported hawks were Shultz and some political appointees at the State Department; McFarlane, his deputy Adm. John Poindexter, and the NSC staff; Pentagon advocates of the special operations forces; and CIA director William Casey. Further problems included inefficiency in interagency coordination on responses to terrorism. The status of the State Department as the lead agency on terrorism met with widespread disapprobation in the government, including the CIA, which was reluctant to forward sensitive intelligence because of the department's reputation for leaks. There was permanent tension between counterterrorism bureaucracies and regional bureaus, the latter resenting the existence of the former. The Middle East attracted the lion's share of attention regarding terrorism, and here came into play the often ugly rivalry between pro-Arab and pro-Israeli government officials. Meanwhile in the Pentagon, U. S. military planning was still overwhelmingly focused on the Soviet threat, to the neglect of confronting terrorism and other forms of "low-intensity conflict."[17]

The Lebanon terrorist attacks prompted Reagan and some of his advisers again to speak periodically in public about reprisal against terrorism. According to administration formulations, retaliation when it took place was to be "proportionate," not indiscriminate, not directed at civilians (or, sometimes, not even putting them at risk), but directed at "those responsible," or "the perpetrators," or targets associated with them. The administration therefore tacitly required itself to have very precise intelligence about terrorist acts; such actions as the Israelis sometimes took in striking one PLO faction after an attack from another PLO faction were obviously ruled out. Whether punishing a terrorist group or a state sponsor was envisioned was not always clear, but the former seemed more often to be the case. Many statements seemed to suggest the clumsy scenarios of using air strikes to execute vigilante justice on specific gunmen or specific terrorist leaders like Abu Nidal. Although the administration viewed all forms of state support for terrorism as aggression, its officials made it clear that a government would have to be found to have ordered or participated in a specific action in order to become a candidate for military retribution from the United States. This unfortunately seemed to encourage outlaw regimes to give vital aid and generalized guidelines to terrorists while leaving them to choose the specific targets, but it was the only politically realistic position for the administration in the circumstances, given the widespread reluctance (even among many terrorism experts) to hold governments accountable for specific acts. Repeatedly talking in public about reprisals had its costs: the administration thereby made itself subject to increased pressure from domestic commentators to act and made itself look weaker vis-à-vis the terrorists when it did not act. Nonetheless, speaking publicly about retaliation first was necessary in the U. S. political context if the administration had any intention of ever carrying out such action.

President Reagan had promised after the Marine headquarters bombing in 1983 to deal justice to those who had directed it, and the counterterrorism hawks in the government seemed to have overcome the opposition of Weinberger and the Joint Chiefs of Staff when bombs were actually loaded on Navy planes for a joint strike with France, also victimized by a suicide bombing on October 23, against Shi'ite terrorists in the Bekaa valley. However, Weinberger's continuing objections, fears of killing civilians, and Marine commandant Gen. PX. Kelley's fear that his men in Beirut would be worse off afterwards delayed U. S. participation, and the French became impatient. So on November 17, the day after the Israelis had punished the Shi'ites for a third suicide bombing, French jets alone struck targets outside Baalbek. The French characterized the strikes as retaliation on behalf of both themselves and the United States. Although there were civilian casualties,[18] the raids drew very little international condemnation or even attention. France's retaliation neither worsened nor lessened the problem of Shi'ite terrorism.

National Security Decision Directive 138, signed by the president on April 3, 1984, established in principle a U. S. policy of preemptive and retaliatory strikes against terrorists, but actually implementing such a policy was another thing altogether. Shultz in his frustration launched a campaign of speeches aiming "to get the American people on board" for retaliation against terrorism.[19] The high point of Shultz's oratorical campaign was his speech "Terrorism and the Modern World," delivered in a New York synagogue on October 25, 1984. The secretary of state declared that terrorism "is a contagious disease that will inevitably spread if it goes untreated,"[20] praised the example of the Israeli people's commitment to the fight against terrorism,[21] and asserted that experience showed that "one of the best deterrents to terrorism is the certainty that swift and sure measures will be taken against those who engage in it."[22] He went on to say:

The outcome may be that we will face a choice between doing nothing or employing military force. . . .

The public must understand *before the fact* that there is potential for loss of life of some of our fighting men and the loss of life of some innocent people.

The public must understand *before the fact* that some will seek to cast any preemptive or retaliatory action by us in the worst light and will attempt to make our military and our policymakers—rather than the terrorists—appear to be the culprits. . . .

If we are going to respond or preempt effectively, our policies will have to have an element of unpredictability and surprise. And the prerequisite for such a policy must be a broad public consensus of the moral and strategic necessity of action. We will need the capability to act on a moment's notice. There will not be time for a renewed national debate after every terrorist attack. We may never have the kind of evidence that can stand up in an American court of law. But we cannot allow ourselves to become the Hamlet of the nations, worrying endlessly over whether and how to respond. . . . Fighting terrorism will not be a clean or pleasant contest, but we have no choice but to play it.

. . . If terrorism is truly a threat to Western moral values, our morality must not paralyze us; it must give us the courage to face up to the threat.[23]

The immediate response to the speech well illustrated the administration's divisions over retaliation against terrorism. George Bush referred to Reagan's recent remark in a presidential debate that "we want to retaliate, but only if we can put our finger on the people responsible and not endanger the lives of innocent civilians."[24] Responding to Shultz's statement about the potential for loss of life, the vice-president said: "I don't agree with that. I think you have to pinpoint the source of the attack. We are not going to go out and bomb innocent civilians. . . . I don't think we ever get to the point where you kill 100 innocent women and children just to kill one terrorist."[25] The president first endorsed Shultz's speech, then appeared to distance himself from it, and then was supportive again all in the same day. Comments to the *New York Times* by State Department and Pentagon sources were strikingly different in tone.[26] Bush and much of the news media seemed to think that Shultz was advocating recklessness, but the secretary of state was actually seeking to cultivate public support for retaliation that incorporated a realistic understanding of the nature of an act of war.

Weinberger, meanwhile, made a speech in November that seemed to be at least partially a response to Shultz's synagogue speech. He warned that "employing our forces almost indiscriminately and as a regular and customary part of our diplomatic efforts would surely plunge us headlong into the sort of domestic turmoil we experienced during the Vietnam war, without accomplishing the goal for which we committed our forces."[27] He laid down what came to be known as the "six commandments" for guiding decisions on using force; many generals applauded them, but some complained that if rigorously followed the guidelines would prevent any U. S. military action short of World War III.[28]

MORE QADDAFI ADVENTURISM, 1984–85

Meanwhile, Washington had continued watching Libya with concern, and 1984 was a particularly strong year of Qaddafi outrages. In December 1983 Algeria had rejected his plea for admission to its Maghreb friendship treaty with Mauritania and Tunisia on the basis of Libya's refusal to settle its border dispute with Algeria. Qaddafi's response came in the form of a commando attack launched from Libyan territory on the Algeria-Tunisia gas pipeline on January 9. The colonel's displeasure with King Hussein's moves relative to the Palestinian issue was expressed in the burning of the Jordanian embassy in Tripoli on February 18; Hussein responded by severing diplomatic relations with Libya. On March 10, during a stopover in Ndjamena, Chad, two bombs probably intended to detonate in mid-flight exploded aboard a French passenger jet, injuring 25 people; the incident was traced to Libya. Six days later a Libyan jet attempted to bomb a radio station in Omdurman, Sudan, which had given air time to anti-Qaddafi Libyans; the bombs hit nearby buildings rather than the radio station, killing five people. At the request of Egypt and Sudan, the United States again sent AWACS planes to Egypt. Around this period, the Jamahiriyah acquired the services of an Iraqi named Ihsan Barbouti to put together a chemical weapons manufacturing plant.[29]

Soon after a series of Libyan terrorist bombings in Great Britain, a diplomat inside the people's bureau in London, acting on specific orders from Tripoli, sprayed submachine-gun fire upon an NFSL demonstration, killing Constable Yvonne Fletcher and injuring ten others on April 17. Britain therefore broke diplomatic relations with Libya, and the Qaddafi regime arrested six Britons in Libya as hostages. During the prolonged standoff at the People's Bureau, the Associated Press reported the recent Libyan annexation of northern Chad; Libyan flags, currency, and identity cards as well as people's committees were imposed, arousing the resentment of the local populace.[30] In his annual June 11 speech commemorating the evacuation of Wheelus Field, Qaddafi called the Americans "the sons of bitches"[31] and urged people "to ally even with the devil against America."[32] Making the unsubstantiated claim that the United States had planned the NFSL's assault on the Bab al-Aziziyya barracks, he declared, "We are capable of exporting terrorism to the heart of America. We are also capable of physical liquidation, destruction, and arson inside America. . . . As for America, which has exported terrorism to us, we will respond likewise."[33]

The next month known Libyan terrorists were refused entry to the United States as Olympics journalists, prompting the Jamahiriyah's withdrawal from the Los Angeles Olympics. Earlier, two Libyans had been arrested in Pennsylvania for trying to buy handguns with silencers, the Qaddafi regime's weapon of choice for assassination. At the same time, mines laid from a Libyan ship, apparently with the motivation of making difficulties for Egypt, were damaging a total of nineteen merchant vessels in the Red Sea, prompting an international uproar in which the United States and other Western countries, as well as the Soviet Union, sent minesweeping vessels to the area.[34]

In August Saudi Arabian authorities aborted a plan for over eight hundred Libyan revolutionary committee members to seize the Grand Mosque in Mecca during the Hajj, in spite of the ostensible rapprochement between Libya and Saudi Arabia at that period; the "pilgrims" were disarmed and sent back to the Jamhiriyah. In September the government of Chad discovered a Libyan plot to kill President Habré and his cabinet with an attaché case bomb. The year 1984 was a major one for the campaign against Libyan exiles, and the Qaddafi regime suffered a major embarrassment in November, when it publicly boasted of its "execution" of Libyan exile leader and former Prime Minister Abdul Hamid Bakoush in Egypt. Cairo promptly announced that it had intercepted Qaddafi's hit squad (which also had orders to kill high-ranking Egyptian officials and to bomb vital installations in the capital) and had shown Libyan agents fake photographs of Bakoush shot and bleeding. The captured terrorists told of Libyan plots to murder heads of state. Embarrassingly, the Libyan announcement concerning Bakoush had come even while President Mitterrand held meetings with Qaddafi on Crete concerning the fact, exposed by Washington, that Libya, unlike France, had not honored a recent agreement to withdraw troops from Chad. Qaddafi promised yet again to withdraw troops from Chad, but he subsequently doubled them instead. Despite his bad behavior, Qaddafi held his third meeting in four months with a NATO leader, visiting Spanish prime minister Felipe Gonzalez in December in Majorca, at which time he with characteristic manners publicly warned his hosts of "hell and destruction" should Spain remain in NATO.[35]

After making an arrest in February 1985, Italian authorities discovered a Libyan plot to assassinate the American, Egyptian, and Saudi Arabian ambassadors to Rome.[36] In a March 3 speech in Tripoli, Qaddafi warned foreign countries, including the United States, Great Britain, and West Germany, that they would face terrorist attacks if they stood in the way of the Jamahiriyah's "legitimate and sacred action—an entire people liquidating its opponents at home and abroad in plain daylight."[37] In May, an assassination ring plotting to kill Libyan dissidents in four U. S. states was broken up, with sixteen Libyans arrested and a Libyan diplomat at the United Nations declared persona non grata.[38]

In this period Qaddafi's words and deeds indicated that, inspired by the example of how Iranian-sponsored terrorism had humiliated the United States and virtually driven it out of Lebanon, the Libyan leader had developed a renewed enthusiasm for the potential of terrorism for striking blows at the power of the United States and his other enemies. In a March interview with the pro-Libyan Beirut daily *Al-Safir*, Qaddafi lauded the "extremism and suicide operations" of the Lebanese Shi'ites,[39] and stated that if the Arabs did not "stand up for themselves for once and divorce the United States for good, . . ." he would take up his "responsibility and start terrorism against Arab rulers."[40] At the end of March, Qaddafi hosted a terrorist convention, at which the Pan-Arab Command for Leading the Revolutionary Forces in the Arab Homeland was founded, with the colonel himself as leader and with Syrian and Iranian support. At the convention, Qaddafi gloried in the joining together of "the extremist Muslim and the extremist Marxist"[41] and stated that "our task here in this command is to see to it that the individual suicidal operations are transformed into an organized action which will reap fruit, defeat the enemy, and liberate the [Arab] nation."[42] Repeatedly returning to the theme of the Lebanon suicide bombings, he declared: "When a fida'i said I want to die in exchange for 300 Americans in Lebanon, it was carried out and America, with all its might, with 50 warships close to Lebanon's shores, could not prevent this. . . . We want to resurrect this spirit in this nation, the spirit of martyrdom. We want every one of us to say. 'I have decided to die just to spite America."[43] The command's own statement called for consolidating ties with the Soviet Union and for its members "to confront imperialism, especially U. S. imperialism, and work toward liquidating its military bases and foil its schemes and strike at its positions and interests wherever they might exist."[44] In an April 1 speech Jalloud extolled the Shi'ite terrorists, who had decided that their "only communication with the Zionists, the Americans, and the enemies of the Arab nation will be through T.N.T. and car bombs," and announced Libya's determination to bring about similar "heroic operations."[45] Interestingly enough, on May 22 Egyptian authorities sealed off streets and foiled a plot by Libyan intelligence to destroy the American embassy in Cairo with a truck bomb. Egyptian officials characterized the incident as part of a broader terrorist campaign by Libya.[46]

ABU NIDAL

The attempted bombing had employed operatives of one of the participants in the new Pan-Arab Command, the terrorist organization of Abu Nidal (aka Sabri al-Banna), known officially as Fatah—the Revolutionary Council (FRC) but using numerous cover names. The Abu Nidal group, highly professional and extremely vicious, was the most active transnational terrorist group of the mid–1980s. It was very much a part of the international terrorist network, maintaining cooperative links with rejectionist groups within the PLO, Hezbollah, the AS-ALA, and European Marxist groups, receiving aid from Syria, Libya, and, to a secondary degree, Iran and South Yemen, and furthermore enjoying a variety of privileges in Eastern European countries, including transit privileges, scholarships for its terrorists in Poland, offices in Poland and East Germany for a profitable network of commercial enterprises, and bases in Bulgaria and in Greece—in the latter case with the permission of the Papandreou government, but unbeknown to Greece's NATO allies.[47]

Abu Nidal was a Fatah chieftain who had created his own terrorist group in 1973, establishing permanent links with Libya very early on; he had fallen out with Arafat in 1974 and was expelled from the PLO for plotting the chairman's assassination. He had gained his reputation as a "terrorist subcontractor" in 1976 through a campaign of attacks against Syria on behalf of its archenemy Iraq. Remarkably, during a period of Iraqi-Syrian rapprochement in late 1978, Abu Nidal was allowed to set up an office in Damascus, and he maintained a foothold in both Syria and Iraq during the next five years, with some fluctuation as to which country was his primary sponsor. Toward the end of 1983, Iraq yielded to pressure from its new moderate Arab friends and from the United States and closed down the FRC's operations in Baghdad.[48]

In 1983 or 1984, Abu Nidal began to move part of his operations to Libya, and the Libyan press periodically reported personal meetings between him and Qaddafi.[49] A convergence seemed quite logical for the Libyan dictator and the reclusive Palestinian terrorist, both known for views which were extreme even by radical Arab standards. By mid–1985 a great mass of mostly clandestinely-derived evidence, including intercepted telephone conversations, had firmly convinced the U. S. government that the main operational base of the FRC as well as Abu Nidal himself had shifted from Damascus to Tripoli, a conclusion which was before long shared by the great majority of the terrorism-watching community abroad as well.[50] The FRC retained its Eastern European assets, an office described as a "skeleton operation" in Damascus and a camp outside the city, an office in Druze territory outside Beirut, a base near Sidon, and at least four camps in Syrian-controlled territory in Lebanon (where it enjoyed close cooperation with agents of Libya, Syria, and Iran), but Qaddafi now, in a fateful move, took up the role of Abu Nidal's primary patron. The FRC enjoyed the full array of Libyan aid, including funding, training, arms, and logistical support, and Tripoli increasingly involved itself in the group's operations.[51] Particularly in the wake of the attempted embassy bombing, Reagan administration officials had cause for concern over the increasingly intimate ties between Qaddafi and the deadliest Palestinian terrorist group.

WASHINGTON DECIDES SOMETHING MUST BE DONE

Meanwhile, Shi'ite terrorism had continued to plague the United States. In December 1984 several U. S. citizens had been tortured and two murdered in an Iranian-directed hijacking of a Kuwait Airways plane. After a February Islamic Jihad announcement that an American hostage had been sentenced to death, Shultz sent Tehran warnings of dire consequences if any of the American hostages were killed; U. S. officials were indeed seriously considering the possibility of striking Iran in response to a future terrorist incident. In April and May, bombings in a Madrid restaurant frequented by U. S. soldiers and near a Riyadh, Saudi Arabia, compound housing U. S. military advisers were claimed on behalf of Islamic Jihad; in the Madrid incident 24 persons were killed and 82 injured, including 15 Americans.[52]

In June, the terrorism problem came to seem unbearable. On June 14 Hezbollah terrorists hijacked TWA Flight 847; the hijacking was soon taken over by Hezbollah's rival Amal, and 39 Americans were held in Beirut in what seemed like a repeat of the Iranian hostage crisis. On June 19 a bomb exploded at the international airport in Frankfurt, West Germany, killing a man and 2 children and injuring 42 people, including 1 American; suspicions that the Abu Nidal group was responsible would be confirmed by West German authorities in 1988. On the same day El Salvadoran guerrillas murdered 13 people at adjoining sidewalk cafes in San Salvador, including 2 U. S. businessmen and 4 marine embassy guards in civilian clothes. On June 23, Sikh terrorists in almost simultaneous bombings killed 2 baggage handlers at a Tokyo airport and destroyed an Air India jet over the North Atlantic Ocean, killing 329 persons, including 19 Americans, in one of the worst terrorist incidents in history.[53] Statistical

evidence, meanwhile, bore out the general impression that terrorism was increasing in volume and lethality.

After the June 19 attacks Reagan called terrorism "a war against all of civilized
society" and declared that "our limits have been reached,"[54] but he nonetheless
followed Weinberger's advice and decided against a proposal for a military strike
inside Nicaragua in response to the San Salvador murders upon being informed
by McFarlane that civilian deaths would be likely.[55] A broad clamor for military
retaliation for the TWA hijacking arose in the United States, while the president
was forced to admit his helplessness and frustration in the situation. Joy over
the ultimate release of the hostages was tempered by the widespread perception
that the administration had caved in to the terrorists; neo-conservative Norman
Podhoretz fulminated against "surrender . . . betrayal . . . loss of nerve . . .
shame."[56] There were reports that Libya had played some role in abetting the
TWA hijacking, but if so it was apparently not a major role.[57]

The trauma of the TWA hijacking was later credited by administration officials
for the forging of the political will needed to make possible eventual military
action against Libya in 1986. Even as the hostages prepared to return home, a
White House official told the *Washington Post* that "the base for sustaining firm
action in the coming months"[58] against terrorism was emerging within the administration. In a July 8 speech aiming at increasing public support for counterterrorist action, Reagan said Americans "are not going to tolerate intimidation,
terror, and outright acts of war against this nation and its people"; denouncing
the international terrorism network and specifically citing Libya, Iran, North
Korea, Cuba, and Nicaragua, he declared: "We are especially not going to
tolerate these attacks from outlaw states run by the strangest collection of misfits,
Looney Tunes, and squalid criminals since the advent of the Third Reich."[59] In
late June the Task Force on Combatting Terrorism to be headed by Bush was
created, and one of the issues it was to consider was military retaliation against
terrorism.[60] Intense discussions on retaliation against terrorism took place within
administration circles, and an official informed the *Post* that "the difference now
is that everyone recognizes that we're going to have to hit back at the terrorists."[61]

In the 1984–85 period, the NSC staff had viewed U. S. policy toward the
increasingly aggressive Qaddafi as stagnant. The president had authorized it on
April 30 to lead an interagency review of Libya policy. With the whole phenomenon of terrorism under review in the wake of the TWA episode, the heightened sensitivity to it gave McFarlane an opportunity to attempt to break the
bureaucratic deadlock on Libya policy. Addressing a meeting of the National
Security Planning Group (NSPG)—the president, and his top foreign policy
advisers—shortly before Reagan's colon cancer surgery on July 13, the national
security adviser declared that diplomatic and economic measures had failed to
stop Qaddafi and that stronger action by the United States would be necessary.
The president, Casey, Shultz, and Weinberger all heartily agreed. Assignments
therefore were passed out: the CIA was ordered to plan possible covert action
against Qaddafi, the State Department was to develop further plans for economic

and political pressure, the Pentagon was to develop contingency plans for possible U. S. strikes on Libyan targets, and the NSC staff and the CIA were to explore possibilities for joint U. S.-Egyptian military action, which had reportedly come close to occurring in 1983, as mentioned above.[62] All in all, "the door was considered open for new ideas on how to deal with Qaddafi."[63] Although McFarlane found a consensus for toughening policy toward Libya, this did not imply inexorable commitment to military action against Libya regardless of Qaddafi's behavior. In subsequent weeks, Poindexter and McFarlane promoted an astonishing plan for an immediate Egyptian invasion of Libya with U. S. air support, but opposition to the plan by the Pentagon and by Shultz—who, despite his enthusiasm for counterterrorism, called it "crazy"—prevailed, and it never reached the president's desk.[64]

WHAT ABOUT SYRIA AND IRAN?

One of the lesser controversies surrounding the later April 14 air strikes against Libya was the assertion that Washington punished the Jamahiriyah and not Syria and Iran because the latter two countries were more potent military foes and attacking them would bring a far greater risk of provoking the Soviet Union to action. While there was some degree of truth in this, the situation was much more complex than such critics suggested. Similarly, some observers claimed that Libya was much less involved with terrorism than Syria, or than Syria and Iran, which was also a misconstruction of a fairly complex reality.

Evaluation of the three countries' roles in terrorism is complicated by their often interlocking nature. For example, concerning Palestinian terrorism there was in the 1980s an informal division of labor between Tripoli and Damascus: Libya provided the bulk of funding for the hard-line Palestinian groups, while Syria was comparatively poor and therefore expended far less money on terrorism; the two countries shared the arming and training; Syria played host to the headquarters of most of these groups after the Israeli invasion of Lebanon in 1982; and Syrian intelligence apparently tended to work more closely with the groups than did Libyan intelligence, whose technical expertise was no match for that of the Syrians. Libya's contribution to the overall infrastructure of international terrorism was greater than that of Syria and Iran and possibly of any other country. The Qaddafi regime was the closest thing in existence to a missionary society for world terrorism; the role of Syria and Iran with terrorists originating outside of the Middle East was much smaller. In the matter of fomenting specific acts, Iran and Syria had both played a greater role than Libya in the three years before mid–1985. Both countries were relative newcomers to the top ranks of state-sponsored terrorism, but their reputations were indelibly established by the Islamic Jihad bombings of 1983, whose impact surpassed that of any previous operations by Libya or any other government.

The issue of just how deeply Syria was involved in terrorism was a matter of deep dispute within Western governments. One school of thought saw Hafez

Assad as, in effect, the "grand maestro" of Middle Eastern terrorism. Nearly all Middle Eastern terrorist organizations other than Fatah were portrayed as being under the control of Syria. Syrian intelligence was seen as normally selecting their targets and closely supervising their lethal operations. Libya and even Iran were portrayed as comparatively peripheral sponsors.[65] Other analysts agreed that Syrian support of terrorism was a serious problem and that Damascus deserved far more public censure than what little it was receiving in the West (all of it from Washington), but they saw Assad as more cautious in terms of specific operations: it was felt he did not desire to provoke a serious confrontation with the West (or even Israel) and that he only preferred to use terrorism for his own selective tactical purposes, caring little about how well the terrorist subculture flourished. Whether it should have or not, Syrian involvement in an attempt to blow up an El Al airliner leaving London in 1986 genuinely amazed Western intelligence analysts.[66] There was a consensus that the ostensibly Palestinian group Saiqa was (despite its membership in the PLO) a mere appendage of the Syrian government, but no consensus concerning supposed Syrian control of other organizations. (Events in the 1986–88 period, including the rapprochement of allegedly Syrian-controlled, Damascus-based groups with Arafat and radical PLO groups' struggle against Syrian-backed Amal, demonstrated exaggeration on the part of the grand maestro theorists.) In 1985 the U. S. government was on record as portraying the worst terrorist threat in the Middle East as being not Syria or Libya but rather Iran.[67]

According to a former State Department official familiar with U. S. terrorism policy deliberations in the latter half of 1985, there was plenty of focus on sponsors of terrorism other than Libya, contrary to some reports. Vigorous debates over how to respond to Syrian support of terrorism were held. Many officials pressed for a harder U. S. line: not an immediate military attack, but moving up the escalation ladder in verbal and other pressure. In the immediate aftermath of the TWA hostage release, other U. S. officials did not want to appear ungrateful to Assad, who had used his influence to bring the crisis to an end; therefore Syria was not explicitly mentioned in the president's "Looney Tune" speech. Assad promised to do his best to gain the release of the remaining U. S. hostages held by Hezbollah, and some U. S. officials became very hopeful, but as time passed these hopes faded in the minds of most officials. Nonetheless, the U. S. assessment in this time period was that Syria was serving more as a constraint than an abettor on terrorism in Lebanon, apart from the Israeli "security zone," not because Damascus wanted to please the West, but because it felt its own interests threatened by too much turmoil in Lebanon. Proponents of a hard line against Syria pointed to Assad's continuing support for groups operating outside Lebanon, including the FRC, but other officials countered that Syria was not being particularly aggressive in terrorism against the United States per se. Though there were numerous terrorist acts in this period for which Syria was thought to be responsible, they were almost all directed against Jordanians, against the PLO, or in southern Lebanon against the Israelis and their allies.

Assad was not perceived as being on an ideological crusade against the West. There was not the slightest enthusiasm among European allies for confronting him, and the prevailing view in the U. S. government was that an aggressively punitive policy against Syria at this time would probably backfire. Military contingency plans for another strike against Syrian troops in Lebanon were held in reserve, but in view of Soviet guarantees Syria itself was regarded as off limits.[68]

The hostage issue was even more central in the case of Iran. In 1984 concern had grown in the NSC staff and with at least one senior CIA official about a projected turbulent succession in Iran and the possibility that the Soviet Union would be able to exploit the situation, while Washington's influence was non-existent. In Iran the faction of speaker of the parliament Hashemi Rafsanjani had spurred a decision to bolster the Islamic Republic's war effort by repairing its relations with various countries, including the United States, and feelers were sent out. On June 17, 1985, McFarlane sent Shultz, Weinberger, and Casey a draft on Iran policy that included a proposal to encourage Western countries to sell arms to Iran in order to revive Western influence within the country. Two days later, Rafsanjani, perceiving the way to Reagan's heart, sent a message expressing Iran's desire to do all it could to end the TWA crisis; the Iranians made good on this promise, and the president sent Rafsanjani a message of thanks and expression of hope for better relations with Tehran. About a week before McFarlane's presentation on Libya, he had received an Israeli official, of all people, bringing the message that the Iranians wanted a dialogue with the United States; the possibility of release of Hezbollah-held hostages in Lebanon was held out, but it would probably have to be accompanied by an American concession of reciprocal importance, such as permitting Israel to sell U. S. weapons to Iran. About a week after the presentation on Libya, the national security adviser secured approval to explore the matter further from the still-hospitalized Reagan, who had high hopes that Colonel Qaddafi's two allies could gain the release of the hostages. He did not seem to appreciate the twisting of his terrorism policy that ensued. McFarlane, however, must have felt some personal discomfort with the contradiction between stated U. S. policy and the initiative he was beginning to pursue with Iran, and it seems quite likely that he consciously or unconsciously tried to compensate for this unease by pushing hard for a tougher approach to Libya. A memorandum written by NSC staff member Lt. Col. Oliver North refers to an "understanding" between Iran and the United States on anti-American terrorism dating back to June of 1985, echoed in a memorandum by Poindexter.[69] There was indeed a remarkable abeyance of such acts by Tehran-linked groups from late July 1985, and perhaps earlier, to September 1986.

In retrospect, the Iranians appear to have played their hand very shrewdly with regard to terrorism. According to reports appearing in June 1985, Tehran had become alarmed at the possibility of American military reprisals. Indeed, if Iranian-backed Shi'ite terrorism against the United States had continued indefinitely at levels of the 1983–85 period, Washington policymakers would have eventually felt compelled to make a harsh response. (Later, in the 1987–88 period the United States demonstrated that, although not eager to do so, it was willing to confront Iran if necessary.) When the tactic of hijackings and bombings against the United States had given Iran about as much as it could hope for, Tehran clearly restrained its terrorist allies as a quid pro quo for secret U. S. arms shipments, with the already captured hostages in Lebanon as the primary lever for manipulating the United States. While Iran's sense of timing was perfect, it was the opposite with Libya: just as Tehran prudently altered its terrorist policies, Qaddafi embraced Abu Nidal and stepped into the vacuum, provoking genuine concern in Washington. Seeming to be motivated by the inspiring example of Iran's successful terrorism, he would ironically bring upon himself much of the wrath that successful terrorism had incited in the United States. Middle Eastern terrorism, however, was never Washington's only concern regarding Libya, a fact which many analysts have neglected. Subversion was another major concern. Syria did not undertake serious efforts to overthrow foreign governments (although it did contribute to making Turkey a more violent place than it would have otherwise been), and while Iran had some role in subversion, it did not appear at this point to be as great as that of Libya. Libya's increasing activities in Central America and the Caribbean,[70] its strong bid for influence in previously pro-Western Sudan, and its continuing occupation of northern Chad contributed to the conviction in Washington that something needed to be done about Qaddafi. Additional incentive was provided by the alluring possibility of somehow contributing to his downfall; no other belligerent radical leader in the world seemed so vulnerable.

A TURBULENT AUTUMN

A significant crisis occurred between Libya and its Arab neighbors in August and September 1985. It began with the expulsion from Libya of over thirty thousand Tunisian workers and ten thousand Egyptian workers, many of whom were forced to leave behind their passports, savings, and possessions. Given its already high unemployment, Tunisia was naturally distressed. In response to harsh criticism in the Tunisian press, Qaddafi sent the Bourguiba regime a threat of military action. Libyan warplanes violated Tunisian airspace, a Libyan sabotage team was discovered in a plot to blow up a tourist hotel, and a Libyan diplomat smuggled one hundred letter bombs into Tunisia addressed to journalists; several exploded, wounding two postal workers. Tunis in turn severed trade and diplomatic relations with Tripoli, whereupon Qaddafi froze nearly $10 million of Tunis Air assets. President Chadli Benjedid of Algeria showed support for the Tunisian government, moving troops to the Libyan border and flying on September 2 to Tunis to meet with Bourguiba. There were reports that units of the Libyan armed forces, upon being ordered to penetrate Tunisia, refused and attempted to move against Qaddafi instead. Algeria and Egypt held private consultations on the Libyan threat, and Admiral Poindexter secretly discussed with Egyptian officials in Cairo contingency plans for joint U. S.-Egyptian military responses to Libyan provocations.[71] President Mubarak had publicly warned that the Qaddafi regime would "some day be made to pay dearly"[72] for the expulsions, and there was some loose talk of war in case of a successful anti-Egyptian terrorist attack by Libya.[73]

In his annual coup anniversary speech on September 1, Qaddafi exclaimed: "We have the right to fight America, and we have the right to export terrorism to them."[74] Qaddafi's client, the Abu Nidal group, was meanwhile on a rampage, its terrorist activities at an all-time high. Among its attacks from July through September were at least two assassinations; bombings of two cafés in Kuwait on July 11, with 15 people killed and dozens wounded; and five major attacks upon tourists in Western Europe, including a grenade assault upon a tour group of handicapped Britons. In September Scotland Yard intercepted anti-personnel grenades meant to be used in an Abu Nidal assault, probably on passengers at London's Heathrow Airport, and Libya was directly implicated. Apparently this discovery was what led the Spanish police to uncover the close links between the Libyan embassy in Madrid and Abu Nidal's pivotal network in Spain. On the prompting of U. S. intelligence, the government of Greece arrested six Abu Nidal gunmen en route to South America to attack a U. S. embassy. At the same time the Abu Nidal group was working to set up a terrorist network within the United States itself. U. S. officials were particularly alarmed by Abu Nidal's indiscriminate attacks against Western civilian targets, which were an abrupt departure from his previous pattern (aside from his fondness for attacking European synagogues) and were felt to be contrary to the Syrian modus operandi. They had evidence of Libyan support for these attacks and felt it was no coincidence that this new pattern of activity had emerged after he moved his headquarters to Libya.[75]

After Israel's October 1 air raid against PLO headquarters in Tunis in retaliation for the murder of three Israeli tourists in Cyprus by Fatah terrorists, the United States received "overwhelming information" that if it vetoed a UN security council resolution condemning the raid, Libya would have a major opportunity to foster turmoil in Tunisia, perhaps leading to the destruction of the American embassy and even the overthrow of the Bourguiba regime. The administration did indeed abstain, despite its reserving itself the right to carry out actions along the same principles against terrorism.[76] Not long afterward there were intelligence reports that Libya was targeting the U. S. embassy and ambassador in Tunis. In the month of October there began a general pattern of Libyan collection of intelligence about U. S. facilities overseas, and U.S. intelligence intercepted messages from Tripoli ordering preparation of terrorist attacks against American targets. In November the State Department issued a travel advisory urging U. S. citizens to avoid Khartoum and recalled the U. S. ambassador for urgent consultations because of the presence there of known Libyan terrorist agents, whom Qaddafi had been pouring into Sudan since the overthrow of Nimeiry in April. To the distress of Washington, the new Sudanese military regime had signed a military assistance agreement with the Jamahiriyah and even allowed Libyan troops to occupy portions of the country.[77]

A pivotal event in the administration's struggle with terrorism was the October 7 seizure of the Mediterranean cruise ship *Achille Lauro* by terrorists of the pro-Arafat Palestine Liberation Front (PLF) faction headed by Abu Abbas, a member of the PLO Executive Committee; there would be rumors of a Libyan role in the affair. The United States prepared to storm the ship with its Delta Force team, but before such action could be taken, the Egyptian and Italian governments had made a deal with the terrorists, giving them safe conduct in exchange for the release of the passengers. However, as the Voice of Lebanon and Associated Press had already reported, the gunmen had murdered a passenger: it turned out to be Leon Klinghoffer, a wheelchair-bound sixty-nine-year-old Jewish American, who had been shot and dumped overboard. The American public was outraged, and Reagan's revulsion at the ruthlessness of the terrorists fueled his desire for militarily punishing terrorism. Available intelligence pinpointed the movement of the terrorists, and an NSC staff plan to intercept the Egyptian getaway plane was developed and implemented over the objections of the traveling Weinberger, who feared the impact on United States-Egypt relations. The successful capture of the terrorists brought euphoria to the administration, Congress, and the American people, and it boosted the president's confidence in the viability of applying military force against terrorism.[78]

Despite all the turmoil in the region surrounding the Tunis air raid, the *Achille Lauro* hijacking, and the U. S. interception of the getaway plane, Egypt, Tunisia, and Algeria continued in October and November to coordinate pressure against Libya. Around early October, President Reagan had signed a finding authorizing covert CIA military assistance to Libyan exile organizations seeking Qaddafi's overthrow; such aid was to be coordinated with states already aiding the exiles—Egypt, Algeria and Iraq. Shultz was reportedly the strongest proponent of the plan. Likewise in October the president issued orders for the CIA to increase its intelligence gathering on terrorist organizations and for the NSA to increase its monitoring of the communications of the governments of Libya, Syria, and South Yemen. During his Washington visit shortly after the *Achille Lauro* episode, Israeli prime minister Shimon Peres met with Casey, and thereafter Washington and Jerusalem significantly increased their exchange of intelligence on terrorism. The Israelis perceived that the Reagan administration was awaiting the right occasion to inflict a blow against terrorism.[79]

On November 3 the *Washington Post* published a front-page Bob Woodward story on the CIA Libyan project, which was leaked to the reporter of Watergate fame by Congress (as the FBI determined) and possibly also by bureaucratic opponents of covert action, with whom Woodward maintained a strong symbiotic relationship. The story related that narrow majorities of the two intelligence committees had supported the plan, but David Durenberger (R-Minn.) and Patrick Leahy (D-Vt.), chairman and vice-chairman respectively of the senate committee, had raised strong objections over possible violations of the prohibition on assassination, although there was no plan for the CIA to assassinate Qaddafi or encourage others to do so. Libya's neighbors reportedly withdrew from the plan upon its being publicly revealed, and the Reagan administration was livid over the leak, which greatly damaged its relations with the congressional committees. Qaddafi was quick to seize upon the very mention of assassination. He increased his verbal attacks on the United States and sought to use the Woodward story to rally support for himself in Libya and the Arab world.[80]

In the second week of November after a gun battle with police, four Libyan hit men seeking to kill prominent exile leaders were arrested south of Alexandria, Egypt. Shortly afterwards, Egyptian officials on the basis of interrogation of the captured terrorists warned of Libyan terrorist plotting in several countries, including Great Britain, Italy, and Austria.[81] On November 21, the "Libyan Revolutionary Officers, anxious to clash with the enemies of the revolution" after meeting with Qaddafi, issued calls for "the striking of American interests in the Arab homeland, . . . alliance with the live forces in Egypt," and "coming to settle accounts with . . . the traitorous ruler of Egypt."[82]

Two days later the same EgyptAir plane that had been recently intercepted by U. S. Navy jets was hijacked while making an Athens-to-Cairo flight by Abu Nidal terrorists using the cover name Egypt's Revolution. The plane landed in Malta, where the hijackers shot Israeli and American passengers; it was the first instance of women passengers being singled out for slaying and was apparently the first instance of a U. S. citizen being targeted and killed by the Abu Nidal group.[83] Shultz speaking on "Meet the Press" heatedly rejected the notion that firmness against terrorists would only lead to more terrorism and declared: "These people are not worth the time of day. . . . the way to get after these people is to get after them with both barrels."[84] President Mubarak sent troops to the Libyan border and sent to Malta an antiterrorist commando unit, but the unit's rescue effort was inept, and fifty-seven more people died from various causes. Egypt accused Libya of responsibility for the episode, an accusation that was generally believed in diplomatic and intelligence circles; according to a former State Department official, there was no particular controversy over it within the U. S. government. Intercepted Libyan conversations convinced U.S. officials that the Jamahiriyah was involved in the operation. Three of the four terrorists had flown to Athens aboard a Libyan jetliner, which was also suspected of carrying their weapons. The grenades hurled by the terrorists at the passengers during the Egyptian assault were later definitely traced to Libya. Sentiment in Washington for action against Libya was naturally increased by the episode.[85]

Meanwhile the United States was closely watching Libyan-Soviet relations. In an August 19 speech McFarlane had cited Moscow's support of Libya and Cuba as obstacles to improvement to superpower relations. Washington officials had undoubtedly been gleeful when Qaddafi's visit to the Soviet Union in October did not produce a friendship treaty and went poorly in general. The new Soviet leader, Mikhail S. Gorbachev, was reportedly repelled by Qaddafi's arrogance, and among numerous points of friction was the Soviets' demand for repayment of Libya's mounting debts in hard currency. At the November Geneva summit, marking the end of the six-year New Cold War, Reagan mentioned Libya to Gorbachev as one of the sources of U. S. distrust of the Soviet Union.[86]

A source of concern for U. S. policymakers at this time was the installation in Libya of its first Soviet SA–5 surface-to-air missiles, which were capable of shooting down U. S. reconnaissance aircraft, B–52 bombers, submarine hunters, and commercial aircraft (the fact that Qaddafi had not been above trying to sink the *Queen Elizabeth II* could not be forgotten). U. S. officials privately expressed to the Soviets their concern that the supply of SA–5s might encourage Qaddafi to take risks to which the United States would have to respond. The Soviets rebuffed these protests, after which the State Department on December 20 publicly denounced the SA–5 transfers, which stimulated increased tension between Washington and Tripoli and, reportedly, accelerated U. S. contingency planning for action against Libya.[87]

THE ROME AND VIENNA MASSACRES

In late December U. S. intelligence was hearing yet more reports of imminent actions by Libyan-linked terrorist groups, and these warnings were passed on to Western European officials. On the morning of December 27 in virtually simultaneous attacks at Rome's Leonardo da Vinci Airport (the site of previous Libyan- sponsored attacks in 1973 and 1981) and Vienna's Schwechat Airport, FRC terrorists attacked travelers with AK–47 assault rifles and hand grenades, firing indiscriminately although emphasizing the ticket counters of the Israeli airline El Al, and, in the Rome airport, the TWA counter as well. In the two attacks over 110 people were wounded and 20 were killed, including 5 Americans, 4 Greeks, 2 Mexicans, 2 Austrians, 1 Italian, 1 Israeli, 1 Algerian, and 4 of the Palestinian terrorists. One of the American victims was eleven-year-old Natasha Simpson, who after being blasted to her knees received an additional burst of gunfire aimed directly at her head; she became a symbolic martyr of terrorism. Within hours of the massacres, an Arab caller in Spain claimed responsibility for them on behalf of the Abu Nidal group, and this was soon confirmed by the surviving terrorists. Vivid television footage showed corpses and huge pools of the victims' blood on the airport floors, and President Reagan and the American people were enraged.[88]

During the terrorists' training in Abu Nidal's camps in the Bekaa valley they had been told they would mount a series of attacks that would start a world war. In both attacks, it was soon learned, the plans had included the seizure of hostages and forced flight of El Al planes to Tel Aviv, over which the aircraft were to be exploded. Another attack had been planned for the Madrid airport but was not executed. Two Arab terrorists who arrived in Brussels the day after the Rome and Vienna attacks and who were followed to an arms cache, were suspected of planning an assault at Brussels airport. The week before, a heavily-armed Palestinian trio reported to belong to the FRC was arrested in Greece; it was later thought to have possibly been a "backup team" for the Rome and Vienna attacks. The Italian newspaper *Il Tempo* reported that the lone surviving terrorist in Rome had said that the Abu Nidal group had prepared an airport attack for Paris also. Two days after the airport massacres French security agents captured three men preparing to bomb a Paris synagogue on behalf of Libya. The authorities soon secretly captured the men's leader, Farid Hassan, head of an Arab terrorist group named the Call of Jesus Christ, and they recruited him as a double agent to gather information on Libyan terrorism in Europe.[89] It appears that an almost unprecedented terrorist assault upon the West and Israel was intended for the 1985–86 holiday season.

The airport attacks immediately touched off an international crisis. The Israeli government swiftly issued harsh threats of retaliation, raising the tension. On December 29, to the shock and revulsion of the Italians and Austrians in particular, Libya's state news agency JANA reproached pro-Western Arab regimes for condemning the massacres and termed them instead " heroic operations," a description it continued to use for the next two weeks. That same day, U. S. spokespersons called attention to Libya's support for the Abu Nidal group. The next day, they issued stronger denunciations of Libya, noted the latter's praise for the airport attacks, called for other governments to join in diplomatic and economic pressures against Qaddafi, and also, without referring to Libya, made statements interpreted as giving Jerusalem a green light to retaliate for the massacres and reiterated the United States' right to respond with the military option if deemed appropriate.[90]

The administration's decision to reproach Libya in connection with the Rome and Vienna massacres was from the first subject to much criticism, but that was not really logical in view of the circumstances. Washington was certain that Libya had become Abu Nidal's chief patron, was working intimately with the group in terrorist activities in Europe, and had been involved in the Malta hijacking. Furthermore, it was a matter of public record that the popular German weekly *Der Spiegel* had recently published an interview granted by Abu Nidal at a villa near Tripoli, Libya, under his Fatah—the Revolutionary Council flag,[91] with the Palestinian terrorist declaring that he and Qaddafi "are linked by a deep and strong friendship . . . . He is a great help to us," and "If we have the chance to inflict the slightest harm to the Americans, we will not hesitate to do it. . . . In the months and years to come the Americans will think of us."[92] Abu Nidal himself was seen in a suburb of Tripoli on the day after the airport attacks. The first hard evidence of governmental support for the airport attacks emerged on December 30 when the Tunisian government revealed that the terrorists had used Tunisian workers' passports, which had been very recently confiscated by the government of Libya (apparently with such purposes in mind); this was quickly confirmed by Interpol in Paris. One of the surviving terrorists in Vienna stated that he worked for the "Al-Assifa" office of the FRC, which Austrian officials noted was in Libya;[93] *Il Tempo* reported that the surviving Rome terrorist had stated, "We have support from Qaddafi and maybe Syria."[94]

Journalists and West European governments intent upon inaction managed to put the focus on the question of a Libyan connection not to the Abu Nidal group but to the specific Rome and Vienna attacks themselves. Actually, since the passports did in fact establish a Libyan connection to the airport attacks, the question was, in effect, did the Qaddafi regime have foreknowledge of those specific actions? The indisputable fact of Libyan prescience of Abu Nidal's general policy of terrorist attacks in Europe was treated as irrelevant by many commentators. When Qaddafi made the decision to support the Abu Nidal group he knew full well that it was not a guerrilla army fighting the armed forces of any nation, but rather a gang of assassins and wanton murderers; therefore the Libyan dictator logically bore a clear responsibility when the Abu Nidal group engaged in its normal and indeed only type of activity.

Libyan foreknowledge of the Rome and Vienna massacres is virtually certain although proof of it has not yet been made public. U. S. officials have claimed to have such information, a body of evidence of Libyan sponsorship of the attacks beyond just the Tunisian passports, but have refused to divulge it publicly. Some officials have, however, privately stated that a Libyan people's bureau was involved and that Libya funded the Rome and Vienna gunmen.[95] A September 1985 meeting between Qaddafi and Abu Nidal had been reported by the Libyan news agency, and intelligence sources would claim that the two had agreed on a price list for different kinds of terrorist acts and that U. S., British, Israeli, and Egyptian citizens and installations would be attacked. Deputy Secretary of State John C. Whitehead stated in late January that Libya "paid for" the Rome and Vienna massacres, and *Newsweek's* April 7 issue cited Western intelligence sources to the effect that the colonel had paid a bonus of five to six million dollars for the attacks. *Newsweek* also reported that the surviving Rome terrorist had been in Libya three months before the attacks took place. Italy charged the Jamahiriyah with "financing logistical support" for the Rome attack. Libya was believed to have supplied weapons, which were not picked up until the terrorists were in Europe; as with the Malta hijacking, grenades used by the terrorists were later traced to a batch bought from Bulgaria by Libya in 1983.[96]

After several contradictory reports, on January 10, 1986, the interior ministers of Italy and Austria stated that the airport terrorists had been trained in the Bekaa valley of Lebanon and flown to Europe via Damascus; therefore, the Assad regime was early on under strong suspicion of having at least acquiesced in the attacks.[97] On January 24, State Department spokesman Bernard Kalb reiterated that evidence existed for Libyan support for the "individuals involved and the incidents" but noted that Abu Nidal appeared to have "drawn on" his "resources" in Syria and the Syrian-controlled Bekaa valley in the attacks. Kalb declared, "We believe that Syria should rid itself of Abu Nidal."[98] After mid-April 1986 the jailed Rome terrorist reportedly became more cooperative with his interrogators and a welter of contradictory press accounts concerning his supposedly implicating Syria ensued; the most persistent story was that one or more Syrian air force intelligence officers participated in the gunmen's training in Lebanon.[99] The Italian and Austrian governments never publicly confirmed that story or otherwise accused Syria of direct involvement in the assaults, but Italian authorities did assert that the final planning of the operations by Abu Nidal and one of his deputies before the terrorists' departure for Europe in November 1985 took place during one of the FRC leader's sojourns in Damascus. The notion of some commentators that the Rome and Vienna massacres were carried out by Abu Nidal at the behest of Syria remains entirely unsubstantiated, but there seems little reason to doubt Syrian culpability. This does not in turn exonerate Libya, and a number of sources have asserted joint Libyan-Syrian sponsorship of the attacks.[100]

WASHINGTON FASHIONS ITS RESPONSE

Admiral William J. Crowe, Jr., Chairman of the Joint Chiefs of Staff, took the initiative after the Rome and Vienna massacres to order planners to prepare military options in case the president decided upon a strike against Libya or Middle Eastern terrorists; an interagency group convened at the White House for similar duties. The Joint Chiefs sent to the vacationing commander-in-chief the essentially political recommendation that only targets in Libya associated with Abu Nidal be struck if a reprisal were ordered.[101] Speaking with aides in California, Reagan reportedly said, "I want to punish the right people. I don't want to lay waste the buildings of an area or a whole city and not know that we have hit the perpetrators"[102] and, "We ought to get them if we can, but let's not start World War III over it."[103]

On New Year's Eve Peres issued denunciations of Libya even more scalding than any ever issued by the Reagan administration.[104] On New Year's Day Qaddafi broke his silence in a fairly bellicose press conference. He called the activities of Palestinian terrorists "the most sacred action on earth," dared the United States and Israel to attack Libya, and declared that if they did, it would mean endless war in the Mediterranean, with not even trade and merchant ships left safe.[105] Furthermore, Libya would "pursue U. S. citizens on their streets and Jews in the streets of occupied Palestine."[106] Qaddafi seized and clearly relished the opportunity to hold almost daily sessions with Western correspondents; he hurled insults at Reagan, and a colorful war of invective between the two men ensued for a couple of weeks. Meanwhile his threat to carry out terrorist attacks in the United States stimulated much attention and concern there, and the FBI tightened its surveillance of Libyan nationals in the country.[107]

After press leaks about the U. S. contingency planning on January 1, the *New York Times* reported two days later that the Navy had moved planes to the aircraft carrier *Coral Sea* in case military action was ordered, and the next day there were reports of Navy EA–6B planes for eavesdropping and radar-jamming being sent from the United States to Sigonella, Sicily. Air Force F–111 fighter-bombers based in Great Britain secretly practiced for an attack on Libya with nonstop nightime runs to Canada and to Turkey. Libya went into a state of high military alert, while a wave of anti-Qaddafi jingoism began to sweep the American people, abetted by local radio announcers and T-shirt vendors. Meanwhile the Israelis were responding to hints from the United States (and reportedly Europe as well) favoring a strike on Libya by letting it be known that they were offended by the notion that they needed other countries' permission to strike against terrorism and that they should do the dirty work for such countries. They were not satisfied with their intelligence on terrorist targets on Libya and moreover were preoc- cupied with problems in their own vicinity and not inclined to open up a new front with ruthless Libya.[108]

In the U. S. government the consensus on retaliating against terrorism that had reportedly been reached the previous summer seemed to have broken down. After the Joint Chiefs of Staff had previously advised striking only targets linked to Abu Nidal, it was now found that they were unable to determine which targets in Libya were linked to him. Weinberger was opposing a strike for a number of mostly political reasons. Shultz disagreed with the insistence on a target linked to Abu Nidal and emphasized that the United States must no longer appear to be paralyzed in the wake of terrorist attacks. The National Security Council staff was the most enthusiastic lobby for action against Libya throughout this period, but, despite the impression later left by the Iran-Contra scandal, it was not dominating foreign policy.[109]

On the flight back to Washington on January 3, Reagan reviewed the military options with Shultz, White House Chief of Staff Donald Regan, and new national security adviser John Poindexter. The president made it clear that he was inclined toward economic rather than military retaliation on this occasion. The leading considerations were said to be fear that Qaddafi would take hostages from among the six hundred to fifteen hundred Americans in Libya (which Reagan would soon openly admit) and lack of a target linked to Abu Nidal. Other concerns were the possibility of killing Libyan and other civilians (especially important to the president); the possibility of killing Soviet advisers manning antiaircraft missiles as well; the possibility of U. S. planes being downed, and even having captured pilots be paraded in public by the Qaddafi regime; the responses of Arab governments, populaces, and terrorists; and, for Weinberger, world opinion in general.[110]

When President Reagan finally met with all his chief defense and foreign policy advisers on January 6, several decisions were taken. The only one that would be publicly announced was for further economic sanctions against Libya. Additionally, orders were given for more money and manpower for the CIA covert program to undermine Qaddafi, with more emphasis on cultivating dis- sident elements in the Libyan military. Reagan authorized expanding contingency plans to include U. S. support for an Egyptian attack of a preemptive nature on Libya, as well as the sending of another secret envoy to Egypt for discussion of such contingencies. In place of an immediate attack on Libya, the president said he wanted Qaddafi "to go to sleep every night" wondering what the United States might do; therefore the U. S. naval forces in the Mediterranean were to continue movements calculated to intimidate the Libyan leader.[111] Also around this time the decision was made to emphasize public and private diplomacy to call attention to Qaddafi's misdeeds in order to prepare the international climate for isolating him and for a U. S. military clash with Libya that might well come about before long; a State Department white paper on Libya which had been in preparation for several months was hurried into print without the planned stylistic polishing. A satellite was reportedly moved from an orbit over Poland to one over North Africa, for increased monitoring of Libyan communications, and Washington's allies were pressed for greater vigilance in monitoring Libyan diplomats, agents, and diplomatic pouches.[112]

There was another ironic juxtaposition of Reagan policies on Iran and Libya. A month earlier the arms-to-Iran policy seemed to have been killed at the NSPG level, but Israeli contacts with Poindexter and North had revived it only in the last few days. Amiram Nir had been sent to coax the Reagan administration, according to secret Israeli documents, because of Jersualem's fear (probably unwarranted) that efforts by Fatah would succeed in persuading Hezbollah to release the American hostages and therefore earn the PLO an entirely new standing in Washington. Earlier on January 6, Reagan signed a draft finding presented by Poindexter for another arms-for-hostages deal. Perhaps the Iran angle was on Regan's mind when he remarked during the meeting on Libya that the administration had no antiterrorism policy, drawing an angry rebuff from Shultz. Shultz felt obliged to defer to the president on the Iran contradiction in U. S. terrorism policy, while determinedly doing his utmost to make that policy vigorous in every other respect.[113]

After having listened to his advisers' disagreements over Iran policy earlier in the day, President Reagan in a news conference on January 7 announced that there was "irrefutable evidence" of Libya's role in the Rome and Vienna massacres and stated:

By providing material support to terrorist groups which attack U. S. citizens, Libya has engaged in armed aggression against the United States under established principles of international law, just as if he [*sic*] had used its own armed forces. . . .

Civilized nations cannot continue to tolerate in the name of material gain and self-interest, the murder of innocents. Qaddafi deserves to be treated as a pariah in the world community. We call on our friends in Western Europe and elsewhere to join with us in isolating him.[114]

Reagan called on all Americans to leave Libya and announced economic sanctions banning trade between the United States and Libya apart from import of news materials and export of humanitarian supplies, banning credit on loans to Libyan government entities, banning U. S. labor in Libya and transactions pertaining to travel between the United States and Libya except for journalistic purposes, and prohibiting economic transactions between Americans and the Libyan government, all upon pain of civil and criminal penalties. This meant the withdrawal of U. S. firms, which pumped three-fourths of Libya's oil and marketed at least one-third of its oil exports. The next day all Libyan assets in U. S. banks would be frozen.[115] Reagan made his warning to Qaddafi clear enough. The final statement of his speech was, "If these steps do not end Qaddafi's terrorism, I promise you that further steps will be taken,"[116] and in an interview three days later he said he was acting to remove "potential hostages" so as to "untie our hands with regard to whatever action might be necessary in the future."[117]

On January 8 Qaddafi, to a gathering of Western European ambassadors in Tripoli, emphasized Libya's "common interests" with Europe and dangled economic carrots; he also hinted that he might respond to U. S. pressure by drawing closer to the Soviet Union, and he warned, "If it comes to war, we will drag Europe into it" and "close our eyes and ears and hit indiscriminately . . . with suicide squads against towns, ports, etc."[118] Two days later, Reagan's good friend Prime Minister Margaret Thatcher of Great Britain served up a double no to the United States: she rejected economic sanctions on the ground that they "don't work" and characterized retaliatory strikes against terrorism as "against international law" and likely to cause "much greater chaos."[119] Meanwhile Reagan's deferral of military action was causing many observers to claim that the United States had shown itself a paper tiger[120] and that its bluster against terrorism was counterproductive when not backed up by action. On January 15 Qaddafi referred to the "receding threat of American military action"; he felt comfortable enough to condone the Rome and Vienna massacres more clearly than he had before and to state concerning various Arab groupings present in Tripoli, "I declare that we shall train them for terrorist and suicide missions and allocate . . . all the weapons needed for such missions."[121]

On the same day Shultz delivered an eloquent speech in which he declared, "We are right to be reluctant to unsheath our sword," but nonetheless "we can not opt out of every contest."[122] He warned of the consequences of allowing states like Qaddafi's Libya to acquire immunity in the pursuit of terroristic warfare and asserted that "state-sponsored terror will increase through our submission to it, not from our active resistance."[123] He raised the specter of state support leading to acquisition of far more deadly weapons, perhaps even nuclear weapons, by terrorists. Drawing upon State Department legal adviser Judge Abraham Sofaer, he made an obvious rejoinder to Thatcher as he vigorously asserted the legality of military strikes against terrorism.[124] The next day, while seeking to downplay differences with Shultz, Weinberger publicly criticized those who called for "instant gratification from some kind of bombing attack without being too worried about the details" and stated that any proposals for attacks should satisfy "the basic question of whether what we are doing will discourage and diminish terrorism in the future."[125]

THE ALLIES PRECLUDE NONMILITARY OPTIONS

Geoffrey Kemp, the senior Middle East specialist on the NSC staff from 1981 to 1985, recalling his travels with other administration officials, stated:

Although there was consensus within the administration, the Congress and amongst our European allies and Arab friends that Qaddafi was a menace and that his activities should be curtailed, the consensus evaporated when it came to recommendations about specific actions.

During private sessions, Arab and European statesmen were usually outspoken in their venom toward the Libyan leader. . . .

. . . European attitudes changed over the years from mild amusement about our "thing" over Qaddafi to cautious agreement that he was a problem and some remedy had to be found. Yet whenever it came down to the bottom line of "what shall we do about the man?" the silence was stunning.[126]

True to form, European governments one by one began ruling out diplomatic and economic sanctions almost as soon as U. S. officials publicly called for such measures, and the fact that the United States obliged their wishes by not attacking Libya made no difference. Italy's government did announce a ban on weapons transfers to Libya on January 9, and the conservative governments of Canada and Norway endorsed the call for sanctions against Libya. Canada's prime minister Brian Mulroney, a friend of Reagan, cited the "moral issue" and took three limited economic measures against Libya, but Norway decided to act only in concert with its European neighbors. In spite of the rebuffs already received, on January 15 the Reagan administration sent John Whitehead and State Department counterterrorism ambassador Robert Oakley on a tour of NATO capitals to present further evidence of Qaddafi's guilt, to press for partial economic and diplomatic sanctions, and to remind allies that terrorism as well as sanctions carried economic costs. The outlook for Whitehead and Oakley's mission was from the start bleak, an especially disgraceful situation in the context of concurrent well-publicized Interpol alerts about possible imminent attacks by Libyan-backed Abu Nidal squads on U. S. and Jewish targets in Scandinavia and the Netherlands.[127]

A number of reasons and excuses for the allies' reluctance to impose sanctions against Libya emerged. (Genuine doubt that Libya was promoting terrorism in Europe was *not* among them.) The leaders of West Germany and Great Britain did not want to increase the pressure upon themselves to impose sanctions upon South Africa. The need to keep Western doors open to Qaddafi so as not to drive him into the arms of the Soviets was cited,[128] though this was one of the least frequently heard arguments for refusing sanctions. The Europeans had long deluded themselves that their economic ties with Libya served to counterbalance the Soviet Union's military ties, but it has been noted that "Libyan willingness to purchase equipment from Western sources has nothing to do with political sympathies.''[129]

A likely unspoken factor in resistance to sanctions was a problem inherent in the structure of an alliance between a superpower and a number of much smaller democracies: opposition parties and a significant portion of the public in allied countries were prone to view cooperation by their governments with the United States as subservience.[130] Oakley testified later that efforts to obtain international cooperation against terrorism met with responses along the lines of ''Oh, this is an American crusade; this is an American obsession.''[131] In January and more often after the later U. S. military encounters with Libya, Europeans could be heard saying that rather than giving lectures, Americans, who had never faced terrorism on their own soil, should learn from their more expert allies. In fact, in the 1970s terrorist incidents had been more frequent in the United States than almost anywhere in the world,[132] and part of the credit for the tremendous reduction in terrorism on American soil in the 1980s went to the FBI, regarded by some as the best domestic terrorism-fighting agency in the world. As for the Europeans, they had obtained some notable successes in determined campaigns against domestic terrorist groups, but their abysmal record up to that point in dealing with Middle Eastern terrorism provided little worthy of imitation.

Even as the Qaddafi regime felt motivated to lobby vigorously against the imposition of European sanctions, European governments were declaring repeatedly that economic sanctions were ineffective and ''never worked,'' although the extent to which this idea truly motivated their reluctance was debatable. An exhaustive 1985 study had found that sanctions had been successful in 36 percent of cases overall and were yet more successful in destabilizing governments. Countries in economic distress were found to be particularly vulnerable to sanctions,[133] and Libya in the midst of the oil glut was just such a country. Experts believed that dramatic effects would be produced by the sudden withdrawal of the thousands of Western European technicians in Libya or by a boycott of Libyan oil, which accounted for more than 99 percent of Libya's exports, by Western Europe, which purchased more than 90 percent of that oil.[134]

Another frequently invoked argument against sanctions was that they would force the governments of the Arab world to rally around Qaddafi (as though such gestures were truly consequential) and produce a united front hostile to the West. Though they had long smugly congratulated themselves for understanding the Middle East better than did the Americans, many of the Western Europeans erroneously viewed their relations with Arab countries as indivisible and seemed not to understand that nothing was going to make the murderous Libyan dictator popular with other Arab leaders; their taking serious economic action against the West on his behalf was inconceivable even under different oil market conditions. In contrast to the Europeans' mental image of easily triggered Arab solidarity was the reality that the Arabs had really never united for anything since 1973; even the Israeli invasion of Lebanon in 1982 had only provoked more quarrels among them. Nonetheless, the Europeans found it hard to break out of their pattern of obsequious behavior toward the Arab world; this difficulty related to their having been intimidated, first by the fierce onslaught of Palestinian terrorism in the early 1970s and, second and more importantly, by the 1973 oil embargo, which had affected Europe more severely than it had the United States.

Another excuse was the assertion that Qaddafi would become more reckless and dangerous were he to be isolated. Beyond doubt, the fear that he would take hostages from among their nationals in Libya weighed upon the Europeans' minds; Qaddafi's willingness to do so was well established. Chancellor Helmut Kohl openly admitted this motivation; Qaddafi had taught him a lesson in 1983 when he had obtained the release of two Libyans charged with torturing Libyan dissidents in Bonn by arresting eight West Germans in Libya on trumped-up espionage charges.[135]

The reason why Europe's governments had so many potential hostages in Libya was the reason generally considered most important in their rejection of sanctions: greed. Libya was the sixteenth leading buyer of EEC exports; a British firm even sold execution chambers to the Qaddafi regime.[136] The pattern of placing economic interests ahead of combatting terrorism was nothing new for the Europeans,[137] and while the oil glut had increased Libya's vulnerability to economic sanctions, it had also increased the Europeans' incentive to remain in Libya because the Qaddafi regime had accumulated many millions of dollars in arrears for their completed work, and they wanted to be sure they would collect.[138]

When the EEC foreign ministers finally met on January 27, they promised that their governments would do all they could to insure that their nationals did not take advantage of U. S. economic withdrawal from Libya (Japan had made a similar promise).[139] They also emptily declared that "states that favor or protect terrorists cannot expect indulgence nor can they expect to have normal relations"[140] with EEC members, and the foreign ministers vowed not to sell arms to countries "clearly implicated" in support of terrorism. Whether the arms embargo was taken seriously or not is open to question, and the failure to name Libya explicitly as a terrorism-sponsoring state resounded as a snub to the United States.[141]

If perhaps some of them thought that sanctions against Libya would have only symbolic value, the Western Europeans seemed not to understand the ramifications of the symbolism involved in refusing to apply sanctions, ramifications that were quite evident in the case of the Reagan administration's South African policy and the images it generated. In the Libyan case, Qaddafi was encouraged to believe that because of their economic entanglement with the Jamahiriyah, the Western Europeans were in a sense on his side in his confrontation with the United States.[142] In the United States, the Europeans took a major beating in both liberal and conservative editorial opinion. The Reagan administration was determined not to have an open feud with the allies as in the Siberian pipeline controversy of 1982, so U. S. government officials maintained a polite public tone throughout, but their private feelings were well expressed by the diplomat who complained, "We can't get the Europeans to do much more than sweep up the blood.''[143] As a German journalist later noted, ''Few [European] politicians were farsighted enough then to realize . . . that America left on its own, would act on its own.''[144]

SOVIET AND ARAB RESPONSES IN EARLY 1986

In the first half of January the Soviet Union increased its survellance of U. S. Navy movements in the Mediterranean and stationed two destroyers and an intelligence-gathering ship off the coast of Israel, evidently to give early warning to Libya of any possible Israeli strike. Soviet spokesmen kept up a steady stream of denunciations of the United States in connection with the Libya crisis. However, they sidestepped the issue of whether the Soviet Union would defend Libya in the event of a conflict.[145]

Qaddafi was able to obtain from the Arab League and the Islamic Conference Organization a number of unanimous resolutions supporting Libya and condemning the United States in January. The Middle East experts and like-minded diplomats giving background briefings to reporters hastily declared that a foolish U. S. policy of confrontation had united the Arab world behind the colonel. Nonetheless, the Qaddafi regime's efforts to secure economic sanctions against the United States by Arab and Islamic states failed more dismally than Washington's efforts with its allies.[146] The degree of genuineness of the support for Libya was further illustrated at the meeting of the Arab Interparliamentary Union in Amman, Jordan, in March. A Libyan delegation was intercepted at the airport and stranded at a hotel outside Amman until a vote of nine to four had been taken to defer the Jamahiriyah's application to join the Union, whereupon the Libyans were ''hustled onto the first flight to Syria.''[147] Even the Libyan people themselves seemed not to be roused by the crisis to genuine fervor on Qaddafi's behalf, contrary to the experts' scenario.[148] During this period Qaddafi's chauffeur was believed to have died in an assassination attempt, and there was reportedly also a coup attempt by disgruntled military officers.[149]

CONTINUING TENSION, JANUARY-MARCH

Behind the scenes in January Qaddafi was pursuing two sharply contrasting courses regarding the United States. In January he met with a Francoist Spanish colonel and two organizers of the violent far-right Fuerza Nueva movement: he promised them financial support for a projected political party that would aim to withdraw Spain from NATO and the European Communities, sever its freshly begun diplomatic ties with Israel, and promote terrorist attacks against American and other targets in Spain and elsewhere in Europe. A Libyan intelligence captain visited Istanbul for about fifteen days to scout American targets for terrorist attacks. Libyan agents were observed staking out a U. S. diplomatic mission in South America. Two Italians were arrested in Sicily while waiting to meet Libyan agents to deliver documents and photographs of a U. S. missile base. Arab sources reported that Libya was working to form dummy U. S. firms to bring personnel and equipment into the United States to give Qaddafi capability to deliver on his threats to inflict terrorism within the United States.[150]

Even as he escalated terrorist planning, Qaddafi sought to use several European and Arab countries as intermediaries with the United States (and with Italy). The Reagan administration, however, spurned direct or indirect dialogue with the Qaddafi regime, all the more so because of the signs of continuing Libyan terrorist plotting.[151] As one official put it, "There is no one here who would trust his word."[152] Qaddafi was said to be "an expert at 'getting people lulled to sleep' with talk of peace and reasonable behavior and then 'doing whatever he pleases.' "[153] His 1984 double-cross of France in Chad was remembered. In September 1981 the colonel had sent an envoy to Washington with peaceful words even as he plotted the assassination of Ambassador Maxwell Rabb and apparently of President Reagan himself.[154]

At a January 21 meeting of the National Security Council, President Reagan approved air and naval maneuvers in the Mediterranean north of Libya, and the operations began three days later with the involvement of the aircraft carriers *Coral Sea* and *Saratoga* and their over one hundred aircraft and at least twenty-three auxiliary vessels. Spokesman Bernard Kalb mentioned the intention of demonstrating U. S. resolve to operate in and over international waters, and administration officials in background briefings referred to the "war of nerves" with Qaddafi and the need to make him understand what he would face if he promoted more terrorism. Libyan jets and ships were operating in the same general area, and Soviet ships shadowed the U. S. fleet. U.S. Navy pilots would be unimpressed with the performance of the Libyan pilots and their Soviet aircraft.[155] On January 25, Qaddafi, in a theatrical appearance before Western reporters, boarded a Libyan patrol boat to sail into the Gulf of Sidra for a "confrontation" with the Sixth Fleet and declared the parallel 32° 30' north latitude to be the "line of death where we shall stand and fight with our backs to the wall."[156] Qaddafi threatened to fire his new SA–5 missiles at U. S. Navy planes that overflew the Gulf of Sidra; intelligence reports stated that the Soviet advisers in Libya had cautioned Qaddafi against that, but Qaddafi had replied that he would decide when to use the missiles. At the end of a week of conflicting press reports about whether U. S. forces were going to cross the "line of death," they had come close but had not crossed it.[157]

At the beginning of February Qaddafi hosted the second "terrorist convention" of the Pan-Arab Command and made implicit appeals for violence against the United States. At the same time, on February 2, the Reagan administration kept the pressure on Libya by passing word that a new set of maneuvers in the vicinity would begin in about a week. On February 4 Israeli jets intercepted and diverted to an Israeli airport a Libyan airliner that was thought to be carrying Palestinian terrorist leaders returning from the convention but instead contained only Syrian leaders and Lebanese militia officials. The U. S. publicly deplored the interception, and Shultz and other U. S. officials privately considered it quite irresponsible, but Washington vetoed a UN Security Council condemnation of it, remembering "exceptional circumstances" like the *Achille Lauro* episode. Libya vowed to intercept Israeli airliners; Syria said it would teach the perpetrators of the interception an unforgettable lesson; and Ahmed Jabril, leader of the Popular Front for the Liberation of Palestine–General Command, who had originally been scheduled to be aboard the Libyan airliner,[158] declared in Tripoli on behalf of six Palestinian groups (including the Abu Nidal group), "Tell those who will be traveling on U. S. or Israeli airliners that from now on we will not be merciful to any traveler even if he is a civilian."[159] All of these parties accused Washington of collaboration with the Israeli interception.[160]

In a remarkably audacious move on February 10, the day before the second set of U. S. maneuvers, Qaddafi unleashed Libyan troops and their GUNT allies in new attacks south of the French-drawn Red Line in Chad.[161] Libya had also begun its own Mediterranean maneuvers on February 8, and a diplomat was quoted as saying: "Libya and the United States are pacing around each other like two snarling dogs, each waiting for the other to start a fight."[162] Paris felt obliged to help President Habré, sending troops and a jet squadron back to Chad; the U. S. supplied C–141 transport planes to fly in hardware, including tanks, for the French. France bombed a Libyan airbase in northern Chad used for supplying the offensive, and Mitterrand threatened to destroy the airbases in southern Libya if Qaddafi continued to attack south of the Red Line. Tripoli, with typical mendacity, declared the airbase was a civilian airport used for famine relief, and the Libyan air force ineffectually bombed the airport in Ndjamena, the capital of Chad. The Reagan administration, enthusiastic about France's anti-Libyan intervention, moved to expedite U. S. military aid to Chad and coordinated its efforts with the governments of Chad and France but sought to avoid giving Chad the appearance of a U. S.-Libyan issue. Qaddafi meanwhile did not neglect to exploit the terrible rioting in Egypt in late February through radio broadcasts calling for revolt against Mubarak.[163]

On March 3 Libya's General People's Congress issued a call for suicide squads to attack "U. S.-Zionist" embassies and other interests. On March 15, Qaddafi hosted a convention of 258 leftist organizations, including separatists, pacifists, terrorists, and guerrillas. Representatives from the Soviet Union, Cuba, Bulgaria, North Korea, Nicaragua, and Iran, as well as demagogue Louis Farrakhan of Chicago, were also in attendance. Actual terrorist training seminars were conducted at the conference, and the Libyan dictator spoke of an "international fighting force" to strike against the United States if it clashed with Libya. On March 19, gunmen in Cairo attacked Israeli diplomats, killing one woman and wounding three other persons; the Egyptian Revolution claimed responsibility, and Libya was thought to be responsible.[164]

After a two-week lull, more fighting had erupted in Chad in the first week of March, and around the same time Libya undertook another intervention that drew Washington's criticism. At the request of the Sudanese government, Libya sent weapons to Sudan on army trucks manned by hundreds of Libyan soldiers who remained to set up a Libyan base for operations against Chad, and the Libyan air force bombed southern Sudan towns held by the black guerrillas previously supported by Qaddafi. Meanwhile, despite the public pan-Arab rhetoric, Egypt had in late February secretly received a U. S. general for discussion of contingency plans for joint U. S.-Egyptian action against Libya, including the new preemptive strike plan. The discussions were productive, but it would soon be other Libya contingency plans that the United States would utilize.[165]

NOTES

1. "Freed American Hostages," *Weekly Compilation of Presidential Documents* 17 (2 Feb. 1981):50.

2. Alvin H. Bernstein, "Iran's Low Intensity War against the United States," *Orbis* 30 (Spring 1986): 150–53; U. S. Department of Defense, *Terrorist Group Profiles* (1989), pp. 15–17; *Washington Post* (hereafter cited as *WP*), 12, 14 Feb., 2 Mar. 1986; Martin C. Arostegui, "Special Reports of Risks International," *Terrorism* (New York) 7 (1985):422; *Facts on File*, 2 Dec. 1983, p. 903; Neil C. Livingstone, "The Impact of Technological Innovation," in Uri Ra'anan et al., *Hydra of Carnage: The International Linkages of Terrorism and Other Low-Intensity Operations; The Witnesses Speak* (Lexington, Mass.: Lexington Books, 1986), p. 140; Bob Woodward, *VEIL: The Secret Wars of the CIA, 1981–1987* (New York: Simon & Schuster, 1987), p. 379; *Facts on File*, 26 Oct. 1984, p. 796.

3. *WP*, 4 Feb. 1986, 22 Feb. 1987; *Christian Science Monitor* (hereafter cited as *CSM*), 26 Feb. 1987.

4. Benjamin Netanyahu, ed., *Terrorism: How the West Can Win* (New York: Farrar, Strauss & Giroux, 1986), p. 205.

5. One pertinent example is the Iran hostage rescue mission of 1980, which was strongly condemned in the Arab and Muslim worlds, while in the United States generally the only regrets were about its lack of success.

6. *New York Times* (hereafter cited as *NYT*), 16 Feb. 1986; *WP*, 2 Feb. 1986; Netanyahu, p. 207; Brian M. Jenkins, *Future Trends in International Terrorism*, Rand Paper Series, no. P-7176 (Santa Monica, Calif: Rand Corporation, 1985), p. 19.

7. Fouad Ajami column, *NYT*, 17 Apr. 1986.

8. "The President's News Conference of January 29, 1981, " *Weekly Compilation of Presidential Documents* 17 (2 Feb. 1981):66.

9. Alexander M. Haig, Jr., letter to the editor, *Policy Review*, no. 37 (1986), p. 88.

10. It was, of course, the internal threat to King Hussein's throne that actually provoked him to drive the PLO out of Jordan in 1970, but the threat of Israeli retaliation was obviously the reason why no resumption of PLO attacks from Jordan was permitted after Hussein and Arafat were reconciled.

11. Tony Hodges, *Western Sahara: The Roots of a Desert War* (Westport, Conn.: Lawrence Hill, 1983; London: Croon Helm, 1983), pp. 245–55. France launched several more air attacks against Polisario even after the release of the hostages because it had the further motive of supporting its embattled traditional client Mauritania.

12. Michael E. Ledeen, *Perilous Statecraft: An Insider's Account of the Iran-Contra Affair* (New York: Charles Scribner's Sons, 1988), p. 2.

13. Morton Kondracke, "Out of the Basement," *New Republic*, 5, 12 Jan. 1987, pp. 12–13; *WP*, 3, 4 Feb. 1986; Ledeen, *Perilous Statecraft*, pp. 1, 8–9.

14. *WP*, 16 Apr. 1986.

15. Kondracke, pp. 12–13. The NSC staff's gung-ho attitude applied to diplomacy as well as to military action (ibid., p. 13).

16. *Los Angeles Times* (hereafter cited as *LAT*), 29 Mar. 1986; *WP*, 4 Feb. 1986.

17. *WP*, 12, 18 Jan., 16 Apr. 1986, 22 Feb. 1987; *NYT*, 27 Oct. 1984, 24 Jan. 1986; "Countdown to Retribution," *U. S. News & World Report*, 28 Apr. 1986, p. 23; Ledeen, *Perilous Statecraft*, pp. 169–74; David C. Martin and John Walcott, *Best Laid Plans: The Inside Story of America's War against Terrorism* (New York: Harper & Row, 1988), p. 193; "The Sound of Spinning Wheels," *U. S. News & World Report*, 23 Mar. 1987, p. 21.

18. *WP*, 2 Apr. 1985, 7 Jan., 4 Feb., 27 Apr. 1986; *Facts on File*, 2 Dec. 1983, pp. 902–3.

19. *WP*, 4 Feb. 1986.

20. George P. Shultz, "Terrorism and the Modern World," *Terrorism* (New York) 7 (1985):436.

21. Ibid., pp. 441–42.

22. Ibid., p. 442.

23. Ibid., pp. 444–45.

24. *WP*, 27 Oct. 1984.

25. *NYT*, 27 Oct. 1984.

26. *NYT*, 28 Oct. 1984. A Pentagon source told the *Times*, "One has to proceed with caution and with a lot of thought about unintended consequences from the use of force," while a State Department source said, "There will be a war on terrorists. You just watch and see."

27. Martin and Walcott, p. 159.

28. *NYT*, 9 Oct. 1987.

29. Martin Sicker, *The Making of a Pariah State: The Adventurist Politics of Muammar Qaddafi* (New York: Praeger, 1987), p. 78; "Bread, the Stuff of Repression," *Arabia: The Islamic World Review*, no. 30 (Feb. 1984), p. 14; *NYT*, 11 Mar. 1984; interview with Terrell E. Arnold, 24 June 1989; *Facts on File*, 23 Mar. 1984, p. 197; "The Mysterious 'Doctor B.,' " *Time*, 27 Feb. 1989, p. 40.

30. *Times* (London), 10 Sept. 1986; J. A. Allan, "Libya," in *Britannica Book of the Year, 1985* (Chicago: Encyclopaedia Britannica, 1985), p. 492; "Libya's Ministry of Fear," *Time*, 30 Apr. 1984, pp. 36–38; *New Orleans Times-Picayune*, 26 Apr. 1984 (AP); *NYT*, 26 Feb. 1984; *Middle East Contemporary Survey*, vol. 8:*1983–84*, ed. Haim Shaked and Daniel Dishon (Tel Aviv: Dayan Center for Middle Eastern and African Studies, The Shiloah Institute, Tel Aviv University, 1986), p. 590 (hereafter cited as *MECS* 8). Both the United States and France intercepted messages from Tripoli ordering the London shootings.

31. *Foreign Broadcast Information Service, Daily Report*, Middle East & Africa (hereafter cited as FBIS-MEA), 12 June 1984, p. Q8.

32. Ibid., p. Q3.

33. Ibid., pp. Q6, Q11. Qaddafi also blamed the NFSL attack on Tunisia, Great Britain, Sudan, the Muslim Brotherhood, and even the Yasir Arafat-led Fatah organization

(Mohamed A. El-Khawas, *Qaddafi: His Ideology in Theory and Practice* [Brattleboro, Vt.: Amana Books, 1986], p. 110; *MECS* 8:599).

34. *WP*, 26 Mar. 1986; Martin and Walcott, p. 261; Blundy and Lycett, pp. 154–55; Larry Pressler, "Libya," *Department of State Bulletin* 87 (Jan. 1987): 88.

35. *CSM*, 13 Dec. 1984; Arostegui, p. 423; U. S. Department of State, *Libya under Qadhafi: A Pattern of Aggression*, Special Report No. 138 (1986), pp. 1–2; *NYT*, 18, 19 Nov. 1984, 5 Jan. 1986; George Henderson, "Red Faces," *Middle East International*, no. 238 (23 Nov. 1984), p. 11; *Washington Times* (hereafter cited as *WT*), 5 Dec. 1985; *Facts on File*, 31 Dec. 1984, p. 966.

36. *WP*, 27 Apr. 1986; *Chicago Tribune*, 22 Apr. 1986.

37. Ariel Merari et al., *Inter 86: A Review of International Terrorism in 1986* (Boulder, Colo.: Westview, 1987), p. 20.

38. Dept. of State, *Libya under Qadhafi*, p. 1; *WT*, 9 Jan. 1986.

39. FBIS-MEA, 29 Mar. 1985, p. Q2.

40. Ibid., 22 Mar. 1985, p. Q2.

41. Sicker, p. 130: FBIS-MEA, 1 Apr. 1985, pp. Q10–Q13.

42. FBIS-MEA, 1 Apr. 1985, p. Q11.

43. Ibid., p. Q13.

44. Ibid., p. Q14.

45. FBIS-MEA, 2 Apr. 1985, pp. Q2–Q3.

46. *WP*, 24 May 1985; *NYT*, 26 Nov. 1985; *Facts on File*, 2 Aug. 1985, p. 578; *WSJ*, 19 June 1985.

47. "Fatah Revolutionary Council (FRC)," *TVI Report* 8 (1988): 5–6; Walter Laqueur, *The Age of Terrorism* (Boston: Little, Brown, 1987), p. 288; U. S. Department of State, "Patterns of Global Terrorism: 1984," *Terrorism* (New York): 9 (1987):415; *NYT*, 25 Jan. 1988; Nathan M. Adams, "Greece: Sanctuary of International Terrorism," *Reader's Digest*, June 1989, pp. 204, 207.

48. Yossi Melman, *The Master Terrorist: The True Story of Abu Nidal* (New York: Adamd Books, 1986), pp. 194, 201; Xavier Raufer, *La Nébuleuse: Le Terrorisme du Moyen-Orient* (Paris: Fayard, 1987), pp. 314–322; *Jerusalem Post*, 12 Sept. 1986; "Iraq and Abu Nidal," *Foreign Report*, 24 Nov. 1983, p. 3.

49. *WSJ*, 15 Oct. 1987; *NYT*, 11 Jan. 1986.

50. Melman, 126–27; "Fatah Revolutionary Council (FRC)," p. 5; "International Terrorism," *Department of State Bulletin* 86 (Aug. 1986):7; *WP*, 30 Dec. 1985; *WT*, 1, 2 Jan. 1986; *NYT*, 28 Apr. 1986; *Sunday Times* (London, hereafter cited as *ST*), 14 Sept. 1986; Jean-Pierre Langellier, "Hand of Abu Nidal Seen behind Airport Massacres," *Guardian Weekly*, 12 Jan. 1986, p. 13; interviews with former Department of State officials, summer 1989. There were some experts who continued to believe that Abu Nidal's main headquarters was in Syria, but they were in the minority.

51. Melman, pp. 126–27; *NYT*, 19 Jan., 8 Sept. 1986; Raufer, pp. 18–19; *WT*, 4 Apr. 1986; Laqueur, *The Age of Terrorism*, p. 284. Abu Nidal himself lived in fear of assassination by such enemies as Fatah, Mossad, or the CIA, and while he spent the greatest amount of time in Tripoli, his paranoia drove him back and forth among Libya and Lebanon, Syria, South Yemen, Bulgaria, and Poland ("Reagan's Choice: Boycott Qadhafi," *U. S. News & World Report*, 20 Jan. 1986, p. 17; Melman, p. 131; *NYT*, 5 Jan. 1986; *WSJ*, 15 Oct. 1987).

52. Nathan M. Adams, "Destination Teheran: Anatomy of a Hijacking," *Reader's Digest*, Oct. 1985, pp. 71–80; *WP*, 3, 15 Apr. 1985, 12 Jan. 1986; U. S., President's Special Review Board, *The Tower Commission Report: The Full Text of the President's Special Review Board*, (New York: Bantam Books and Times Books, 1987), p. 113 (hereafter cited as *Tower Commission*); Facts on File, 28 June 1985, p. 486.

53. *Facts on File*, 28 June 1985, p. 486; "An Attack on Civilization," *Time*, 1 July 1985, p. 8; *WP*, 29 July 1988; U. S. Department of State, *Patterns of Global Terrorism: 1986* (1988), p. 16.

54. *Facts on File*, 21 June 1985, p. 461.

55. The proposed target was a training base in Nicaragua linked to the gunmen of the June 19 attack. The administration instead delivered a strong threat to the Sandinistas concerning any further assassinations of U. S. citizens in Central America (*NYT*, 24 July 1985; "Weighing a Retaliatory Raid," *Time*, 5 Aug. 1985, p. 23).

56. *WP*, 9 Oct. 1985.

57. *LAT*, 21 Feb. 1987; *Focus on Libya*, Oct. 1987.

58. *WP*, 1 July 1985.

59. *Facts on File*, 12 July 1985, p. 506. Presumably any of these three epithets could have been inspired by Qaddafi.

60. George Bush, "Prelude to Retaliation: Building a Governmental Consensus on Terrorism," *SAIS Review* 7 (Winter/Spring 1987): 1–9.

61. *WP*, 12 July 1985.

62. Martin and Walcott, pp. 262–65; *WP*, 21 Dec. 1985, 26 Mar., 2 Apr. 1986, 20 Feb. 1987; Woodward, pp. 409–12; *LAT*, 29 Mar. 1986.

63. *WP*, 26 Mar. 1986.

64. Interview with a former Department of State official, 1 July 1989; *WP*, 20 Feb. 1987; *LAT*, 21 Feb. 1987.

65. This is a representation of the overall drift of the grand maestro theory on Syria and not of the views of specific analysts, for which it would be oversimplified.

66. In December 1986 the State Department asserted that "available evidence indicates that Syria prefers to support groups whose activities are generally in line with Syrian objectives rather than to select targets or control operations itself" ("Syrian Support for International Terrorism: 1983–86," *Department of State Bulletin* 87 [Feb. 1987]:73).

67. In 1985 the State Department referred to Iran as "currently the world's leading supporter of terrorism" (Dept. of State, "Patterns of Global Terrorism: 1984," p. 413), and William Casey said Qaddafi was "not in the Ayatollah Khomeini's league" (William J. Casey, "The International Linkages—What Do We Know?," in Ra'anan et al., p. 7). U. S. officials did not state that Muammar Qaddafi was the "grand maestro" of Middle Eastern terrorism, nor did they believe such a thing. However, that impression was likely to be gleaned from their rhetoric in early 1986 by citizens who had not habitually followed official pronouncements on Middle Eastern terrorism.

68. Interviews with a former Department of State official, 1, 6 July 1989; *WP*, 14 May 1986; interview with a former senior CIA official, 23 Mar. 1989; "Reagan's Hostage Crisis," *U. S. News & World Report*, 1 July 1985, p. 21.

69. *Tower Commission*, pp. 20–26, 105–7, 112–17, 126, 128, 131–34; Martin and Walcott, pp. 222–23, 227–28; Memphis *Commercial Appeal*, 20 Dec. 1986; "From Many Strands, a Tangled Web," *Time*, 8 Dec. 1986, p. 28; Donald T. Regan, *For the Record: From Wall Street to Washington* (San Diego: Harcourt Brace Jovanovich, 1988), pp. 17, 19–21; *LAT*, 13 July 1987, *NYT*, 28 Feb. 1987.

70. "An American Reprisal?" *Foreign Report*, 6 June 1985, pp. 4–5; "Get Tough: The Reagan Plan," *Newsweek*, 20 Jan. 1986, p. 17.

71. *Facts on File*, 4 Oct. 1985, p. 724; *WP*, 13 Sept., 6, 17 Nov., 21 Dec. 1985, 26 Mar., 2 Apr. 1986, 20 Feb. 1987; *NYT*, 23 Aug. 1985, 21 Feb. 1987; *CSM*, 26 Sept. 1985; "Reagan's Choice," p. 17; Dept. of State, *Libya under Qadhafi*, pp. 2–3; *Middle East Contemporary Survey*, vol. 10: *1986*, ed. Itamar Rabinovich and Haim Shaked (Boulder, Colo.: Westview, 1986), p. 518 (hereafter cited as *MECS* 10); *Chicago Tribune*, 20 Apr. 1986; "Qadhafi-Chadli Meet," *Arabia: The Islamic World Review* 5 (Mar. 1986):16; *WSJ*, 3 Apr. 1986; *LAT*, 21 Feb. 1987.

72. *CSM*, 26 Sept. 1985.

73. *WP*, 17 Nov. 1985.

74. FBIS-MEA, 3 Sept. 1985, p. Q9.

75. Melman, pp. 201–7; *Times* (London), 16 Sept. 1986; *Jerusalem Post*, 28 Sept. 1986; *WSJ*, 15 Oct. 1987; *FBIS*, 30 Dec. 1985, p. I3; Nathan M. Adams, "Profiteers of Terror: The European Connection," *Reader's Digest*, Aug. 1986, p. 53; interviews with former Department of State officials, summer 1989.

76. *NYT*, 7 Oct. 1985. Libya at this time renewed radio broadcasts urging the massacre of the Tunisian Jews, and at least one Tunisian security officer apparently responded, opening fire on a synagogue and killing a number of people (*Facts on File*, 6 Dec. 1985, p. 903; *WP*, 10 Oct. 1985).

77. *WP*, 3 Nov. 1985, 18, 21 Apr. 1986; *NYT*, 17 Apr., 14 June 1986; *WT*, 26 Nov. 1985.

78. *WP*, 11 Oct. 1985, 5 Jan. 1986, 16 Apr. 1986; *NYT*, 8 Apr. 1986; *Oxford Eagle* (Miss.), 8 Oct. 1985 (AP); "O.K., Muammar, Your Move," *U. S. News & World Report*, 7 Apr. 1986, p. 25; "Hitting the Source," *Time*, 28 Apr. 1986, p. 23.

79. *WP*, 3, 17 Nov. 1985, 26 Mar. 1986; *NYT*, 4 Nov. 1985; Woodward, pp. 417–18; Martin and Walcott, p. 266; *WT*, 21 July 1987; Rowland Evans and Robert Novak, "Congress Is Crippling the CIA," *Reader's Digest*, Nov. 1986, p. 101; Melman, pp. 178–80, 183; "The Price of Success," *Time*, 28 Oct. 1985, p. 29.

80. *WP*, 3, 27 Nov. 1985; Woodward, pp. 17–19; Walcott and Martin, p. 266; *WT*, 21 July 1987. Durenberger and Leahy had threatened to disclose the operation to the press. Poindexter cited the Libya leak to the president as a reason not to inform Congress about the first arms shipment to Iran (ibid.).

Coincidentally, the first U. S. covert action to overthrow a foreign head of state had taken place in Libya in the administration of Thomas Jefferson. Desiring that the United States pay more tribute than it had been paying, the pasha of Tripoli had declared war on the United States, and he came into possession of American prisoners of war in 1804. The U. S. consul to Tunis organized a multinational force to replace the corsair-sponsoring pasha with his exiled brother. The consul's force captured the Libyan city of Derna in 1805, and the pasha was prompted to release the prisoners and negotiate a settlement with the United States more favorable than those Tripoli had with European states.

81. *NYT*, 12 Nov. 1985; *Times* (London), 18 Nov. 1985.

82. FBIS-MEA, 21 Nov. 1985, pp. Q2–Q3.

83. *NYT*, 26, 28 Nov. 1985; Melman, pp. 128–29, 201–7; *WP*, 22 Apr. 1986; U. S. Department of State, *International Terrorism*, Selected Documents No. 24 (1986), p. 2.

84. *NYT*, 25 Nov. 1985.

85. *NYT*, 29 Nov. 1985; 28 Apr. 1986; *WSJ*, 25 Nov. 1985; interview with former Department of State official, 1 July 1989; *WP*, 22 Apr., 5 May, 1986; Martin and Walcott, p. 267; *ST*, 1 Dec. 1985, 14 Sept. 1986; *Times* (London), 30 Apr. 1987. Abu Nidal biographer Yossi Melman, perhaps relying on Israeli intelligence sources, stated that Libyan intelligence agents and Ahmad Qaddafi, nephew of Muammar, had directed the

actions of the skyjackers and that Abu Nidal had received a several-million dollar down payment for the operation (Melman, pp. 128–29).

86. *Facts on File*, 30 Aug. 1985, p. 644; *Times* (London), 26 Mar. 1986; "Libya, USSR—A Change of Climate?," *Arabia: The Islamic World Review* 5 (Dec. 1985):37; *WP*, 17 Nov. 1985; *NYT*, 8 Jan., 2 May 1986.

87. *WP*, 10 Nov., 21 Dec. 1985, 8, 15 Jan., 25, 26 Mar. 1986; "Hitting Back at Libya: How the U. S. Might Do It," *Newsweek*, 21 Apr. 1986, p. 23; *LAT*, 8 Apr. 1986; Memphis *Commercial Appeal*, 17 Apr. 1986; "Sailing in Harm's Way," *Time*, 7 Apr. 1986, p. 16.

88. *NYT*, 25 Jan., 8 Apr. 1986; *LAT*, 7 Apr. 1986; "Terrorist Attacks Force Greater Airport Security," *Aviation Week & Space Technology*, 124 (6 Jan. 1986):33; *Times* (London), 28 Dec. 1985; "An Eye for an Eye," *Time*, 13 Jan. 1986, p. 26; Rod Nordland and Ray Wilkinson, "Inside Terror, Inc.," *Newsweek*, 7 Apr. 1986, p. 25.

89. *NYT*, 2 Jan. 1986, 6 Feb. 1987; *Times* (London), 2, 4, 13 Jan. 1986; Nordland and Wilkinson, p. 28; *WT* 1 Jan. 1986; *ST*, 25 May 1986.

90. *WP*, 31 Dec. 1985, 1 Jan. 1986; FBIS-MEA, 30 Dec. 1985, p. Q1; *NYT*, 11 Jan. 1986; Memphis *Commercial Appeal*, 31 Dec. 1985.

91. Melman, p. 129; *WP*, 1 Jan. 1986.

92. FBIS-MEA, 18 Oct. 1985, pp. A8, A3. The FRC leader also gave an interview while flanked by high-ranking Libyan officials in Tripoli, published by the Kuwaiti newspaper *Al-Qabas* on September 21, 1985 (*ST*, 1 Dec. 1985; FBIS-MEA, 24 Sept. 1985, pp. A1–A5).

93. *WT*, 1 Jan. 1986; *WP*, 31 Dec. 1985, 1 Jan. 1986; Nordland and Wilkinson, p. 27. Some of the terrorists had Moroccan passports, which may also have been supplied by Libya, which was known to keep a large stockpile of stolen and forged Moroccan and Tunisian passports (*Times* [London], 28 Dec. 1985; *Middle East Policy Survey* [hereafter cited as *MEPS*], no. 141, 6 Dec. 1985).

94. *WT*, 1 Jan. 1986.

95. *MEPS*, no. 144, 24 Jan. 1986; *NYT*, 25 Jan. 1986; *WP*, 22 Apr., 5 May 1986; interviews with former Department of State officials, summer 1989. That evidence was not publicly divulged should not be taken, as some would, as a sure sign that the evidence was nonexistent or worthless. The public disclosure of intelligence information is always extremely controversial within the government, due to the risks to intelligence sources and methods; this was true in the few instances, including the Soviet destruction of a Korean airliner in 1983, in which such public disclosures were made by the Reagan administration (*NYT*, 2 June 1986). It is difficult to exaggerate the vehemence with which intelligence officials resist such disclosures; their attitude is epitomized in the observation of former CIA official George Carver, Jr., in this context that "in World War II whole cities were sacrificed to protect intelligence sources" ("Intelligence Gathering—At a Price," *National Journal* 18 [10 May 1986]:1104).

Accordingly, it is quite abnormal for governments to publicly disclose intelligence information on terrorism derived from ongoing sources and methods. (Interrogation of captured terrorists is obviously a different matter.) For one example, the United States never publicly disclosed any of the intelligence behind its condemnation of Iran and Syria for the 1983 Marine barracks bombing. In the case of the Rome and Vienna massacres, there was no compelling political reason to disclose intelligence information, given the facts that no decision for military retaliation was taken and the Europeans speedily announced their unwillingness to impose sanctions. The fact that Libya was not mentioned in the terrorists' subsequent trials in Italy and Austria is irrelevant concerning the case gathered by the United States. Intelligence agencies are not in the business of providing information to foreign judicial systems, being reluctant enough to provide such information within their own countries. The context described here is essential for a proper understanding of the events under review, and it has been widely overlooked or willfully ignored in discussion of them.

96. Melman, p. 127; New Orleans *Times-Picayune*, 20 Apr. 1986 (UPI); *NYT*, 25 Jan., 23, 25 May 1986; Nordland and Wilkinson, pp. 25, 27; "Gaddafi and Terrorism," *World Press Review*, June 1986, p. 25; Robert Oakley, "International Terrorism," *Foreign Affairs* 65 (1987): 617; *Times* (London), 30 Apr. 1987. An interesting piece of circumstantial evidence concerns Rasmi Awad, an organizer of FRC terrorist attacks in Europe, who was arrested in London in September 1985 for the previously mentioned plot involving Libyan intelligence. British officials came to the opinion that this Libyan/FRC plot was intended to involve an airport massacre at Heathrow Airport simultaneous to the Rome and Vienna massacres. They noted that Awad's Spanish passport had recent immigration stamps from Rome and Vienna (*Jerusalem Post*, 28 Sept. 1986; *WSJ*, 15 Oct. 1987). In the latter city the Libyan embassy had in 1985 been the residence of FRC leaders in town to negotiate secretly with France (Raufer, p. 78).

97. *WP*, 11 Jan. 1986.

98. *NYT*, 25 Jan. 1986.

99. Cf. *NYT*, 21, 22, 23, 25, 29 May, 10, 15 June 1986, 6 Feb. 1987; *WP*, 22, 24, 25, 28 May 1986.

100. *Times* (London), 16 Dec. 1987; *NYT*, 13 Feb. 1988. "Terrorism: What's Next," *Foreign Report*, 24 Apr. 1986, p. 2; Blundy and Lycett, pp. 5, 159; Taheri, p. 259.

101. *WP*, 3, 7 Jan. 1986; Memphis *Commercial Appeal*, 1 Jan. 1986; *NYT*, 12 Jan. 1986.

102. *NYT*, 12 Jan. 1986.

103. *WP*, 1 Jan. 1986.

104. Ibid.

105. FBIS-MEA, 3 Jan. 1986, pp. Q1–Q3.

106. FBIS-MEA, 6 Jan. 1986, p. Q7.

107. *NYT*, 8 Jan., 23 Apr. 1986.

108. *WP*, 1, 4, 7 Jan. 1986; *NYT*, 3, 5, 6 Jan. 1986; Martin and Walcott, p. 274; Memphis *Commercial Appeal*, 5 Jan. 1986; *MEPS*, no. 143, 10 Jan. 1986.

109. *NYT*, 8, 16, 21 Jan. 1986; *WP*, 12 Mar. 1986.

110. *NYT*, 7, 8, 9, 12 Jan. 1986; *WP*, 3, 4, 7 Jan. 1986; Woodward, p. 431; "Slapping Back at Gaddafi," *Time*, 20 Jan. 1986, p. 17; "Reagan's Choice," p. 17; *CSM*, 10 Jan. 1986.

111. *WP*, 7, 24 Jan. 1986; "Get Tough," p. 16; *MEPS*, no. 145, 7 Feb. 1986; *NYT*, 21 Feb. 1987.

112. "Get Tough," p. 16; Seymour M. Hersh, "Target: Qaddafi," *New York Times Magazine*, 22 Feb. 1987, p. 71.

113. *Tower Commission*, pp. 37, 182–201, 213–14; Memphis *Commercial Appeal*, 2 Apr. 1989 (*Newsday*); *NYT*, 12 Jan. 1986; *WP* 3 Feb. 1986; *WSJ*, 20 Feb. 1987.

114. *NYT*, 8 Jan. 1986.

115. *NYT*, 8, 9 Jan. 1986; "Getting Americans Out of Libya: Is It Legal?," *Newsweek*, 20 Jan. 1986, p. 19; *WP*, 8 Jan. 1986. One State Department official called the American workers in Libya "economic soldiers of fortune" (*WT*, 9 Jan. 1986).

116. *NYT*, 8 Jan. 1986.

117. "Sanctions against Libya," *Weekly Compilation of Presidential Documents* 22 (20 Jan. 1986):42.

118. *WP*, 10 Jan. 1986.

119. *WP*, 11 Jan. 1986.

120. For example, *German Tribune*, 19 Jan. 1986.

121. *NYT*, 16 Jan. 1986. Shultz was prompted to declare, "Qaddafi is his own smoking gun" (*WP*, 17 Jan. 1986).

122. George P. Shultz, "Low-Intensity Warfare: The Challenge of Ambiguity," *Department of State Bulletin* 86 (Mar. 1986):15, 17.

123. Ibid., p. 17.

124. Ibid.; "George Shultz's Feisty Lawyer," *Time*, 6 Apr. 1987, p. 31.

125. *NYT*, 17 Jan. 1986.

126. *WP*, 12 Jan. 1986.

127. *WP*, 4, 11, 14, 16 Jan., 2 Feb., 1986; *NYT*, 10, 11, 17, 23 Jan. 1986; Memphis *Commercial Appeal*, 14 Jan. 1986; "Reagan's Choice," p. 18; *Times* (London), 13, 15 Jan. 1986.

128. *NYT*, 9, 10 Jan., 5 May 1986; Richard B. Parker, *North Africa: Regional Tensions and Strategic Concerns* (New York: Praeger, 1984), p. 134.

129. Pedro Ramet, "Soviet-Libyan Relations under Qaddafi," *Survey* 29 (Spring 1985): 112.

130. For example, West Germany (*NYT*, 13 Apr. 1986).

131. *NYT*, 7 Apr. 1986.

132. The United States was the second most popular location for terrorist bombings in the period 1977 to 1983, after France (Paul Wilkinson, "State-Sponsored International Terrorism: The Problems of Response," *World Today* 40 [July 1984]:197). According to Risks International, the United States was the third leading location for terrorist incidents from 1970 to 1978, after Italy and Spain. In the same period, seventy-two deaths from terrorism in the United States ranked it ahead of Great Britain without Northern Ireland and West Germany, the latter a reputed hotbed of terrorism (James B. Motley, *US Strategy to Combat Domestic Political Terrorism*, National Security Affairs Monograph Series, no. 83–2 [Washington, D.C.: National Defense University Press, 1983], pp. 14, 22).

133. Gary Clyde Hufbauer and Jeffrey J. Schott assisted by Kimberly Ann Elliot, *Economic Sanctions Reconsidered: History and Current Policy* (Washington, D.C.: Institute for International Economics, 1985), pp. 43, 80, 83.

134. "Why U.S. Allies Won't Follow," *U. S. News & World Report*, 20 Jan. 1986, p. 18; John K. Cooley, *Libyan Sandstorm* (New York: Holt, Rinehart & Winston, 1982), pp. 286–87; Richard H. Shultz Jr., "Can Democratic Governments Use Military Force in a War against Terrorism?," *World Affairs* 148 (Spring 1986):209; *WP*, 10 Nov. 1985; *NYT*, 12 Jan. 1986. As a potential target of sanctions, undeveloped Libya, with its one-product economy, is a polar opposite to industrialized, economically strong South Africa, a fact that was often overlooked in analogies about effectiveness.

135. *WP*, 1 Jan., 22 Apr. 1986; *NYT*, 10 Jan., 10 Apr. 1986 *Facts on File*, 20 May 1983, p. 362.

136. Anthony Lejeune, "A Friend in Need," *National Review*, 23 May 1986, p. 27; "Look What We're Doing," *Economist*, 26 Apr. 1986, p. 48.

137. Paul Wilkinson, the leading British terrorism expert, had said in 1980, "It is primarily the responsibility of each individual Western government to clean out the Augean stable of modern 'diplomatic terrorism.' . . . It is their prerogative . . . to expel diplomats . . . to sever diplomatic relations. In my view the European governments, both individually and collectively, have been appallingly weak and irresponsible in failing to use these powers. They have allowed international law to be contemptuously defied by foreign states and nations. They have all too often backed down or turned a blind eye rather than put at risk some tempting export contract or access to oil or other valuable commodities. Such pathetic weakness inevitably invites further humiliations and further undermining of already fragile international laws and conventions" (Paul Wilkinson, "Proposals for Government and International Responses to Terrorism," *Terrorism* [New York] 5 [1981]:184–85).

138. Edward Schumacher, "The United States and Libya," *Foreign Affairs* 65 (Winter 1986/87):344; *WP*, 20 Apr. 1986.

139. *NYT*, 28 Jan., 28 Apr. 1986.

140. *WP*, 15 Apr. 1986.

141. *NYT*, 28 Jan. 1986; Cal McCrystal, "Malta: Caught in the Crossfire," *Sunday Times Magazine*, 26 Oct. 1986, p. 36; Adams, "Profiteers," p. 51; *WT*, 7 Apr. 1986; *WP*, 16 Apr. 1986. Great Britain and West Germany advocated naming Libya, while Spain, Italy, Denmark, Greece, and France were said to have opposed it (*German Tribune*, 9 Feb. 1986; *NYT*, 28 Jan. 1986). Nonetheless, it was reported a few days later that Italy had frozen negotiations by its parastatal enterprises on new contracts with Libya (*NYT*, 2 Feb. 1986), and the West German and Italian governments privately promised to begin cutting back on purchases of Libyan oil (*MEPS*, 7 Feb. 1986).

142. *WP*, 10 Jan. 1986; *Times* (London), 25 Apr. 1986.

143. "Washington Whispers," *U. S. News & World Report*, 20 Jan. 1986, p. 14.

144. *German Tribune*, 13 Apr. 1986.

145. *NYT*, 7, 14, 17 Jan. 1986.

146. *NYT*, 9, 10 Jan., 1 Feb. 1986; *CSM*, 13 Jan. 1986; *WP*, 31 Jan. 1986. At an Arab League conference called for Libya at the end of the month, only eight of twenty-one foreign ministers bothered to attend, and the Algerian minister left for another engagement only moments after the opening (ibid.).

147. *CSM*, 26 Mar. 1986.

148. *Times* (London), 15 Jan. 1986; "Beyond the Barracks Gates," *Time*, 27 Jan. 1986, p. 31: *NYT*, 18, 19 Jan. 1986.

149. Blundy and Lycett, p. 215; *WSJ*, 26 Mar. 1986.

150. "A Tale of Two Colonels," *Economist*, 17 May 1986, p. 54; *WP*, 30 Apr., 11, 13 May 1986; Memphis *Commercial Appeal*, 29 Jan. 1986; *WT*, 8 Oct. 1986; *CSM*, 31 Mar. 1986.

151. *WP*, 2 Apr. 1986; *NYT*, 23 May 1986.

152. *NYT*, 29 Jan. 1986. Certainly, Qaddafi was anything but a man of his word. His rapprochements with foreign governments had usually not brought his support of terrorists opposing those governments to a halt. Even after he entered into his Arab-African Union with King Hassan in 1984, he had continued to fund and host a Moroccan underground group, and it was allowed to join his Pan-Arab Command (*NYT*, 28 Apr. 1986).

153. *WP*, 29 Apr. 1986.

154. *WP*, 2 Apr. 1986; "Searching for Hit Teams," *Time*, 21 Dec. 1981, p. 22. Unsuccessful secret diplomatic discussions between the United States and Libya in January

and April 1983 in Geneva and London have been reported (*Focus on Libya*, Mar. 1984; Blundy and Lycett, p. 163). There may have been no authorized direct contacts after that period. U. S. Vatican envoy William Wilson engaged in secret contacts with Libyan officials from 1982 to 1986; most, though not all, accounts portray these diplomatic forays as authorized by neither the State Department nor the White House. In his January 10 interview with European correspondents Reagan said that he recalled past proposals by intermediaries for dialogue with Qaddafi, but that "before anything could be done, why, he would do something else that made it rather impossible" ("Sanctions against Libya," p. 44). Indirect contact, however, had continued through what has been described as an "alternative network of dealings . . . facilitating a measure of economic and diplomatic relations. . . . under the table, through third parties," particularly businessmen, Europeans, and Arabs (*Focus on Libya*, Sept. 1988; interview with Joseph Churba, 25 May 1989).

155. *NYT*, 24 Jan. 1986; Parks, p. 44; *Fort Worth Star-Telegram*, 25 Jan. 1986; *WP*, 24 Jan., 3 Feb. 1986; "Cat and Mouse with Gaddafi," *Time*, 3 Feb. 1986, p. 18; Memphis *Commercial Appeal*, 25 Jan. 1986; Daniel P. Bolger, *Americans at War: 1975–1986, An Era of Violent Peace* (Novato, Calif.: Presidio Press, 1988), pp. 389–92.

156. *NYT*, 26 Jan. 1986.

157. *WP*, 30 Jan. 1986; *NYT*, 28 Jan. 1986.

158. *NYT*, 3, 4, 5, Feb. 1986; *Facts on File*, 7 Feb. 1986, p. 68; *MEPS*, 7 Feb. 1986; *WP*, 8 Feb. 1986; Melman, p. 166.

159. FBIS-MEA, 6 Feb. 1986, p. A1.

160. Ibid., pp. A1, H2; *NYT*, 5 Feb. 1986.

161. *NYT*, 11, 16 Feb. 1986.

162. *NYT*, 9 Feb. 1986.

163. *NYT*, 17, 18, 23 Feb. 1986; *WT*, 18 Apr. 1986; Aharon Levran and Zeev Eytan, *Middle East Military Balance, 1986* (Boulder, Colo.: Westview, 1988), p. 51; *WP*, 27 Mar. 1986; *MEPS*, no. 146, 21 Feb. 1986.

164. *WP*, 5, 27 Mar. 1986; Schumacher, p. 337; *CSM*, 31 Mar. 1986; *Times* (London), 26 Mar. 1986; *WT*, 8, 15 Apr. 1986; Merari et al., p. 86; *MECS* 10:77.

165. *NYT*, 6 Mar. 1986; *WP*, 28, 29 Mar., 15 Dec. 1986; "Sudan: Kaddafi Calling," *Newsweek*, 14 Apr. 1986, p. 30; "A Hearty Appetite," *Economist*, 29 Mar. 1986, p. 28; *WT*, 24 Mar. 1986; Woodward, pp. 435–36.

4

Operation Prairie Fire

INCEPTION AND PREPARATION

In mid-January Qaddafi had declared before a people's congress in Libya that "if war comes I believe it will be in the sea hundreds of miles away from land,"[1] and so it would roughly be, by his choice and the choice of the Reagan administration. Among the many military contingencies reviewed by Washington planners in the wake of the Rome and Vienna massacres were plans for Sixth Fleet exercises extending into the Gulf of Sidra. Shultz and Poindexter saw already scheduled Mediterranean exercises involving three aircraft carriers (the first appearance of three carriers in the Mediterranean since 1984) as an opportunity to punish Qaddafi, not an original idea, of course. Although American forces had entered the Gulf of Sidra a number of times without drawing fire since Qaddafi's air fiasco in August 1981, the secretary of state and the national security adviser apparently believed that if the United States penetrated the gulf in a grand enough fashion, Libya would attack and give the Navy an opportunity to respond again. Weinberger and the Navy were quite willing to reassert America's right to navigate the Gulf of Sidra, in accordance with Washington's long-standing policy of challenging unreasonable nautical claims, a policy to which the Reagan administration had made an increased commitment. They were not so enthusiastic about a major clash with Libya, however.[2]

Accounts have varied as to when it became settled within the U. S. government that a foray into the Gulf of Sidra would be made. By late January, there was argument over whether to proceed into the gulf with forces from the two carriers available or to wait for the third carrier to arrive in March. Sixth Fleet commanders were willing enough to rely on two carriers, but Weinberger and U. S. NATO commander Gen. Bernard Rogers wanted three carriers: the logic was said to be having one carrier from which to launch aircraft, a second on which to land them, and a third in case of emergencies. Administration hard-liners bitterly complained of the Navy's unwillingness to disrupt its rotation schedule by sending a carrier to the Mediterranean early and more broadly accused the Pentagon of repeated efforts to hamstring the Gulf of Sidra operation. Meanwhile, Qaddafi's swaggering declaration of a "line of death" during the exercises provoked two responses among U. S. officials: outrage, with the feeling that he had to be challenged, and glee at the enhanced prospect that he would bring a drubbing upon himself if the navy entered the Gulf of Sidra.[3]

For Reagan the decision to confront Qaddafi in the Gulf of Sidra was by some accounts sealed definitively in February when he and his advisers received CIA reports of Libyan agents casing numerous U. S. overseas installations as potential terrorism targets. The conclusion was that Qaddafi had still not gotten the message to refrain from terrorism against the United States and that it was just a matter of time before another major attack came. Around this time, according to *Newsweek* sources, Navy aircraft began making unannounced crossings of the "line of death" for thirty-two consecutive days, forcing constant alert for Libyan air defenses;[4] one military officer, apparently referring to those flights, mentioned "poking them in the ribs . . . to keep them on edge."[5]

The U. S. government did not prefer to confront Libya unilaterally and so sought to involve some of its allies. On February 25 Reagan contacted Mitterrand and invited him to send a French carrier to join the U. S. maneuvers coming in the Gulf of Sidra in late March. Ironically, the French were reported to have concluded a secret deal with Libya in February for the sale of "urgently" needed Exocet antiship missiles. When U. S. Ambassador to the United Nations Vernon A. Walters secretly visited Paris at the beginning of March, Reagan's invitation was declined. The French also declined to join Washington in covert action against Qaddafi after having previously seemed to show interest; their explanation was that U. S. action against Qaddafi would be counterproductive since it would not be designed to bring a complete end to him.[6]

At about the same time, Israeli journalist Yossi Melman has stated, Casey visited Israel to present a proposal for joint United States–Israel military action against Libya of a nature not specified by Melman. This is remarkable in light of the well-attested view of senior officials in the Pentagon and other agencies that such a collaboration would have catastrophic consequences for the United States in the Arab world, where it would be viewed as anti-Arab rather than antiterrorist. After intense discussions, Melman claimed, Israel's governing coalition refused the proposal on the grounds that Libya was not one of the states that most endangered Israel and that it would be foolish to open up a new front with Qaddafi; intelligence aid was offered to the United States, however. Mossad had also earlier rejected cooperation with the CIA in covert planning against the Qaddafi regime.[7] Jerusalem's attitude on these matters did not lend support to the notion advanced by some that the Reagan administration clashed with Libya in order to do a favor to Israel.

On March 14, the day after the State Department announced the release of an additional $10 million in military aid to Chad, President Reagan and the NSPG met to discuss the rules of engagement for the upcoming naval maneuvers off Libya, which were code-named Operation Prairie Fire.[8] He reportedly asked his advisers some rather prescient questions: "Could this lead into trouble? Could we end up with a less palatable situation than we have now?"[9] He was evidently reassured. Libyan aggression in the Gulf was considered highly probable, and Shultz as well as NSC staffers wanted a major U. S. attack on the Libyan mainland as soon as the Jamahiriyah fired. Weinberger and Crowe wanted the more restrained response suggested by the Navy's manual. Poindexter engineered a compromise according to which, if Libya fired, the Sixth Fleet's commander, Vice Admiral Frank B. Kelso III, would have discretion to return fire under the proportional response doctrine, sometimes termed "tit-for-tat," which many military analysts rued as having served the United States poorly in the Vietnam War. If there were a single U. S. serviceman killed, it was tentatively decided to bomb five coastal airbases and not be inhibited by the risk of Soviet casualties, but Kelso would have to check back with the president first. If Qaddafi launched an all-out attack, U. S. planes were to bomb Libyan oil fields, oil depots, and terrorist training camps inland upon presidential approval. There was reportedly eagerness to inflict humiliation on Qaddafi.[10]

A number of motives and assumptions underlay the administration's decision to confront Libya in the Gulf of Sidra. The most important motive was to make Qaddafi understand that he would have to pay a price for terrorism and other aggressions. Some administration officials characterized the exercise as Washington's definitive response to the Rome and Vienna massacres. Shultz and Poindexter expressed hope that inflicting defeat upon the Jamahiriyah could prompt its military men to overthrow Qaddafi. Sending a message of resolve to Moscow may have been a subsidiary motive. Some policymakers believed that humbling Qaddafi was necessary for the United States' credibility in the Middle East and was secretly desired by some Arab leaders.[11] Shultz had declared in his above-mentioned January speech:

Striking against terrorism in the Middle East is bound to be controversial. But the worst thing that we could do to our moderate friends in the region is to demonstrate that extremist policies succeed and that the United States is impotent to deal with such challenges. If we want to be a factor in the region—if we want countries to take risks for peace relying on our support—then we had better show that our power is an effective counterweight to extremism.[12]

The U. S. government operated under the assumptions that responding to Qaddafi's fire at U. S. targets would be easily defensible under international law and that international criticism of Washington would be mitigated by the fact that very few countries recognized Libya's claim to the Gulf of Sidra. The maneuvers, it was felt, could provide the sort of military engagement the post-Vietnam American public would accept: one involving quick victory assured in advance, few or no American casualties, and a target viewed as an enemy by a consensus of Americans. Additionally, Libyan civilian casualties seemed unlikely. (Opinion polls had shown support for limited military action but not all-out war against Libya.) Officials believed that the Soviet Union would not intervene on behalf of Qaddafi: they were mindful of the disastrous autumn Gorbachev-Qaddafi meeting and had a general feeling that the "correlation of forces" in the world had shifted back in the United States' favor. After the breakdown of the Hussein-Arafat entente there was little in the way of a Middle East peace process to disrupt, and administration officials did not fear any serious problems in relations with Arab leaders, because of those leaders' dislike of Qaddafi.[13]

THE BATTLE OF SIDRA

Weinberger secretly flew to London to review the rules of engagement with Kelso; one innovation was that once Libyans fired, the Navy would have authority to direct fire at any Libyan forces judged to have hostile intent whether they had opened fire yet or not. U. S. officials informed the Soviets of Washington's intention to cross the line of death, implicitly warning them to take precautions. The third aircraft carrier, the *America*, entered the Mediterranean on March 19; unfamiliarity of its personnel with the Libyan theater actually complicated the Sixth Fleet's task in some ways. The administration publicly maintained then and after the subsequent clashes that the maneuvers were routine exercises not intended to warn Qaddafi, but only to assert free international passage.[14] However, anonymous officials were quite talkative with the press; some said to *Time*, "Tommyrot! Of course we're aching for a go at Gaddafi" and "If he sticks his head up, we'll clobber him. We're looking for an excuse."[15] A supply of "Terrorist Buster" T-shirts sold out aboard the carrier *Saratoga*.[16]

On March 22 U. S. embassies, consulates, and trade missions abroad were placed on heightened alert. The next day a huge armada, including three aircraft carriers, twenty-seven accompanying vessels, over two hundred planes, nuclear-powered attack submarines, and almost twenty-five thousand servicemen, began maneuvers north of Libya.[17] That night U. S. Navy planes began flying sorties across the line of death and at 1:00 P.M. local time on March 24 a surface action group of three U. S. ships sailed across the line. Within two hours two Libyan SA–5 missiles were fired from a site near the port of Surt toward U. S. jets about seventy miles away. About five hours later, the Libyans fired an undetermined number of SA–5 and SA–2 missiles in three separate incidents within thirty minutes of one another. In total, six to twelve missiles were fired and all missed.[18]

Kelso calmly postponed his response to the missile firings, waiting until night, when Libya's pilots rarely flew far. At 10:06 P.M., after the Surt target acquisition radars were reactivated for another firing at U. S. aircraft, two Navy A–7 planes fired HARM missiles at the radar dishes, and their emissions ceased. They used standoff tactics for pilot safety, firing from forty miles away and allowing the missiles to home in on their targets. Only the radars were targeted— "shooting out the tires," it was called—and not the highly explosive missiles, in order to minimize collateral damage, especially to Soviet advisers. When the Surt missile site later began emitting radar signals again, another pair of A–7s launched two more HARMs at the site, and only very brief emissions were subsequently detected.[19]

Less than an hour before the first A–7 attack on the Surt missile site, a Libyan patrol boat heading toward the U. S. surface action group was destroyed by Navy A–6s firing Harpoon missiles and Rockeye cluster bombs. In the next thirteen hours U. S. aircraft attacked several more patrol boats that ventured into the gulf, destroying one more and severely damaging another. Press accounts incorrectly described these attacks as "retaliatory."[20] The patrol boats carried Italian antiship missiles (which were under the maintenance of private British engineers, as were the missile site radar units), and U. S. forces could hardly afford to allow the boats to come within firing range of U. S. ships. Dozens of Libyan sailors died: they were sacrificed by Qaddafi as militarily conventional suicide squads in his vain hope of gaining glory by sinking a U. S. ship should the Americans be so inept as to allow his boats close enough. Libyan aircraft ventured out over the gulf only once during its penetration by the United States; it was reported that six Syrian pilots on loan to Qaddafi had refused to fly out to confront the U. S. warplanes. There were no more aggressive Libyan moves after noon on March 25, and the United States had suffered no casualties or damage to its planes or ships. Congressmen and foreign heads of state declared that the United States had made its point about freedom of navigation in the Gulf of Sidra and expressed the desire that it terminate the naval exercises as soon as possible. On March 27, the Navy withdrew north of the line of death, three days ahead of schedule, to the consternation of administration hard-liners, who privately complained that it was a unilateral decision by Weinberger. John F. Lehman, Jr., secretary of the Navy at that time, was one of the disturbed officials; he later wrote that Kelso had been scheduled to send his forces much closer to the Libyan twelve-mile sea limit, in expectation that Qaddafi would launch his air force, creating a "turkey shoot" which would have hopefully dealt a crushing blow to his position. On March 29 the Navy departed from the Libyan area; the *Saratoga* sailed home, while the *America* and the *Coral Sea* sailed for the northern Mediterranean.[21]

INTERNATIONAL REACTION

The Soviets had taken the U. S. warnings to heart: they had removed their submarines from the area lest they be mistaken for Libyan submarines,[22] and they kept a communication ship anchored at Surt "lit up like a carnival so that the U. S. fleet would know not to shoot it."[23] Qaddafi's efforts against the U.S. forces were said to have been regarded by the Kremlin as a "quixotic venture," against Moscow's best interests, and Soviet ships in the vicinity had relayed information to their headquarters at Sevastopol rather than providing "real-time" intelligence to Libya. Soviet spokesmen predictably condemned U. S. actions: Gorbachev spoke of the revealing of the "imperial-bandit face" of the United States. However, a blow to Soviet prestige in the Middle East and in general was provided by the performance of the SA–5s and by Moscow's unwillingness to confront the United States in order to assist its ally Libya.[24]

The Reagan administration was pleased with the outcome of the Gulf of Sidra maneuvers; Weinberger declared, "It was in every way a successful operation."[25] There was strong bipartisan support in Congress; Dante B. Fascell (D-Fla.), Chairman of the House Foreign Affairs Committee, expressed concerns pertaining to the War Powers Act, but few congressmen joined him. Two opinion polls showed 67 percent and 75 percent respectively of the American public supporting the U. S. military action, but there were concerns about possible increased terrorist attacks and the safety of overseas travel. There were critics, of course, and beyond those pundits who bewailed any American use of military force, there were some commentators who questioned how attacks against Libya's naval craft and a missile site were suited to counterterrorism and expressed doubts about the tactics of proportional response.[26]

Among the United States' allies, Israel and Great Britain strongly supported the U. S. actions in the Gulf of Sidra: Israeli officials called them a blow against international terrorism, and Margaret Thatcher emphasized the rights of self-defense and of free passage in international waters and airspace. The Dutch government sharply criticized Libya for starting the battle. The northern European allies were generally more supportive than the southern European allies, but there were expressions of anxiety and concern all around. While there was a strong consensus that the Gulf of Sidra was international waters, Canada and a number of other allies, without directly criticizing the United States, stated that the dispute over the Gulf of Sidra should be settled by peaceful means.[27] While the government of Greece deplored the clashes without specifically condemning the United States, the Socialist party of Prime Minister Andreas Papandreou bombastically condemned "the armed enforcement of a new Pax Americana. . . . the attempt for a holocaust in the Mediterranean."[28]

On a Shultz tour of Turkey, Greece, and Italy in the days following the clashes, the secretary's hosts rehearsed the standard arguments that the United States' actions were counterproductive because they earned for Qaddafi increased visibility and prestige and expressions of solidarity that he would not have otherwise obtained. Shultz declared in response that "if you let people get away with murder, you are encouraging murder" and said, "The other side of the coin is that when somebody engages in outrageous behavior, if you don't challenge it or do something about it repeatedly then you seem to be going along. And we feel that the right judgment on this is to blow the whistle on it.''[29] When he called upon the president of Italy, Shultz was kept waiting for forty-five minutes by the much displeased Francesco Cossiga. Prime Minister Bettino Craxi had sharply criticized both the United States and Libya and gone out of his way to emphasize that the Gulf of Sidra maneuvers were in no way connected to NATO. The Italians' particularly strong sensitivity was believed to be related to the Sixth Fleet's having sailed out of Italian ports, to Italy's geographic proximity to the conflict, and to the potential for new terrorism; Craxi was also allegedly upset at first hearing of the clash through news agency reports. In Italy there were demonstrations against the United States by young people. There were scattered anti-American demonstrations in other countries, but not on a scale comparable to the demonstrations in Europe in the week following the U. S. air strikes in April.[30]

Tripoli radio's prediction that "the whole Arab nation will soon be racing toward the battlefield and crowding toward the war against America"[31] was stillborn: in fact the reaction in the Arab world to the battle of the Gulf of Sidra was far milder than what the U. S. government had anticipated. There were almost no anti-American demonstrations in the Arab world outside Libya and Syria and no parallels to the violent student rioting in Egypt that had followed the *Achille Lauro* episode. The Arab League's foreign ministers issued harsh unanimous condemnations of the United States, but conservative Arab regimes made sure to excise calls for economic sanctions and diplomatic rupture with Washington.[32] Most Arab governments also individually condemned the United States but with such obvious lack of passion that the state newspaper *Al-Ittihad* in the United Arab Emirates bewailed "this silence in Arab capitals regarding the aggression against Libya."[33] Interestingly, King Hassan of Morocco, after having expressed full solidarity with Libya (with which his country was in nominal union at this time), disregarded both the Middle East experts' script for the confrontation and the feelings of his partner Qaddafi by publicly proposing on March 25 that the Arab leaders choose one of their number to hold a summit meeting with Israel. There were seemingly conflicting reports of Arab officials being privately pleased at Washington's military humbling of Qaddafi and of pervasive dismay at the turn of events among Arab officials. Both responses were no doubt present, with the latter probably more common, but Arab officials who were disturbed over U. S. actions were mostly moved not by sympathy for the Libyan dictator but by fear of the potential repercussions in the Middle East.[34] Meanwhile, on March 25 Prime Minister Mir Hossein Moussavi of Iran expressed full solidarity with Libya against the United States; on the same day an official in his office called the United States and asked why the Americans had not been in contact recently.[35]

Within Libya, Qaddafi sought to exploit the occasion to the fullest: he showed great enthusiasm during a round of speechmaking in which he claimed victory, declaring that Libya had shot down three U. S. planes and claiming that the United States had succeeded only in sinking a fishing boat. The casualties among

Libyan sailors were not publicly acknowledged. There were the usual vague accounts that Qaddafi had been strengthened immeasurably in Libya by U. S. action, as journalists transmitted the long-standing attitudes of the Tripoli diplomatic corps as though they constituted substantive news.[36] More detailed accounts by other journalists painted a far different picture. As one reporter stated it, "Few traces of anti-American sentiment—or even of serious interest in . . . [the] fighting in the Gulf of Sidra—could be found in the streets of . . . [Tripoli] last week."[37] A number of reporters noted how small, artificial, and unenthusiastic the anti-American rallies were and how bored Libyans seemed to be with Qaddafi and his confrontation with the United States. There were unconfirmed reports of a revolt by the Libyan navy and of yet another assassination attempt against Qaddafi in the wake of the fighting.[38]

QADDAFI CALLS ON HIS DIPLOMATS

Whether there ever would have come to pass any of the long-term benefits in the campaigns against terrorism and the Qaddafi regime that the Reagan administration had hoped would issue from the defeat of Libya in the Gulf of Sidra will never be known; the short-term effects were quite contrary to what was desired in Washington. Although it had been Qaddafi's decision to fire antiaircraft missiles and send gunboats against U. S. forces over and on international waters, according to his way of thinking Libya was the victim of an aggression that had to be avenged. From the U. S. standpoint, what was important was not the unimpressiveness of the amount of Libyan military equipment that had been destroyed, but rather that the U. S. military response had been strong enough to anger Qaddafi but not strong enough to intimidate him.

The Libyan leader alarmed the Europeans by making threats to attack NATO bases in Europe.[39] Radio Tripoli issued blistering calls for terrorism against the United States: American "bases" in the Arab world should be stormed, American experts and consultants there should be executed,[40] the Arab nation should transform itself "into suicide squads and into human bombs" to "pursue American terrorist embassies and interests wherever they may be,"[41] and the duty of all Arabs was to make "everything American . . . a military target."[42] Additionally, the Abu Nidal group and the loose Palestine National Salvation Front (PNSF) terrorist coalition announced plans for revenge against the United States.[43]

On March 25, the second day in which fighting had taken place in the Gulf of Sidra, U. S. intelligence intercepted messages from the Libyan government to its people's bureaus in thirty countries ordering terrorist attacks against U. S. targets. (On the same day Turkish police received intelligence leading them to increase security at sensitive spots, including a U. S. officers' club in Ankara, which was indeed the site of an attempted Libyan attack several weeks later.) In the preceding weeks Washington had attained an intelligence breakthrough in managing to intercept regularly the messages emanating from the downtown Tripoli headquarters of the Libyan intelligence service, and the United States continued to intercept from three to five Libyan messages a day discussing terrorist attacks against Americans.[44] One message outlined operational plans for more than ten attacks and called for Libyans and Palestinians working for the Jamahiriyah to "cause maximum casualties to U. S. citizens and other Western people."[45] In recent weeks, the Qaddafi regime had intensified recruitment of European and Palestinian hit men to deflect from Libya the blame for terrorist attacks. Interception of cables by the United States was supplemented by eavesdropping on telephone conversations between Libyans and suspected Palestinian terrorists, and defecting agents of Libya supplied information on plots against Americans. Increased Libyan surveillance of overseas American citizens, businesses, and government posts was observed.[46]

In short order the State Department on March 26 publicly noted the Libyan surveillance operations and pointedly warned that "there are a variety of assets available for a response to international terrorism and the Libyan threat in particular."[47] President Reagan warned in a speech the next day that he would hold Qaddafi accountable for any Libyan terrorist acts against Americans. Military planners went back to work crafting a retaliatory strike for use if Libya did indeed succeed in killing Americans. U. S. officials privately requested increased security for American diplomats in Western Europe and the Middle East, and orders for limiting their movements were issued. Government officials leaked to *Newsweek* contents of highly classified CIA reports on Libyan surveillance of at least thirty-five U. S. targets overseas, including the headquarters of the Sixth Fleet and the homes of its highest officers in Naples. The leak exasperated some U. S. officials dealing with the terrorism problem; it was said to have been motivated by a desire to deter Qaddafi from carrying through with his schemes.[48]

A number of violent ripostes by Libya and its terrorist clients and sympathizers began unimpressively, then developed into something more serious. On March 25 a Libyan-aligned group in Beirut fired shells that missed the U. S. embassy by about a mile, and on the same day Japanese radicals in Tokyo fired homemade rockets at the U. S. embassy and the Imperial Palace, causing no injuries or damage. The next day terrorists in Greece bombed a car with U. S. license plates and a gas station a mile from the hotel where George Shultz was staying; another bomb under the car of an American diplomat was defused. In succeeding days, a stick of dynamite was hurled onto the roof of the U. S. embassy in Bolivia, causing only minor damage, and police in Istanbul arrested two persons who confessed to be agents of Qaddafi planning attacks on American targets in Turkey.[49]

According to *Sunday Times* of London sources in Lebanon, Qaddafi earmarked $6 million for attacks against U. S. and British interests in Lebanon at this juncture, and a Libyan intelligence officer began approaching low-level militia leaders, offering financial rewards for such attacks. American intelligence sources said Libya gave orders to two Lebanese army officers with close links to Syria to activate a plan for killing U. S. diplomats in Beirut. On the evening of March 28 there was an explosion at the American Language Centre in West Beirut, and hours later local hoodlums kidnapped British teachers Leigh Douglas and Philip Padfield, members of the "Daring Diners' Club" of Westerners persisting in West Beirut. The two men were believed to have been abducted on orders from Libyan intelligence and held on Libya's behalf by a group in the area. During the next two weeks Western intelligence sources found that Qaddafi was offering Hezbollah huge sums in exchange for its more than a dozen French and American hostages. Although those efforts would not prove successful, Libyan agents were believed to have purchased Peter Kilburn, the only American hostage not held by Hezbollah.[50] Meanwhile, Qaddafi in an interview threatened terrorist attacks against American targets if "war" resumed between the United States and Libya but sought to distance himself from his and others' current round of plots by saying, "Many, many people in the world support us, and they are angry. They may do anything, but we are not responsible."[51]

Paris was one of the destinations of intercepted messages from Tripoli ordering terrorist attacks, and the French counterintelligence service soon discovered a Libyan plot there. Beginning on April 2, France expelled a number of Arabs, among them two Libyan diplomats. The plan had been for an attack resembling the Rome and Vienna massacres, with terrorists hurling grenades and firing AK–47s at persons waiting in line at the U. S. visa office in Paris. The markings on the weapons, which the terrorists had been observed picking up from the Libyan people's bureau, matched those of weapons used in the airport attacks.[52]

The awful realization that terrorists were back on the offensive struck the public with the April 2 explosion aboard TWA Flight 840 between Rome and Athens. A Colombian-American was immediately killed, and a Greek-American grandmother, her daughter, and her infant granddaughter fell to their deaths over Greece. The Abu Nidal group, under one of its many cover names, claimed responsibility for the incident as a retaliation for Libya's defeat in the Gulf of Sidra. U. S. officials characterized Qaddafi as a suspect in the action but carefully reserved judgment. They played down speculation connecting the explosion with the Gulf of Sidra, and they were almost certainly correct in that, because of the complexity of the operation and the short interval since the Gulf of Sidra battle. There was much inconclusive speculation about what terrorist group and what state might be behind the bombing. In 1988 the State Department would point the finger at the Special Operations Group of Fatah, led by Arafat associate "Colonel Hawari," using alumni of the May 15 group, the Arab terrorist group most proficient at bombmaking.[53] Meanwhile, the most consequential of the terrorist acts of this period was yet to come.

NOTES

1. *Washington Post* (hereafter cited as *WP*), 15 Jan. 1986.

2. *WP*, 8 Jan., 25 Mar. 1986; *Los Angeles Times*, (hereafter cited as *LAT*), 29 Mar. 1986; *Air Force Times*, 7 Apr. 1986; *New York Times* (hereafter cited as *NYT*), 25 Mar. 1986; W. Hays Parks, "Crossing the Line," U. S. Naval Institute *Proceedings* 112 (Nov.

1986): 42–43; "O.K., Muammar, Your Move," *U. S. News & World Report*, 7 Apr. 1986, p. 24; "Targeting a 'Mad Dog,' " *Newsweek*, 21 Apr. 1986, p. 21.

3. John F. Lehman, Jr., *Command of the Seas* (New York: Charles Scribner's Sons, 1988), pp. 367–68; *LAT*, 29 Mar., 15 Apr. 1986; "Kaddafi's Crusade," *Newsweek*, 7 Apr. 1986, p. 24; David C. Martin and John Walcott, *Best Laid Plans: The Inside Story of America's War Against Terrorism* (New York: Harper & Row, 1988), p. 280; *NYT*, 26 Mar. 1986; *Middle East Policy Survey* (hereafter cited as *MEPS*), no. 149, 4 Apr. 1986.

4. "Kaddafi's Crusade," p. 24; "O.K., Muammar," pp. 24–25; *WP*, 25 Mar. 1986; *NYT*, 26 Mar. 1986; *LAT*, 29 Mar. 1986.

5. *LAT*, 29 Mar. 1986.

6. *Times* (London), 29 Apr. 1986; *WP*, 29 Apr. 1986; Nathan M. Adams, "Profiteers of Terror: The European Connection," *Reader's Digest*, Aug. 1986, p. 51; Bob Woodward, *VEIL: The Secret Wars of the CIA, 1981–1987* (New York: Simon & Schuster, 1987), p. 442.

7. Yossi Melman, *The Master Terrorist: The True Story of Abu Nidal* (New York: Adama Books, 1986), p. 183; *WP*, 6, 12 Jan. 1986; Woodward, p. 442. Melman refers to Casey touring the Middle East along with senior State Department officials for counterterrorism purposes in March. If the account is correct, one has to wonder whether Weinberger, who among Reagan's senior advisers was the most pro-Arab as well as the most cautious about military force, was kept uninformed about Casey's proposal, which, were it the case, would hardly be unparalleled in administration dealings.

8. *NYT*, 14 Mar. 1986; Woodward, p. 440; "O.K., Muammar," p. 25.

9. "Sailing in Harm's Way," *Time*, 7 Apr. 1986, p. 18.

10. Ibid., pp. 23–24; Woodward, pp. 441–42; "Kaddafi's Crusade," p. 24; Parks, p. 44; "The Poindexter Doctrine," *Newsweek*, 21 Apr. 1986, p. 24; *WP*, 27 Mar. 1986, 20 Feb. 1987; *NYT*, 10 Apr. 1986.

11. "Sailing in Harm's Way," p. 18; *NYT*, 27 Mar. 1986; *WP*, 24, 26, 27 Mar., 4 Apr. 1986; Woodward, p. 441–42; "O.K., Muammar," p. 22.

12. George Shultz, "Low-Intensity Warfare: The Challenge of Ambiguity," *Department of State Bulletin* 86 (Mar. 1986): 16.

13. *WP*, 26, 27 Mar. 1986; "Week of the Big Stick," *Time*, 7 Apr. 1986, p. 15; *Christian Science Monitor* (hereafter cited as *CSM*), 28 Mar. 1986; Mark Falcoff, "Foes without Hate," *Public Opinion* 9 (Mar.-Apr. 1987): 14; *NYT*, 27 Mar. 1986; *Times* (London), 16 Apr. 1986; "America to World: Have Power, Will Use," *U. S. News & World Report*, 7 Apr. 1986, p. 20.

14. "Sailing in Harm's Way," pp. 18, 23; Martin and Walcott, p. 281; *NYT*, 20 Mar. 1986; Robert E. Stumpf, "Air War with Libya," U. S. Naval Institute *Proceedings* 112 (Aug. 1986):46.

15. "To the Shores of Tripoli," *Time*, 31 Mar. 1986; p. 26.

16. "Kaddafi's Crusade," p. 24.

17. *Air Forces Times*, 7 Apr. 1986; Woodward, p. 442; *NYT*, 25 Mar. 1986; Memphis *Commercial Appeal*, 26 Mar. 1986; "O.K., Muammar," p. 24.

18. "Sailing in Harm's Way," pp. 17, 18; Stumpf, p. 46; *LAT*, 8 Apr. 1986; David M. North, "Merits of U. S., Soviet Weapons Explored in Libyan Conflict," *Aviation Week & Space Technology* 124 (31 Mar. 1986):20.

19. "Sailing in Harm's Way," pp. 20, 17; Parks, p. 45; *NYT*, 28 Mar. 1986; *WP*, 27 Mar. 1986; North, "U. S., Soviet Weapons," p. 21; Stumpf, p. 47.

20. "Sailing in Harm's Way," pp. 16–17; Stumpf, p. 47; Parks, p. 45; *NYT*, 26 Mar. 1986. As noted above, even the two attacks on the Surt missile site had been preemptive in timing.

21. *Sunday Times*, (hereafter cited as *ST*), 6 Apr. 1986; Parks, p. 45; *WP*, 4 Apr. 1986; "Hitting Back," p. 23; "Sailing in Harm's Way," p. 17; *MEPS*, 4 Apr. 1986; Lehman, pp. 370–371; Daniel P. Bolger, *Americans at War: 1975–1986, An Era of Violent Peace* (Novato, Calif.: Presidio Press, 1988), p. 400. Operation Prairie Fire marked the first combat use of the Harpoon and HARM missiles ("O.K., Muammar," p. 23).

22. *NYT*, 28 Mar. 1986.

23. "Sailing in Harm's Way," p. 23.

24. *NYT*, 28 Mar., 1986; "Early Warning," *World Press Review*, May 1986, p. 5; "Sailing in Harm's Way," p. 23; *Philadelphia Inquirer*, 30 Mar. 1986 (NewsBank, International Affairs and Defense, 1986, 27:C14, hereafter cited as NewsBank, INT).

25. "Sailing in Harm's Way," p. 23.

26. *NYT*, 25 Mar. 1986; *WP*, 25, 26, 30 Mar. 1986; "America to World," p. 20; "Kaddafi's Crusade," p. 23. An Arab diplomat observed, "The US allowed Qaddafi to determine the level of action. . . . The US destroyed two Libyan planes in 1981 and two boats now. By the year 2000 Qaddafi may begin to run out of sophisticated weapons" (*MEPS*, 4 Apr. 1986).

27. *WP*, 26 Mar. 1986; *NYT*, 26, 27 Mar. 1986; *Times* (London), 29 Mar. 1986; *Washington Times* (hereafter cited as *WT*), 26 Mar. 1986; *CSM*, 27 Mar. 1986; *German Tribune*, 13 Apr. 1986; "Gulf of Assertion," *Economist*, 29 Mar. 1986, p. 12.

28. *NYT*, 27 Mar. 1986.

29. *NYT*, 29 Mar. 1986.

30. *WP*, 16 Apr. 1986; *NYT*, 26, 27, 28 Mar. 1986; *Times* (London), 29 Mar. 1986; *Facts on File*, 28 Mar. 1986, p. 203; *WT*, 27 Mar. 1986.

31. *WT*, 26 Mar. 1986.

32. *WP*, 27 Mar. 1986; *WT*, 26, 28 Mar. 1986; *NYT*, 27, 28 Mar. 1986. When the Gulf of Sidra clashes broke out, the foreign ministers rejected Libya's request to interrupt the agenda on the Iran-Iraq war, which included complaints about Libya's supplying of arms to Iran (*NYT*, 26 Mar. 1986).

33. *WP*, 27 Mar. 1986.

34. "O.K., Muammar," p. 22; *Times* (London), 26 Mar. 1986; *Foreign Broadcast Information Service, Daily Report*, Middle East & Africa, 18 Apr. 1986, pp. D4–D5; "Kaddafi's Crusade," p. 24; *Wall Street Journal* (hereafter cited as *WSJ*), 26 Mar. 1986; *WP*, 27 Mar. 1986. *U. S. News & World Report* claimed that Saudi Arabia and Egypt "privately applauded the U. S. moves" ("O.K., Muammar," p. 22). Bob Woodward published a leak about the secret U. S.–Egyptian contingency planning in the March 26 edition of the *Post*. For public consumption Mubarak or his aides planted in the semiofficial *Al-Ahram* the erroneous story that the United States had three times attempted to enlist Cairo in a war against Libya and had three times been rebuffed. The Egyptian leader, however, privately told U. S. Ambassador Nicholas Veliotes that Egypt would continue in the contingency planning (*WP*, 26 Mar., 2 Apr. 1986; *NYT*, 21 Apr. 1986; *WSJ*, 3 Apr. 1986; Woodward, p. 444).

35. *NYT*, 26 Mar. 1986; U. S., President's Special Review Board, *The Tower Commission Report: The Full Text of the President's Special Review Board* (New York: Bantam Books and Times Book, 1987), pp. 265–66, 269.

36. *WP*, 26 Mar. 1986; *NYT*, 28, 29, 30 Mar. 1986; *Times* (London), 28 Mar. 1986.

37. *Philadelphia Inquirer*, 30 Mar. 1986 (NewsBank, INT, 1986, 27:C3).

38. Ibid.; *WSJ*, 28 Mar. 1986; *Times* (London), 28 Mar., 1 Apr. 1986; *NYT*, 29 Mar. 1986; "The Browning of the Green Book," *Economist*, 5 Apr. 1986, p. 46; "It Hurt," *Economist*, 19 Apr. 1986, p. 23; *ST*, 27 Apr. 1986.

39. *Philadelphia Inquirer*, 30 Mar. 1986 (NewsBank, INT, 1986, 27:C14); *NYT*, 29 Mar. 1986; *WP*, 29 Mar. 1986.

40. *NYT*, 26 Mar. 1986.

41. *Times* (London), 27 Mar. 1986.

42. Memphis *Commercial Appeal*, 29 Mar. 1986.

43. *WP*, 26 Mar. 1986; "Kaddafi's Crusade," p. 20; *NYT*, 26 Mar. 1986.

44. Robert Oakley, "International Terrorism," *Foreign Affairs* 65 (1987):617; Memphis *Commercial Appeal*, 20 Apr. 1986; Woodward, p. 444; "Washington Whispers," *U. S. News & World Report*, 7 Apr. 1986, p. 13.

45. "Targeting Gaddafi," *Time*, 21 Apr. 1986, p. 20

46. "Kaddafi's Crusade," p. 22; *NYT*, 12 Apr. 1986; "Targeting a 'Mad Dog,' " pp. 25, 20.

47. *WP*, 6 Apr. 1986.

48. *NYT*, 29 Mar. 1986; "In the Dead of the Night," *Time*, 28 Apr. 1986, p. 28; *WSJ*, 10 Apr. 1986; "Kaddafi's Crusade," p. 21; *WP*, 6 Apr. 1986; "Targeting a 'Mad Dog,' " p. 21. The fact of widespread serious Libyan terrorist plotting against the United States in this period received more than adequate piecemeal corroboration from foreign governments, including British interception of messages ordering various terrorist attacks (*Times* [London], 15 Apr. 1986).

49. *WP*, 26, 29 Mar., 16 Apr. 1986; *NYT*, 26 Mar., 21 Apr. 1986; Memphis *Commercial Appeal*, 27 Mar. 1986; *Air Force Times*, 7 Apr. 1986.

50. *ST*, 6, 20 Apr. 1986; "Targeting a 'Mad Dog,' " pp. 20, 25; *NYT*, 18, 19 Apr. 1986; *WP*, 19 Apr. 1986; "Hitting the Source," *Time*, 28 Apr. 1986, p. 19; "Targeting Gaddafi," p. 20; Adams, "Profiteers," p. 55.

51. *WT*, 1 Apr. 1986 (UPI).

52. "Kaddafi's Crusade," p. 21; "Tut Tut, Mostly," *Economist*, 19 Apr. 1986; Richard Mackenzie and Adam Platt, "Furor Explodes over NATO as U. S. Bombs Fall on Libya," *Insight*, 28 Apr. 1986, p. 31; *NYT*, 6, 16, 19 Apr. 1986; *LAT*, 6 Apr. 1986; Oakley, "International Terrorism," p. 617; *WP*, 16 Apr. 5 May 1986.

53. "Explosion on Flight 840," *Time*, 14 Apr. 1986, p. 35; *NYT*, 6 Apr. 1986; "French Court Convicts Palestinian Terrorist," *Department of State Bulletin* 89 (Feb. 1989): 64–65. The department also asserted that the Hawari group engaged in abortive plotting against U. S. facilities in Europe during the summer of 1986.

5

The La Belle Discotheque
Bombing and Its Aftermath

Within days of the battle in the Gulf of Sidra, a senior U. S. official had vowed, ''The next act of terrorism will bring the hammer down'' on Libya.[1] However, as noted, assignment of responsibility for the TWA bombing proved elusive. The prediction would find its fulfillment after an explosion in the divided city of Berlin.

While leaving it to the local people's bureaus to choose specific terrorist targets,the Qaddafi regime was providing general guidance: one intercepted message from Tripoli to Libyan diplomats suggested attacking social gathering places where U. S. military personnel habitually congregated. East Berlin was one of the destinations of orders to ''carry out the plan,'' and Libyan diplomats with known records of terrorist activities were sighted in West Berlin in the first few days of April by U. S. and West Berlin security personnel. American officials had sought and obtained cooperation against local Libyan terrorist plotting from a number of governments, including those of West Germany, France, Turkey, Italy, Switzerland, and Yugoslavia, but they did not find a positive response from Qaddafi's Soviet and East German allies when approaching them about the activities of the Libyan people's bureau in East Berlin.[2]

On Friday evening April 4, the East Berlin people's bureau sent Tripoli a cable declaring, ''We have something planned that will make you happy.[3] . . . It will happen soon, the bomb will blow, American soldiers must be hit.''[4] The message was intercepted, decoded, and routed to the operations center of the U. S. Army brigade in Berlin. U. S. officials moved to alert American soldiers on the streets of West Berlin and in its nightspots, including the La Belle discotheque. However, they were fifteen minutes too late: at 1:49 A.M. local time, a bomb exploded in the La Belle, where about five hundred people were crowded. There was a chaotic scene as walls buckled, part of the ceiling collapsed, and hundreds of screaming patrons fled into the streets. A U. S. GI named Kenneth Ford and his Turkish girlfriend Nermine Hanay were immediately killed; James Goins, another American soldier, was mortally wounded and would die two months later. There were 229 other persons wounded, including 79 Americans, mostly soldiers. It was considered remarkable that more people were not killed.[5]

After the explosion the East Berlin people's bureau reported to Tripoli that the operation had been successful and could not be traced to Libya. Officials in Washington soon possessed the translated messages, and even the most skeptical among them were convinced that they had a smoking-gun against the Qaddafi regime. According to some accounts, the La Belle intercepts that the United States found in its possession were retrieved and decoded by its own National Security Agency. According to other British and U. S. sources, the March 25, April 4, and April 5 Libyan messages were intercepted by the British eavesdropping service GCHQ and speedily transmitted to the Americans. (The NSA and the GCHQ are reported to be intimately entwined, including special radio circuits linking each to the other.) In any case, it is certain that the messages that U. S. officials used to link Libya to the discotheque bombings were intercepted by the British themselves—as British officials implied in statements after the U. S. air strikes concerning their own gathering of information implicating Libya—and not simply shown to Whitehall by U. S. officials. British opposition leader David Steel of the Liberal party affirmed the validity of the evidence shown him by Thatcher's foreign minister, Sir Geoffrey Howe. West Germany also intercepted the Libyan messages: Chancellor Kohl on April 16 told the *Bundestag* that Bonn had "incontrovertible intelligence" of Libyan responsibility for the La Belle bombing, gathered independently of the United States. He mentioned Libyan messages which were clearly the same as the April 4 and 5 messages Reagan cited in his speech after the air strikes. Israeli Prime Minister Peres stated that Libya was "undoubtedly" behind the discotheque bombing, and Israeli officials told the *Chicago Tribune* that Jerusalem had given the United States evidence linking Libya to the incident. Prime Minister Craxi of Italy averred after the air strikes that Washington had offered "absolutely convincing proof" of Libya's guilt in it. In the week after the explosion, American, British, and French officials meeting in West Berlin contemplated sending military policemen to East Berlin to arrest Libyan diplomats suspected in the incident, but decided that such a move would be too provocative; they did, however, ban Libyan diplomats in East Berlin from further crossing into West Berlin.[6]

More than a month after the La Belle discotheque bombing, press reports of an additional Syrian connection to the incident emerged. That information involved the exposure of a fledgling Europe-based group of terrorists for hire called the Jordanian Revolutionary Movement for National Salvation, having links to Syria, Libya, and reportedly also the Abu Nidal group. It was centered around the Hindawi clan, which had fled the Italians in Libya in the 1920s, settled in Palestine, fled the Israelis in the late 1940s, and had become Jordanian citizens. The Hindawi group came to light with the arrest of its leader, Nezar Hindawi, for a Syrian-supported attempt to use an Irish woman to smuggle a bomb aboard an El Al airliner in London on April 17, in what was widely supposed to have been intended as a grotesquely disproportionate revenge for the February Israeli interception of a Libyan airliner carrying Syrian officials. The arrest of Nezar Hindawi led quickly to the arrest in West Berlin of his brother Ahmed Hazi, who was eventually convicted in November 1986 of the March 29 bombing of the German-Arab Friendship Society. The latter action, which injured nine people, was done at the instigation of Nezar and utilized the services of the Syrian embassy in East Berlin. Ahmed—who, according to testimony in his trial, was an ardent admirer of Qaddafi—and Nezar had been frequent visitors to Libya, Lebanon, and Syria in the 1984–85 period. Hazi was originally arrested as a suspect in the La Belle bombing. This came about, according to press leaks in May 1986, after Nezar reportedly told British interrogators that Syrian officials had boasted of their involvement in the disco bombing and that Hazi had been involved at their behest. A number of persons saw Hazi at La Belle the day before the explosion, and a sketch of what could have been the discotheque was found in his apartment. There were other press reports in May that Israel had gathered information linking Syria to the La Belle bombing, to which Whitehead responded by acknowledging their plausibility in view of previous cases of dual Libyan and Syrian involvement in acts of terrorism; he continued to insist that the evidence against Libya was "incontrovertible."[7]

One terrorism expert has privately suggested that Hazi could have separately marketed the La Belle bombing to both the Libyans and the Syrians in order to gain two payoffs for one act. Hazi may not have been that clever; a more likely scenario is that Libyan and Syrian officials consciously collaborated in the episode. The phenomenon of joint state sponsorship of terrorist acts cannot reasonably be denied: the Iranian- and Syrian-sponsored Islamic Jihad bombings of 1983 are only the most famous examples of such incidents. Gen. Ali Douba, a member of Syria's terrorism apparatus, was reported by Robin Wright to have worked with Libya, and according to Yonah Alexander, the secret services of Libya and Syria had formed a working alliance to assassinate opponents of both countries, with a mixed team of Syrians and Libyans known to have attacked a Syrian dissident in West Germany in one instance.[8]

Whether the two terrorist allies consciously collaborated in the La Belle incident or not, the Reagan administration's original conclusion that the La Belle bombing was conceived by the Libyans still seems quite sound. An attack against Americans and against a nightclub fit long-standing Libyan modi operandi, whereas Syria had over the long term shown less inclination to take the terrorism offensive against the United States directly,[9] and Syrian-sponsored anti-American attacks were not known to have occurred outside of countries neighboring Syria. Furthermore, there was the backdrop of the immediate motive of revenge for the Gulf of Sidra defeat, numerous Libyan anti-American plots in other counties, and of sightings of Libyan diplomats in West Berlin, none of which was paralleled in the case of Syria.

As previously noted, Libyan agents had been under order to put layers of deniability between Libya and terrorist attacks by working through Palestinians and other non-Libyans, so they would have a motive to seek to draw the Syrians into the plot. A former Libyan diplomat has testified that Qaddafi sought to involve Damascus in a 1983 plot to kill King Hussein by shooting down his private jet; the Syrian foreign minister warmed to the idea, but Assad rejected it on the grounds that it would make every Arab leader fear for his life whenever he flew in an airplane.[10]

In any case, the insistence of many observers that Syria participated in the La Belle discotheque bombing *instead of* Libya is unreasonable. There appear to be three reasons for this stance. First, some people seem to be sincerely uninformed about the fact that the involvement of one country in a terrorist action or with a specific terrorist does not preclude the involvement of another country, and they see Ahmed Hazi's conviction of bombing the German-Arab Friendship Society under Syrian sponsorship as ruling out a Libyan role in the La Belle attack in which Hazi is strongly suspected.[11] Second, there are some parties who are so passionate about pinning responsibility for terrorism on Syria that they prefer to intensify the Assad regime's guilt by leaving Libya out of the picture. Third, and most widely manifest, the idea that Syria and *not* Libya performed the La Belle bombing is obviously a visceral response of Western intellectuals and journalists, as well as government officials in Europe, expressing their resentment of the U. S. air strikes against Libya, which were justified by citing Libya's complicity in the West Berlin incident. Some of these persons have gone so far as to espouse, without any evidence, a notion of a Reagan administration conspiracy to frame Qaddafi. The idea that such a scheme could be carried off is absurd in view of the sprawling, unwieldy nature of the U. S. government, which is always ideologically heterogeneous and filled with career personnel feeling no peculiar loyalty to the current administration. Moreover, the conspiracy theorists seem to have amnesia about foreign governments' corroboration of Libyan guilt in the discotheque bombing. *After* the evidence concerning a Syrian role emerged, British Minister of State for Foreign and Commonwealth Affairs Timothy Renton declared that "British evidence of Libyan involvement in the West Berlin bombing remained incontrovertible and the British Government had seen nothing to contradict it,"[12] and Kohl declared, "I have not the slightest doubt that the trail of blood from the Berlin disco bombing leads to Tripoli."[13] They have not revoked these assertions. If they fully viewed the facts, the conspiracy theorists would have to try to make a case for a preposterous joint U. S.–British–German–Israeli conspiracy.

THE ADMINISTRATION DECIDES TO RETALIATE

Nonetheless, in the week after the La Belle explosion, the Reagan adminis-tration's deliberations were not complicated by any hints of a possible Syrian connection, which policymakers would probably in retrospect consider fortui-tous. As Reagan returned on April 6 from Easter vacation in California, Shultz, Poindexter, Casey, and Regan had formed a solid bloc in favor of military reprisal against Libya. At this time Bush and Weinberger were touring the Middle East and the Pacific, respectively. The vice-president had declared in an interview that he favored hitting hard at Qaddafi after his next terrorist act. Weinberger offered no opposition this time to the idea of military action in his communi-cations with Washington.[14] Shultz reportedly told the president, "We have taken enough punishment and beating. We have to act."[15] Reagan needed little per-suasion; there was considerable anger with Qaddafi all around. The only wran-gling in the days to come would be over specific targeting and tactics.[16]

Reagan is said to have told his aides on April 7, "Try to make the world smaller for terrorists."[17] He made his initial approval of an attack tentative, but it would have taken a truly major development to prevent it. The decision became more firm but still not irrevocable when the president issued a formal National Security Decision Directive on April 9. Officials were ordered to gather as much evidence as possible against Libya on the La Belle incident and to double-check all of it; this enabled members of the government to tell reporters in the week before the raid that the evidence was still being examined pending a final con-clusion. Reagan directed planners to develop scenarios to minimize the risks to U. S. pilots and to civilians on the ground. Central in the planning were Crowe and the Joint Chiefs of Staff, as well as Kelso and NATO commander Gen. Bernard Rogers, who were brought to Washington for the purpose; more detailed aspects, such as munitions loadings and attack profiles were handled by more junior military commanders in the European theater. Military lawyers were fre-quently consulted. Lt. Col. Oliver North and the NSC staff busied themselves in the preparations, but contrary to the portrayal given by North's partisans and by investigative reporter Seymour Hersh, the NSC staff did not have a controlling role. The president had left the preparations firmly in the grasp of the U. S. military; the NSC staff was reduced to eavesdropping on the Pentagon in order to be able to be fully apprised of what was transpiring, including the military's selection of aim points.[18]

No military option other than air strikes was seriously considered. The pres-ident's guidelines led quickly to the decision that the attack would be made at night, which was heavily influenced by the humiliating memory of the daylight attack on Syrian positions in Lebanon by Navy jets in 1983. A night attack would take advantage of the poor nocturnal flying of the Libyan air force and would reduce the risk to pilots from ground-based antiaircraft fire, in particular virtually eliminating the threat of man-operated weapons, including the shoulder-launched missiles that the Syrians had used to shoot down a Navy jet. Crowe and the Joint Chiefs asserted that more firepower needed to be added to U. S. assets presently in the Mediterranean and suggested that F–111 jets based in Great Britain be used. Therefore, on the evening of April 8 a top-secret telex was sent to Prime Minister Thatcher asking for British endorsement of a U.S strike on Libya and permission to launch planes from the British bases. Days of negotiations ensued.[19]

One of the great controversies surrounding Operation El Dorado Canyon, as the air raids would be called, would be the assertion that the decision for a joint Navy–Air Force strike rather than an all-Navy strike was the product of motivations other than rational military considerations. In view of the fact that most Sixth Fleet contingency plans for large air strikes factored in the British-based F–111s, it cannot be considered bizarre that the U. S. military at this juncture contemplated using them. Some critics alleged that the reason for using the F–111s was to involve Great Britain in the operation. Certainly there was a bias in favor of making the attack as multilateral as possible: reportedly even Portugal was asked to allow overflight of its air space, which seemed to have only symbolic value; that this bias was the decisive factor in favor of seeking to use the F–111s cannot be said for certain. The suggestion that the joint attack was the result of jealousy by the Air Force after the all-Navy Gulf of Sidra battle in March should be dismissed out of hand: in the immediate aftermath of the Rome and Vienna massacres, Chief of Naval Operations Adm. James D. Watkins had taken the lead in promoting the idea of a joint Navy–Air Force strike, and Navy and Air Force theater personnel had begun meeting to prepare such contingencies in January.[20]

More plausible was the view expressed by John F. Lehman, Jr., after he left the post of Secretary of the Navy, that the decisive factor was what he saw as an irrational commitment on the part of the top military brass to "jointness" in military operations, having previously manifested itself in Grenada. Lehman's view is, however, widely contested in the military. Certainly an attack on Libya could have been launched from only the two aircraft carriers in the Mediterranean, but not *any* sort of attack. The criterion of a night attack ruled out using the Navy's A–7s and F/A–18s for bombing runs. Another criterion for the attack was that it had to be punishing, with plenty of "high visibility" damage to the targets. If the United States was going to the trouble of attacking, it had to strike Libya hard enough to give a chance for a deterrent effect upon terrorist opponents including the Qaddafi regime itself. An attack that was widely reported as having only inflicted light damage could even be viewed as a Libyan victory, and inflicting relatively light military damage on the Jamahiriyah in March had obviously not served much useful purpose. Furthermore, to protect pilots' lives planners wanted simultaneous and not successive air strikes; the hypersensitivity of Libyan air defenses in the wake of the April 15 attack would vindicate the wisdom of this criterion. With these things in view, the twenty combat-ready A–6s on the carriers were not enough for a punishing strike on as many as four or five targets. It was argued by some military experts that more A–6s could have been flown to the carriers. Some Navy officers countered this argument with the assertion that such a move would have been detected by the Libyans or their Soviet friends, and therefore would have put the defenders on intensified alert. Furthermore, the F–111 was regarded as attractive because it was the most sophisticated U. S. aircraft of its type. It was faster than the A–6, carried a much heavier bombload, and had superior missile-evading capability. Additionally, Gen. Rogers was reported to have found it desirable to demonstrate to present and future enemies of the United States that there did not have to be an aircraft carrier nearby for them to fear an attack.[21]

CALCULATIONS BEHIND THE DECISION TO ATTACK

A number of factors greatly affected the administration's thinking in the decision to attack Libya; undoubtedly, particular factors carried different weight with different officials. One key consideration was intelligence concerning continuing Libyan terrorist plotting against the United States worldwide. A rocket explosion near the American embassy in Beirut early on April 6 was traced to Libya; there were unclaimed bombings directed against the United States in Bangkok and Stockholm on April 7 and 8, respectively. Libyan plots were discovered for an attack on the U. S. consulate in Munich and for the bombing of the U. S. chancery and embassy and kidnapping of the American ambassador in an African country. Orders from Tripoli were issued for striking U. S. international air carriers, and numerous other plots were in motion for attacks on American embassies and individuals in Europe, the Middle East, Africa, and Latin America, where a car with Libyan diplomatic tags was found to be tailing a bus filled with American school children. Reagan was incensed by these plans. They neutralized in the eyes of Washington officials the standard concern about provoking more attacks by the terrorists: it seemed that the United States had nothing to lose in that respect by hitting Libya and could perhaps deter plots that were already in motion. In addition, it was felt that publicly presenting the attack as being preemptive as well as retaliatory was desirable to bolster the legal case for it.[22]

Especially important was the administration's belief that it was time to strike a blow against terrorism in general and to "raise the costs" for it, as Shultz said. Officials recognized that Qaddafi was not the whole problem but felt that punishing him could help discourage terrorism by others, including his allies, Syria and Iran. It was felt that the evidence on the La Belle bombing was too good to pass up the opportunity to implement the White House's long-announced doctrine of reprisal against terrorism. Credibility was even at stake: by making threats (with the intention of deterring), particularly against Qaddafi, the administration had "burned its bridges."[23] An NSC staffer remarked, "There's no question we created a bit of a Frankenstein's monster. . . . But the monster was supposed to spook Gaddafi."[24] In the La Belle bombing, Qaddafi had called the

United States' bluff. Now, Washington knew that Libya had struck, and after press leaks described below, Qaddafi knew that Washington knew. Given his record of brinkmanship, pushing opponents as far as he possibly could without reprisal, it was felt that to do nothing would be tantamount to conceding to him a "license to kill," and would encourage terrorists in general by proving to them that the United States was impotent against them.[25]

Erroneously divorcing the Libyan raid from this context of war on terrorism would be some observers like Hersh, who in 1987 sought to portray it as an "assassination attempt" against Qaddafi emanating from a wicked NSC staff. The target list did include the spacious Bab al-Aziziyya complex in Tripoli, a site for terrorist training and the "nerve center" of the regime, with communications and intelligence centers, a barracks of revolutionary guards, headquarters for the Libyan Military, and Qaddafi's working and living quarters. Gen. Richard Lawson, deputy US commander in Europe claimed credit for selecting it and the other four targets which Reagan approved. There is little doubt that the administration hoped that the Libyan dictator would be one of the casualties of the air strikes but portraying that as the raison d'être is unreasonable. All persons familiar with the subject of Qaddafi were aware of his habit of constantly shifting offices and sleeping quarters; at least six other sites in Libya were identified as Qadaffi residences. His main command post in times of crisis was said to be an oasis more than a hundred miles inland. U. S. intelligence indicated in the few days before the attack that the colonel was moving three times a day. Even if Qaddafi were at Bab al-Aziziyya on the night of the raid, the U. S. government expected that he would be not in the Bedouin tent where he often received visitors, but in the underground bunker which was his main living quarters in Bab al-Aziziyya. After the attack Kelso responded to a reporter's query by observing that the U. S. planes did not have "ordnance to go after deep bunkers," and Qaddafi's bunker had indeed been built by the East Germans to withstand anything short of a nuclear strike. Obviously, Qaddafi's demise in the air strike had to be seen as a very improbable outcome. According to a report in 1988, a proposal by an NSC staff official to use Qaddafi's British acquaintance Terry Waite as an unwitting agent to manipulate the colonel into place for the raid was swiftly rejected by the administration. Administration officials stated that they desired to hit the intelligence center and the revolutionary guards in the compound in order to make a symbolic point against terrorism and to demonstrate vulnerability on the part of Qaddafi's loyalists so as to encourage his potential opponents inside Libya. Also quite importantly, the administration felt that hitting Bab al-Aziziyya could have an intimidating effect upon Qaddafi whether he was present or not.[26]

Indeed, many of the calculations behind the decision to attack rested on the assumption that the Libyan leader would still be around afterward. A number of officials asserted that the key premise was that Qaddafi's terrorism could be stopped only by striking against Libya until he either retreated or fell in a coup; making it too painful for him to continue was an objective. Some officials declared that the administration believed that with one attack it would not likely "hit the jackpot," that is, bring an immediate end to Qaddafi's support of terrorism or the downfall of his regime; President Reagan's speech after the air raids reflected this. The possibility of subsequent U. S. attacks was very much in the mind of many officials.[27]

Stimulating Qaddafi's overthrow was for most administration officials a subsidiary motive for the raid, and, contrary to the widespread impression, they saw it as a long-term objective rather than expecting an immediate coup. As strongly expressed by Bush, the administration flatly rejected the notion held by Italian and some other European officials, as well as by the Middle East experts, that attacking Qaddafi would only serve to make him a larger-than-life figure in Libya and the Arab world; Bush and others held that it would in fact weaken the colonel in the long run. Some officials reportedly felt that the impression that he was able to act with impunity was what would strengthen Qaddafi. In response to the argument that leaving him alone was more likely to facilitate his downfall, officials argued that the Libyan strongman's repression was so effective that he would not fall without a push.[28]

One key assumption by the administration in preparing the strike on Libya was that the European allies would continue to reject tough nonmilitary measures against the Jamahiriyah. Nonetheless, U. S. diplomats were assigned the task of pressuring the allies for the closing of Libyan people's bureaus and economic sanctions. By most accounts, a drastic breakthrough in terms of sanctions would have probably sufficed to dissuade Reagan from military action. The State Department shared evidence on La Belle and other Libyan terrorist plots with the allies, and they found it persuasive. In spite of that, in spite of warnings from Whitehead and Oakley in their January tour that in the absence of strong collective sanctions Washington would feel free to resort to "other measures," and in spite of fresh hints of military action, the Europeans remained intransigent. Because of the location of the La Belle explosion, the government of West Germany came under the heaviest American pressure, but it swiftly rejected sanctions, and, while it expelled two Libyan diplomats for the Munich consulate plot, it permitted four others who were suspected of terrorist connections to remain. An ancillary motive for the bombing of Libya for some U. S. officials was to shock the Europeans out of their torpid posture, although others who supported the attack feared it could be counterproductive in those respects.[29]

THE COUNTDOWN TO RETALIATION

Events would make Shultz's previously expressed wish that the United States "act on a moment's notice" seem laughable. Action was delayed for a week after Reagan's preliminary decision to strike Libya; accounts concerning the reasons for this delay have been wildly contradictory. Throughout the period a flood of leaks filled broadcasts and newspapers. Beginning the day after the discotheque bombing, anonymous officials revealed that Libya was implicated, and much information about the diplomatic messages and their interception leaked in subsequent days, causing great consternation at the National Security Agency and leading the Libyans to change their code. Ambassador to West Germany Richard Burt angered administration officials[30] by saying on the "Today" show on April 7 that there were "very clear indications that there was Libyan involvement" and, when asked about retaliation, saying that Reagan was "studying this issue right now."[31] "The White House resolved to retaliate against Libya,"[32] declared a headline in the April 9 issue of the *Wall Street Journal*. The *Washington Times* on April 11 reported that the use of F–111s based in Great Britain was possible because Margaret Thatcher appeared to be easing her opposition.[33]

The movements of the Sixth Feet (now down to only two aircraft carriers) received maximum publicity, and its pilots were deeply dismayed to learn that details of target areas and proposed timing were being aired in the American press; many concluded that chances for carrying out the mission without heavy losses had been endangered. Reagan was also angered by the leaks, and by one account they forced a postponement of the operation. The reason for the leaks is not perfectly clear. They seemed not to have resulted from desire to force the president to call off the attack. Perhaps it was simply the sheer irresponsibility of government officials accustomed to talking freely to the press under cover of anonymity and not wise enough to change their habits in time of crisis. Many officials fought against the impact of the leakers with deliberately restrained assessments of the evidence against Libya and by putting out the word that an attack was not imminent after all, or by saying that the president had not reached a final decision yet, which was true only in an extremely technical sense.[34]

In Tripoli, dozens of foreign correspondents were gathering to await the U. S. attack, and Qaddafi was aware of what was being reported. He held a press conference on April 9 announcing that he had just finished a meeting for preparing military plans for an impending U. S. attack[35] and warned, "It is axiomatic that if aggression is being staged against us, we shall escalate the violence against American targets, civilian and noncivilian, all over the world."[36] He threatened to sabotage Mediterranean shipping and attack ports that hosted the Sixth Fleet[37] and spoke of an agreement with the Soviet Union for "consultations and coordinating efforts during dangerous conflicts."[38] According to one report, in the meeting Qaddafi spoke of, preparations were made to prevent a coup d'etat in the wake of a U. S. attack (despite the cliché that an attack could only strengthen the colonel's position), and a participating KGB representative made it clear that Moscow was not going to come to the Jamahiriyah's defense, which was just what Washington officials were assuming.[39] In his press conference later that same day, Reagan called Qaddafi "the mad dog of the Middle East," said that he was a "suspect" in the recent terrorist attacks, sidestepped the question of whether he had made a decision to retaliate, and reiterated that long-declared policy was that if those responsible for terrorism could be identified, the United States would "respond."[40]

Oil prices rose daily as apprehension about a possible U. S. attack against Libya spread. Moderate Arabs privately warned Washington that another clash with Qaddafi could strengthen him in Libya and the Arab world. On his tour of friendly Arabian states, Bush was told that quiet assassination would be a better approach to Qadaffi than overt military action.[41] A high-ranking Algerian official confidentially told U. S. counterparts, "You Americans must realize that Qaddafi will disappear one day, but that the humiliation you inflict on the Libyan people will live on and on."[42] Despite the turmoil, a new alliance of anti-Qaddafi Libyans surfaced in Paris on April 7. Continental NATO leaders publicly expressed misgivings over the possibility of an attack, and Canada's Mulroney cautioned against using a "shotgun approach" but did not indicate that all possible military reprisals should be ruled out. The Continental allies also privately pressured Thatcher not to grant the United States use of British bases in England or Cyprus.[43]

Having received a personal phone call on April 9 from her friend Reagan requesting permission for the F–111s and aerial tankers to fly from bases in England, Thatcher faced perhaps the most difficult decision in her political career. Opinion polls already showed the idea of military retaliation against terrorism to be highly unpopular with the British public, and she had herself proclaimed it contrary to international law as recently as January. She was sagging badly in the popularity polls, and the British public was experiencing a wave of anti-Americanism over recent controversies surrounding multinational corporations; Thatcher herself was entangled in the furor. Furthermore, she shared the fears of other NATO allies about the aftermath of an attack on Libya, and the cabinet was aware that the two new British hostages in Lebanon were under Libyan control. Considerations on the other side of the issue were Libya's substantial support over the years for the IRA, the memory of the killing of Yvonne Fletcher, and the "Falklands factor": the memory of how Reagan had given crucial help to Great Britain in the 1982 reconquest of the Falkland Islands, despite Washington's misgivings over the importance of the islands and the anticipated impact upon opinion in Latin America. The most crucial consideration for Thatcher, however, was concern about the long-term consequences for the Western alliance: if America were totally deserted by its European allies in this operation, it could seemingly cause such anger and disillusionment with NATO in the United States that existing pressure for reversing the massive commitment of ground troops to Europe could prevail. Thatcher's decision to allow use of the bases was smoothed by Reagan's plea that the F–111s were needed to reduce risks to American personnel and Libyan civilians and by Washington's position that the raid was to be self-defense against ongoing Libyan terrorism as well as retaliation for the La Belle incident.[44]

On April 12 Reagan secretly dispatched Vernon Walters, his ambassador to the United Nations, to Europe to seek support against Libya from the allies. Walters' first stop was pleasant because, after agonizing over it, Thatcher had already reached the decision to grant the F–111 request. Discussion therefore centered upon public justification of the attack and how much intelligence should be disclosed. When he crossed over to the Continent and gave leaders strong indications of what Washington was planning, Walters was told that an attack was a dangerous idea, likely to produce more terrorism and trap the United States in a cycle of violence. Prime Minister Gonzalez in Madrid said no to the possibilities of U. S. aircraft overflying Spain or being refueled by tanker aircraft based there. (Italy and Greece had already made it known that their bases could not be used; the administration had made no plans to ask.) Walters pressed the West Germans for sanctions with no success on April 13.[45]

The Reagan administration earnestly desired its planes to overfly France, which lay on the direct route between England and Libya. However, Walters received a negative response when he met with Prime Minister Jacques Chirac on the evening of April 13; Reagan was incensed that even permission to land the F–111s in Corsica after the raid was refused. Reasons cited for the rejection by the French have included their fear that the attack would only incite Qaddafi more, the fear of harm to their efforts to woo his ally Iran in order to win the release of eight Frenchmen held by Hezbollah in Lebanon, and the haste with which a decision was expected upon the proposal.[46]

The most intriguing aspect of Walters's visit to Paris came in his meeting with Mitterrand on the morning of April 14. Echoing earlier Paris sentiments concerning covert action, the French president declared that it was unwise to "do a pinprick" in attacking Libya and suggested that the United States and France discuss a much stronger joint military action that would be certain to bring an end to the rule of Qaddafi in Libya; he later repeated such sentiments in a conversation with West German politician Franz Josef Strauss. It was widely felt that Mitterrand had been striking an advantageous posture in full knowledge that Washington would not consider an invasion of Libya politically viable.[47]

Shrill threats of retaliation in Europe continued to proceed from Tripoli. The kidnapping of the Italian bishop of Tripoli and four Franciscans in Benghazi was linked in speculation to efforts by Libya to deter European support for a U. S. attack or to the impending visit of the Pope to a synagogue in Rome. On April 12 Qaddafi declared that he was moving foreign workers in Libya into military camps targeted by the United States. In a seeming effort to keep the Libyans off balance, Whitehead and Oakley in television appearances on April 13 said that the evaluation of the La Belle evidence was not yet final and spoke of a U. S. military assault as possible but not inevitable.[48]

Monday April 14 was a busy day for the Jamahiriyah. In the morning the Libyan air force bombed another southern Sudanese village, reportedly killing seven people, including children. Two Libyan diplomats in the Central African Republic were presented with notice of expulsion in connection with an explosion that had destroyed a bridge outside the capital of Bangui on April 1.[49] In an interview with Italian television, Qaddafi indicated that he expected a U. S. attack and dodged the question, "Do you count on Soviet support?" by declaring, "We count on the support of the whole world."[50] The foreign ministers of Libya,

Syria, and Iran gathered in Tehran to discuss the possibility of an attack on Libya and, reportedly, intensification of anti-American terrorism. In Libya, the Qaddafi regime put into effect its contingency plan for an air attack. Hospitals were put on alert, missiles and radar were positioned, and Libyan naval vessels were moved alongside merchant ships to force the United States to risk killing foreign civilian seamen if it desired to attack the Libyan navy.[51] At the same time officials in Tripoli anxiously looked to see what the Europeans would do.

The EEC foreign ministers gathered that day in the Hague to try to head off an American attack on Libya but brought with them little of the political will needed for the task. Despite the warnings of Britain's Foreign Secretary Geoffrey Howe that if they were "concerned about the possibility of an American military attack, the Europeans must be able to show a commitment to alternative means,"[52] the ministers overwhelmingly rejected the closure of Libyan people's bureaus; economic sanctions were apparently not even broached. A decision to name Libya as a country implicated in terrorism passed reportedly only over objections from France and West Germany, the two countries that had in recent days expelled Libyan diplomat-terrorists, and from Italy, which had taken the initiative for calling the meeting in the first place. The ministers' final communiqué called for unspecified restrictions in the movements of Libyan diplomats and reductions in the staff of Libyan diplomatic and consular missions, tighter visa requirements for Libyans,[53] and, in an obvious plea to Washington, "avoiding further escalation of military tension in the region."[54] Amazingly, the European foreign ministers expected these long-overdue half measures to mollify Washington sufficiently to prevent an attack. Immediate administration response was negative.[55]

NOTES

1. "Kaddafi's Crusade," *Newsweek*, 7 Apr. 1986, p. 23.

2. Bob Woodward, *VEIL: The Secret Wars of the CIA, 1981–1987* (New York: Simon & Schuster, 1987), p 445; *Washington Post* (hereafter cited as *WP*), 22 Apr. 1986; David Blundy and Andrew Lycett, *Qaddafi and the Libyan Revolution* (Boston: Little, Brown, 1987), pp. 4–5; *New York Times* (hereafter cited as *NYT*), 12, 15 Apr. 1986; *Los Angeles Times* (hereafter cited as *LAT*), 15 Apr. 1986; *Wall Street Journal* (hereafter cited as *WSJ*), 11 Apr. 1986; Robert Oakley, "International Terrorism," *Foreign Affairs* 65 (1987): 617.

3. Seymour Hersh, "Target: Qaddafi," *New York Times Magazine*, 22 Feb. 1987, p. 74.

4. Blundy and Lycett, p. 5; *NYT*, 17 Apr. 1986.

5. David C. Martin and John Walcott, *Best Laid Plans: The Inside Story of America's War Against Terrorism* (New York: Harper & Row, 1988), p. 285; "Seeking the Smoking Fuse," *Time*, 21 Apr. 1986, p. 22; "Targeting a 'Mad Dog,' " *Newsweek*, 21 Apr. 1986, p. 25; *NYT*, 6, 23 Apr., 8 June 1986; *LAT*, 6, 13 Apr. 1986; Memphis *Commercial Appeal*, 6 Apr. 1986; Daniel P. Bolger, *Americans at War: 1975–1986, An Era of Violent*

Peace (Novato, Calif.: Presidio Press, 1988), p. 404; *Washington Times* (hereafter cited as *WT*), 9 June 1986.

6. Larry Speakes with Robert Pack, *Speaking Out: The Reagan Presidency from inside the White House* (New York: Charles Scribner's Sons, 1988), p. 180; *NYT*, 10, 15, 17, 23 Apr., 20 Nov. 1986; *WP*, 15, 17 Apr. 1986; Woodward, p. 445; Blundy and Lycett, p. 405; Martin and Walcott, pp. 285–86; James Bamford, *The Puzzle Palace: A Report on America's Most Secret Agency* (Boston: Houghton, Mifflin, 1982), pp. 315, 317, 331; "Spook Corner," *Economist*, 19 Apr. 1986, p. 24; *Washington Times* (hereafter cited as *WT*), 16 Apr. 1986; *Chicago Tribune*, 17, 20 Apr. 1986; *LAT*, 15 Apr. 1986; New Orleans *Times-Picayune*, 20 Apr. 1986 (AP).

7. *NYT*, 27 Apr., 14 May, 14 Sept., 21 Nov. 1986; "Brothers in Arms," *Newsweek*, 5 May 1986, p. 31; *WP*, 14, 16 May 1986; *LAT*, 14 May 1986; "A Syrian Smoking Gun?" *Newsweek*, 19 May 1986, p. 40; *German Tribune*, 30 Nov. 1986; *WT*, 6 Apr. 1987. Without stating specifics, some U. S. officials have indicated that they think Libya as well as Syria was involved in the Friendship Society bombing (*NYT*, 12 Jan. 1988).

8. *CSM*, 6 Nov. 1986; Yonah Alexander, "Libyan Terrorism: Some Strategic Considerations," in U. S. Congress, Senate Committee on the Judiciary, Subcommittee on Security and Terrorism, *Libyan-Sponsored Terrorism: A Dilemma for Policymakers*, 19 Feb. 1986, 99th Cong., 2d sess., p. 104.

9. *Focus on Libya*, Apr. 1985; Martin and Walcott, p. 372; Daniel Pipes, "Terrorism: The Syrian Connection," *National Interest*, no. 15 (Spring 1989), p. 27.

10. Blundy and Lycett, pp. 147–48.

11. Before the La Belle bombing, Syria may have activated Hazi upon being approached by Libya, or the Libyans may have approached Hazi directly. Journalistic reports portrayed Hazi in a 1985 trip to Libya as having been "fobbed off" with $5,000 before he subsequently received training in Syria. Actually, as one terrorism expert has noted, it is naive to assume that Hazi's relationship with Libya came to an end after his 1985 visit (interview with Terrell E. Arnold, 10 June 1989). The $5,000 payment was much larger than what was given to the Mootz Brothers, two confirmed terrorist "sleepers" for Libya in West Germany (David Th. Schiller, "Two Bombings in Berlin: More than Meets the Eye," *TVRI Report* 7 [1987]:4). Some other things that should be kept in mind are: the fact that it was in Hazi's interest to play down his relationship with Libya since he did not want to be tried for murder in the lethal La Belle incident, and the fact that the Hindawi brothers were not career servants of the Syrian government but mercenaries working for the highest bidder at a given time.

12. *Times* (London), 13 May 1986.

13. *WP*, 30 May 1986. The conspiracy theorists eagerly seized upon several statements by Volker Kähne, spokesman for the West Berlin Justice Department, to the effect that the West Berlin police had been unable to find proof of a Libyan role in the La Belle discotheque bombing. They did not take note of Kähne's statements that the West Berlin authorities also had no proof linking Syria to the bombing and his admission that they had no legal power to obtain information from the West German intelligence agencies, including the material Kohl had referred to on April 17, 1986 (New Orleans *Times-Picayune*, 7 Dec. 1986 [AP]). As for the U. S. evidence, Washington officials confirmed that they had not offered to share the information with West Berlin investigators, which was in keeping with the long-standing U. S. policy of avoiding the sharing of raw intelligence with the government of West Germany because of its susceptibility to penetration by Soviet and East German agents (Memphis *Commercial Appeal*, 12 Jan. 1988; *NYT*, 14 Jan. 1989).

14. "Kaddafi's Crusade," p. 23; "Falling Oil Prices Cut Two Ways," *U. S. News and World Report*, 14 Apr. 1986, p. 27; *NYT*, 15 Apr. 1986; *WP*, 16 Apr. 1986.

15. "Targeting Gaddafi," p. 21.

16. *WP*, 16, 18 Apr. 1986; George Bush, "Prelude to Retaliation: Building a Governmental Consensus on Terrorism," *SAIS Review* 7 (Winter/Spring 1987): 8.

17. "In the Dead of the Night," *Time*, 28 Apr. 1986, p. 28.

18. *LAT*, 16 Apr. 1986; *NYT*, 10 Apr. 1986; W. Hays Parks, "Crossing the Line," U. S. Naval Institute *Proceedings* 112 (Nov. 1986): 46; "Targeting a 'Mad Dog,' " p. 22; *WSJ*, 21 Apr. 1986; *WP*, 18 Apr. 1986; Bolger, p. 418; Martin and Walcott, p. 288. Around this time North was also attempting to arrange meetings with Iranian officials, and Reagan was becoming annoyed with the Iranians' "continual stalling." (U. S., President's Special Review Board, *The Tower Commission Report: The Full Text of the President's Special Review Board* [New York: Bantam Books and Times Books, 1987], pp. 266–77.

19. "In the Dead of the Night," p. 28; *WSJ*, 21 Apr. 1986; Parks, p. 48; "Reagan's Raiders," *Newsweek*, 28 Apr. 1986, p. 26; "U. S. Airpower Hits Back," *Defence Update International* 73 (July 1986): 31; *NYT*, 16 Apr. 1986.

20. "U. S. Demonstrates Advanced Weapons Technology in Libya," *Aviation Week & Space Technology* 124 (21 Apr. 1986): 18; Rick Hornung, "Air Tankers Aid in Raid on Libya," *Military Logistics Forum* 2 (June 1986): 11; *WP*, 20 Apr. 1986; Martin and Walcott, p. 271.

21. John F. Lehman, Jr., *Command of the Seas* (New York: Charles Scribner's Sons, 1988), pp. 300–301, 371; Anthony H. Cordesman, "The Emerging Lessons from the U. S. Attack on Libya," *Armed Forces* 5 (Aug. 1986): 359; *NYT*, 16 Apr., 6 May 1986, 4 Feb. 1987; Bolger, p. 413; *WSJ*, 21 Apr. 1986.

22. *LAT*, 16 Apr. 1986; *WP*, 8, 9, 15, 16 Apr. 1986; "Targeting a 'Mad Dog,' " pp. 20, 25; *NYT*, 8, 9, 15, 16 Apr. 1986; *WSJ*, 10 Apr. 1986.

23. *NYT*, 12, 18 Apr. 1986; *WSJ*, 11, 16 Apr. 1986; "Targeting Gaddafi," p. 21.

24. "Targeting Gaddafi," p. 21.

25. *NYT*, 20 Apr. 1986; *LAT*, 14 May 1986; interview with a former Department of State official, 13 June 1989.

26. Hersh, p. 17 ff.; *WP*, 16 Apr. 1986; Pedro Ramet, "Soviet-Libyan Relations under Qaddafi," *Survey* 29 (Spring 1985): 109; Martin and Walcott, p. 286, 296; Michael Ledeen, "The Shame of It," *American Spectator*, May 1987, p. 31; Woodward, p. 276; *Sunday Times* (London), (hereafter cited as *ST*), 20 Apr. 1986; David M. North, "Air Force, Navy Brief Congress on Lessons from Libya Strikes," *Aviation Week & Space Technology*, 2 June 1986, p. 63; *NYT*, 15, 17, 18 Apr. 1986; *WT*, 16 April (AP), 15 Aug. 1986 (UPI); Speakes with Pack, p. 181.

27. *LAT*, 3, 6 Apr. 1986; New Orleans *Times-Picayune*, 18 Apr. 1986 (UPI); *NYT*, 16 Apr. 1986.

28. *NYT*, 16, 20 Apr. 1986; "Falling Oil Prices," p. 27; *LAT*, 13 Apr. 1986.

29. *NYT*, 9, 10, 13, 14, 15, 24 Apr. 1986; " Targeting a 'Mad Dog,' " pp. 21, 25; "Hitting the Source," *Time*, 28 Apr. 1986, pp. 26–27; *Times* (London), 16 Apr. 1986; *WP*, 15 Apr. 1986; interview with a former Department of State official, 1 July 1989.

30. *NYT*, 12, 15 Apr. 1986; "Targeting a 'Mad Dog,' " p. 20; *LAT*, 16 Apr. 1986; "Reagan's Raiders," p. 27; "Targeting Gaddafi," p. 21; *WP*, 18 Apr. 1986; "U. S. Demonstrates," p. 18; Woodward, p. 445; Memphis *Commercial Appeal*, 11 Apr. 1986; "Seeking the Smoking Fuse," p. 22.

31. *NYT*, 8 Apr. 1986.

32. *WSJ*, 9 Apr. 1986.

33. *WT*, 11 Apr. 1986.

34. Robert E. Stumpf, "Air War with Libya," U. S. Naval Institute *Proceedings* 112 (Aug. 1986):48; "Targeting Gaddafi," pp. 21–22; *LAT*, 16 Apr. 1986, 1 May 1987; *NYT*, 12 Apr. 1986; John Weisman, "Betrayal and Trust: The Tricky Art of Finding—and Keeping—Good TV News Sources," *TV Guide*, 7 Mar. 1987, p. 4. There was no evidence that either these officials or the leakers were being orchestrated. The leakers tried to rationalize their behavior by saying they were trying to dissuade Qaddafi from further attacks (*WSJ*, 8 Apr. 1986). According to some journalists, beyond efforts to mislead Qaddafi through the press, some erroneous information came from officials who were not well informed but no less talkative for it (*NYT*, 12 Apr. 1986; "Targeting a 'Mad Dog,' " p. 20; cf. Woodward, p. 445).

35. "Secret Sharers," *Time*, 27 July 1987, p. 19; *NYT*, 10 Apr. 1986.

36. *NYT*, 10 Apr. 1986.

37. Ibid.

38. *NYT*, 13 Apr. 1986.

39. "Libya Was Ready," *Foreign Report*, 24 Apr. 1986, pp. 2–3; *NYT*, 16 Apr. 1986. According to *Foreign Report*, at that meeting it was decided that 3,500 Soviet-bloc servicemen would be flown to southern Libya, Soviet reconnaissance aircraft based in Benghazi would be flown to Eastern Europe, and Soviet warships and freighters would leave Libyan waters ("Libya Was Ready," p. 3).

40. *NYT*, 10 Apr. 1986.

41. *WSJ*, 11 Apr. 1986; "Can Reagan Make Qadhafi Cry Uncle?," *U. S. News & World Report*, 21 Apr. 1986, p. 6; *Middle East Policy Survey*, no. 150, 18 Apr. 1986.

42. *WP*, 20 Apr. 1986.

43. *Foreign Broadcast Information Service, Daily Report*, Middle East & Africa (hereafter cited as FBIS-MEA), 8 Apr. 1986, p. Q7; *WP*, 12, 14 Apr. 1986; *NYT*, 12, 13 Apr. 1986; *LAT*, 14 Apr. 1986; *Times* (London), 14 Apr. 1986.

44. *LAT*, 13, 16 Apr. 1986; *NYT*, 9 Mar., 8, 16, 27 Apr. 1986; *ST*, 20 Apr. 1986; *Times* (London), 24 Apr. 1986.

45. *ST*, 20 Apr. 1986; *WP*, 16 Apr. 1986; "Why Europe Is Angry," *Newsweek*, 28 Apr. 1986, p. 34; "Raid Sparks European Protests, Special NATO and EEC Sessions," *Aviation Week & Space Technology* 124 (21 Apr. 1986):25; *NYT*, 14 Apr. 1986. There were leaks in the British press also about the impending use of the F–111s against Libya, but in an apparent case of indirection similar to some of what was coming from Washington, the word was put out that Thatcher had refused Reagan's request, which story was discussed in Parliament and duly reported in the London *Times* (*Times* [London], 14 Apr. 1986).

46. "Look What We're Doing," *Economist*, 26 Apr. 1986, p. 48; *NYT*, 18, 24 Apr., 8 May 1986; "Hitting the Source," p. 26. France had already turned down the overflight request on April 12, but the White House had soon made an urgent plea for reconsideration (*WP*, 29 Apr. 1986).

47. *NYT*, 18, 22, 23, 24, 25 Apr., 1 May 1986; *WP*, 22, 27 Apr. 1986; *Times* (London), 23 Apr. 1986.

48. *NYT*, 13, 14 Apr. 1986; *LAT*, 13, 14, 16 Apr. 1986; *Times* (London), 14, 15 Apr. 1986; *WP*, 14, 15 Apr. 1986.

49. FBIS-MEA, 17 Apr. 1986, p. Q17, 15 Apr. 1986, p. S1.

50. FBIS-MEA, 17 Apr. 1986, p. Q9.

51. "Gaddafi and Terrorism," *World Press Review*, June 1986, p. 25; *Times* (London), 15 Apr. 1986; *NYT*, 15 Apr. 1986.

52. *WP*, 15 Apr. 1986.

53. *NYT*, 15 Apr. 1986; *Times* (London), 15, 16 Apr. 1986.

54. *Times* (London), 16 Apr. 1986.

55. *LAT*, 14, 15 Apr. 1986; *Times* (London), 15 Apr. 1986.

6

Operation El Dorado Canyon
and Its Aftermath

THE AIR STRIKES

Operation El Dorado Canyon was initiated at 5:13 P.M. British time on April 14 as twenty-eight KC–10 and KC–135 tanker aircraft, some of them newly arrived from the United States, began launching from Royal Air Force bases at Mildenhall and Fairford in England. Among the tankers' crew members were seven women; aboard the lead KC–10 was Col. Sam Westbrook, the commander of the 48th Tactical Fighter Wing at Lakenheath. At 5:36 twenty-four F–111 fighter-bombers at Lakenheath and five EF–111 Raven radar-jamming craft at Upper Heyford began departing on a five-thousand-nautical-mile round trip to Tripoli via the Strait of Gibraltar. It was a route almost twice as long as that which a flight over France would have afforded, but contrary to the impression many people had after the attack, F–111 pilots were trained for missions that grueling. Four nighttime refuelings of the F–111s, carried out in radio silence, were necessary on the way to Libya; after the first one, six F–111s and one EF–111, which had been brought along as spares, turned and flew back to England. At about the same time that the Air Force planes were taking off from England, the aircraft carriers *Coral Sea* and *America* in waters off Sicily began a dash southward toward Libya. With high velocity and electronic silence they were able to escape the surveillance of Soviet naval vessels and two Soviet spy planes that had taken off from a base near Tripoli.[1]

  The administration's steadfast silence concerning Libya on Monday suggested to reporters that something important was afoot. At 4:00 P.M. Washington time (11:00 P.M. in Libya) congressional leaders assembled in the Executive Office

Building to discuss the Libya operation with Bush, Shultz, Weinberger, Casey, Crowe, Poindexter, and Reagan, who arrived ten minutes later. The president said the United States had "the goods on" Qaddafi, citing the La Belle bombing and the thwarted Libyan plot in Paris, before turning the presentation over to Poindexter. The legislators found the evidence on La Belle persuasive[2] and supported the idea of attacking. However, several complained that with the F–111s already aloft, they were being notified rather than consulted, whereupon Poindexter replied that the air raids could still be called off if they objected; none did so. The legislators had been asked for security purposes to maintain public silence until after the attack, but Sen. Robert Byrd (D-W.Va.) and Sen. Claiborne Pell (D-R.I.) proceeded to reporters' microphones after the session and announced that the president would speak to the nation at 9:00 P.M.; the 6:30 network news duly noted this sign of imminent action. Reagan was infuriated, and Republicans complained that the Democratic senators had tipped off the Qaddafi regime. However, Sen. Richard Lugar (R-Ind.) had told the press on Sunday that Shultz had invited him to a Monday afternoon meeting with the president on responding to Libya;[3] if the Libyans had been attentive and intuitive, they could have prepared for a Monday night attack.

The Air Force armada's procession toward the Jamahiriyah went smoothly, apart from refueling problems that put three F–111s and their tanker escorts twelve minutes behind schedule; they therefore departed from their planned route over the Mediterranean and violated the air space of Algeria and Tunisia. At 12:20 and 12:45 A.M. Libyan time the *Coral Sea* and the *America*, respectively, began launching more than seventy Navy and Marine Corps aircraft, including fourteen A–6s for bombing runs, as well as six each of A–7s and F/A–18s for firing missiles at radar. Portuguese radar operators, and apparently French and Spanish ones as well, had detected the F–111s but had done or said nothing. As the Air Force planes reached the central Mediterranean, an Italian operator radioed them for identification and received no response. According to Prime Minister Mifsud Bonnici of Malta, the Italians then notified Malta that unidentified aircraft were approaching the island, and the Maltese in turn notified the Libyans of unidentified planes heading toward North Africa thirty minutes or more before the U. S. attack began.[4]

As the clock approached 2:00 A.M. Libyan time, an impressive joint Air Force-Navy aerial armada approached the coast of Libya, and the Soviet chargé in Washington was summoned and informed that an attack was taking place and that it was in no way directed against the Soviet Union, but rather against Libyan terrorism. At 1:54 defense suppression began from offshore: the EF–111s and EA–6B Prowlers started their jamming against Libyan radar and communications, which triggered the previously quiescent Libyan radars into activity, whereupon the A–7s and F/A–18s began firing Shrike and HARM missiles respectively, which rode the radar beams back to their sites. Before the air raids were finished, they would pummel Libyan surface-to-air missile (SAM) sites with forty-eight antiradiation missiles, destroying more than a dozen sites.[5]

With remarkable synchronization, the F–111s and A–6s were over their targets around Tripoli and Benghazi and ready to bomb at 2:00 A.M.. American journalists in their Tripoli hotel were ready, several waiting with open telephone lines.[6] Astonishingly, the Qaddafi regime was not ready, even in spite of the warning from its Maltese allies. The lengthy buildup of tension since the discotheque bombing, as one analyst noted, "did not produce increased Libyan vigilance but fatigue."[7] The pilots were amazed to see that the street lights were on in both cities; they remained on throughout the attack. Runway lights shone, as well as floodlights around the principal buildings and the minarets of the central mosque in Tripoli, which provided a beacon for the U. S. planes. No air raid alarms sounded, no instructions on what to do in an air attack had been given to the populace, there was no curfew, and cars were driving with their headlights bright. Undoubtedly, the expedient of flying in low had helped preserve surprise for the attacking aircraft. The Libyans would later say that they had been thinking in terms of an attack from the carriers in the Mediterranean and not from Britain, but Libya's media had earlier taken note of a CBS News report that an attack might be launched from NATO bases.[8] Qaddafi would later try to blame his military for all of this incompetence, but it only seems appropriate that the colonel himself should bear the brunt of the responsibility for such a colossal failure of leadership.

The F–111 crews, flying at nine miles a minute, and the A–6 pilots operated with two major constraints. First was the strict rules of engagement laid down by Kelso, the designated commander for Operation El Dorado Canyon. For the crews' safety, each plane was limited to a single run on its target and was not even to enter Libyan airspace if self-defense chaff for confusing SAMs and other secret gear used to create false targets were not working. For the sake of avoiding collateral damage, especially civilian casualties, the crews were forbidden to drop their bombs unless they could make redundant positive target identification on multiple aiming systems; additionally, the use of standoff tactics to avoid risking the crews' lives in flight over the targets was rejected in order to minimize civilian casualties.[9]

The second major constraint was the Libyan air defense system. It was slow to activate, but once it began, there was unleashed a spectacular barrage of ZSU–23 artillery fire and SA–2, SA–3, SA–6, SA–8, and *French* Crotale missiles.[10] Although there was said to be "no more dense and capable air system outside the Soviet Union, and very few in the Soviet Union,"[11] the Libyan Arab Air Defense Command itself was grossly understaffed, characterized by poor equipment maintenance, and probably leaving much to be desired in quality of training. Even given those deficiencies, the tactic of flying low underneath the SAM operating envelopes and the effective defense suppression by Navy, Marine, and Air Force planes doubtless saved American pilots' lives. Radars that were not struck by HARMS or Shrikes were turned off to forestall such a fate; unguided SAMs went hopelessly wild. The Surt SA–5 site did not activate until after the bombing runs, its operators apparently having learned their lesson in the March battle. When the Surt air base commander was ordered to launch his aircraft, he suggested that the air base at Benghazi respond instead.[12]

U. S. Air Forces Europe (USAFE) had drawn up plans to attack the Bab al-Aziziyya compound with nine F–111s each dropping four two-thousand-pound laser-guided "smart" bombs designed for precision.[13] The Pentagon later stated that "inasmuch as the entire complex was, in one way or another, related to Qaddafi's command and control of terrorism, the entire complex was considered targetable."[14] Each F–111 had been given an aim point within the complex selected not by the NSC staff, but by the USAFE command in West Germany; at least seven different buildings are reported to have been targeted. Finding Bab al-Aziziyya was complicated not only by the attack coming at night, but also by the fact that the complex did not show up well on radar; therefore military planners had assigned specific docks on the Tripoli waterfront as "off set" points to guide each crew, with the exact distance and direction to the compound programmed into the plane's computer. As it turned out, much less firepower was brought to bear against Bab al-Aziziyya than planned: one plane lost its generator twenty seconds from the target, scrambling all its electronics; one plane's crew withheld their bombs because their infrared camera would not work; one plane missed its off set point and therefore did not bomb; and one plane reportedly took a mistaken off set point and dropped its bombs one and a half miles northeast of the complex. Earlier, one F–111 had missed the air strike because while it refueled in radio silence, the tanker crew had not realized that the last of their F–111s was not yet finished and so had prematurely turned north to await the return flight. The F–111 crew had not perceived this change of direction and therefore after finishing its refueling had flown the wrong direction without realizing it until it was too late to participate in the strike. Another F–111 had turned back while still over the water because a bleed air duct in its engine cracked, and the plane manned by Fernando Ribas-Dominicci and Paul Lorence crashed in the water before reaching the target. Many military officers later held the opinion that the lost F–111 had crashed without being hit by Libyan fire, but Westbrook believed that it had been hit, because pilots he interviewed had witnessed it burning fiercely before hitting the water.[15]

Only two F–111s, therefore, bombed the Bab al-Aziziyya complex, and one of those violated the rules of engagement in that its infrared camera was inoperative. Contrary to some journalists' impressions, the large Bedouin tent in which Qaddafi received visitors was not an aim point; the tent was prominently visible in a film of the attack shown by the Pentagon two days afterward, but a nearby building was in the crosshairs. The bombs did not entirely flatten any buildings in the complex but did wreak entirely heavy damage—impressive enough for Qaddafi to leave it unrepaired as an outdoor museum of U. S. aggression. It is generally believed that Qaddafi was in Bab al-Aziziyya as the bombing took place, which surprised some administration experts who expected greater caution on his part. The ever-imaginative colonel would later claim that during the attack he was valiantly rushing to his family's defense and that heavenly angels and Libyan soldiers together saved his life from an assault of thirty-three aircraft. However, according to the most reliable accounts, he was safe underground in his bunker at the time. (This means that assertions that Qaddafi narrowly escaped death or that his life may have been saved by the malfunctions experienced by several of the fighter-bombers are apparently erroneous.) One intriguing fact is that in an interview with United Press International correspondent Marie Colvin before the air raids, Qaddafi said that he believed Bab al-Aziziyya was on the U. S. target list, which may have been due to leaks in Washington mentioning the compound as a possible target.[16] Qaddafi's failure to evacuate himself and, by most accounts, his family from the complex suggests that despite his professed expectations of a U. S. attack, on some psychological level he still could not grasp that an hour of retribution for his regime's crimes was finally coming.

Simultaneously with the attack on Bab al-Aziziyya, three F–111s likewise armed with sets of four one-ton laser-guided bombs flew against a naval commando training complex in the area of Sidi Bilal about fifteen miles west of Tripoli, a site where Palestinian terrorists had trained in activities including ship seizures and underwater demolitions and that was linked to the Libyan mining of the Red Sea. The second and third attackers were hampered by smoke from the first F–111's bombs, but, contrary to early press accounts, the training complex did receive direct hits. Furthermore, the F–111s also hit three adjacent military targets: a secondary naval academy, a Palestinian terrorist training camp where Abu Nidal's son had reportedly been training (the Palestinians themselves had evacuated two days earlier), and a large maritime academy whose construction was almost complete before the air raid. The official Pentagon press release made no mention of the latter two sites; the damage to the new academy was estimated at $10 million to $15 million.[17]

Six F–111s had been assigned to strike at the military side of Tripoli Airport: their main objective was to smash on the parking apron Soviet-made IL–76 transport jets that the Pentagon identified as having been used to transport terrorists and their weapons. Each plane was to drop twelve 500-pound Snakeye retarded delivery "dumb" bombs, which parachuted to their targets in order to keep the bombers from being blasted by their own ordnance. One F–111 aborted its mission before arrival at the target because of failure of its terrain-following radar. The remaining five entered Libyan territory east of Tripoli and circled to attack the airport coming from south of the city. At 2:06 A.M. they began bombing, inflicting major damage on several buildings, destroying at least two IL–76s, and severely damaging three others, in the Pentagon's estimate based on aerial photography. European diplomats on the ground reported that at least ten IL–76s were badly damaged and ten to fifteen helicopters were disabled.[18]

One of the two targets for the navy A–6s was the Jamahiriyah Barracks in Benghazi, described by the Pentagon as an alternate terrorist command and control headquarters and a billeting area for Qaddafi's palace guard; it also housed members of the Islamic Legion and served as a terrorist training facility. One of its intended attackers had aborted on the deck; in the face of heavy antiaircraft fire, the other six A–6s dropped Snakeye bomb loads like those used on Tripoli Airport. The barracks was heavily damaged, half destroyed according to the account of one journalist on the ground, and an adjacent warehouse was also hit, with four MiG jets destroyed and a fifth damaged in their shipping crates.[19]

Simultaneously, five A–6s armed with a dozen five-hundred-pound Rockeye cluster bombs each and one A–6 armed with a dozen Snakeyes attacked Benina Airfield east of Benghazi; two other A–6s meant to attack there also aborted with equipment problems under the rules of engagement. The United States' avowed purpose for striking Benina was to prevent its MiG–23 pilots (which included the only Libyan pilots who had shown any proficiency at night flying during the Sixth Fleet's surveillance of the previous several months) from scrambling against the U. S. forces, although American officials would also point out that the base had been used to supply Libyan fighters in Chad. The airfield itself was cratered; one of Libya's new SA–5 sites was destroyed, as were a storage and support building and three smaller buildings; two hangars were significantly damaged; at least three and perhaps as many as fourteen MiG–23s were destroyed, as well as two Mi–8 helicopters, an F–27 transport plane, a small straight-wing aircraft, and a twin Otter propeller-driven plane; two Boeing 727s were damaged. By 2:13 A.M. the U. S. planes were back over water, with their $50-million mission concluded, even as the Libyans continued their furious but futile anti-aircraft barrage.[20]

Americans tuned in to NBC Nightly News listened to the Tripoli air raid as correspondent Steve Delaney held the receiver of his telephone outside his hotel room window. (Some observers would insist that the military operation was timed for the evening news; at the same time, it should be noted that the timing set by Kelso made good sense from a military standpoint. Military manuals have long recommended that a night attack be launched between midnight and 3:00 A.M. in the theater of action in order to catch the defenders at the period of their bodies' peak drowsiness.) Shortly thereafter, Larry Speakes went to the White House briefing room to deliver the official announcement of the U. S. attack on Libya. On his way he stopped by Poindexter's office and found Poindexter and Shultz together in a mood not of jubilation, but of "quiet satisfaction."[21]

In his televised address to the nation at 9:00 P.M. Eastern Standard Time, Reagan paraphrased intercepted Libyan messages of March 25, April 4, and April 5 linking the Jamahiriyah to the La Belle discotheque bombing. (Intelligence professionals would be greatly dismayed by the president's revealing of this intelligence information, but government leakers had already given the press more information than Reagan disclosed. Political officials considered the disclosure essential for gaining public support for the military action.)[22] The president also mentioned "solid evidence" of planning by Qaddafi for other attacks against American targets, specifically referring to the plot that had been aborted in Paris. He noted that ignoring Qaddafi as some commentators suggested had already been shown to be counterproductive and declared, "For us to ignore by inaction the slaughter of American civilians and soldiers, whether in nightclubs or airline terminals, is simply not in the American tradition. When our citizens are abused or attacked anywhere in the world on the direct order of a hostile regime, we will respond so long as I'm in the Oval Office. Self-defense is not only our right, it is our duty.''[23]

Reagan characterized the Libyan people as ''decent people caught in the grip of a tyrant.'' He mentioned that the United States had tried without success ''quiet diplomacy, public condemnation, economic sanctions, and demonstrations of military force.'' He emphasized that the U. S. air strikes were not merely punitive in intent but were ''preemptive actions against terrorist installations'' meant to ''diminish Qaddafi's capacity to export terror'' and to ''provide him with incentives and reasons to alter his criminal behavior.'' Yet the president said he had ''no illusion that tonight's action will bring down the curtain on Qaddafi's reign of terror'' but hoped the attack would ''bring closer a safer and more secure world for decent men and women.'' He warned that ''if necessary, we shall do it again. It gives me no pleasure to say that and I wish it were otherwise.''[24]

Already the Navy aircraft were all safe on deck again, and four and one-half hours later all the F–111s had landed safely (with the plane having a cracked lead bleed duct diverting to the Rota base in Spain due to its overheated engine) except for the plane flown by Lorence and Ribas-Dominicci; nearly thirteen hours of search and rescue efforts, unhampered by the Libyans, proved fruitless. The loss of one F–111 crew was disconcerting to American military leaders, though losing one of over a hundred aircraft used in the operation was not seen as a heavy toll. The initial reports of damage to the targets seemed unimpressive, and some officials advocated a second attack. However, later photographs from British-based U. S. SR–71 reconnaissance aircraft were not so impeded by cloud cover as earlier photographs, and it was seen that all five targets had in fact been severely damaged. There was no doubt that the Air Force-Navy coordination in Operation El Dorado Canyon had been superb. The cottage industry of perfectionist critics of U. S. military operations particularly seized on the high number of aborted bombing missions: six out of seventeen F–111s, apart from the crashed jet, and three out of fifteen A–6s. Military leaders were disappointed by this failure rate, but they would have been far more surprised by no aborts at all. Redundancy had, in fact, been built into the mission. Military men felt that both equipment malfunction and pilot disorientation were made far more likely by the French refusal to permit overflight; they also pointed out that in full-scale war, rules of engagement would have been less strict, and therefore more bombs would have been dropped.[25]

COLLATERAL DAMAGE

Military analysts credited the U. S. strike aircraft with a high overall rate of accuracy, particularly in comparison with Vietnam air raids. However, there were bombs that were not accurate, some having tragic results. Stray U. S. bombs in Benghazi destroyed a gas station and a dispensary and damaged a schoolhouse, all unoccupied, and crushed two houses, killing five civilians. A number of unexploded bombs intended for the Tripoli airport fell on two farms two miles off target, probably due to parachutes of some Snakeyes not opening, which can cause their ballistics to go wildly wrong. A hay shed was wrecked and three hundred chickens were allegedly killed; the only human casualty was a boy who received a slight shrapnel wound. Fortunately, no bombs appeared to have strayed into civilian housing surrounding the Bab al-Aziziyya complex and adjacent to the Sidi Bilal naval commando center.[26]

The foreign journalists in Libya were given detailed tours of the sites with collateral damage. Only three hours after the attack, they were rushed off to see the Bin Ashur district of Tripoli, scene of the great majority of the civilian casualties in Libya. The back of the French embassy was demolished, but the one individual inside it at the time was unhurt; several other embassies received lesser damage. In the neighborhood facing north of the French embassy, the reporters saw sights they would probably never forget: dazed residents in their pajamas stumbling through the rubble, pools of blood, blood-stained sheets and mattresses, pieces of flesh, wrecked automobiles, and a young father staggering with grief as the digging up of rubble uncovered the corpse of his eighteen-month-old daughter. The Libyan government also took the journalists to see corpses in a morgue and injured persons in a hospital. Seventeen was the high figure cited for Bin Ashur deaths. The reporters noted the irony that Bin Ashur was a habitation of the Libyan middle class, some of the very people Washington hoped would help overthrow Qaddafi.[27]

The foreign correspondents considered it highly likely that the intended target of the bombs that fell on Bin Ashur had been Al Arafiq, the headquarters of the Libyan intelligence service about a hundred yards southeast of the French embassy. American officials freely admitted that they had contemplated attacking this headquarters but insisted they had ruled it out; Crowe stated that it had been a list of alternate targets he had shown Reagan on April 8 but that he had recommended against striking it because the likelihood of civilian damage was too high. It may be noteworthy that the most renowned leak-finding U. S. reporters have not found officials who disputed these assertions off the record. On May 8, the Defense Department conceded that stray U. S. bombs had hit the two houses in Benghazi and stated tersely that bombs from one F–111 had apparently fallen in the area of the French Embassy. General Rogers and others in the military claimed that one of the F–111s that was intended to hit Bab al-Aziziyya one and a half miles to the southeast picked the wrong set of docks for its radar off set point and ended up mistakenly dropping bombs over Bin Ashur.[28]

The Pentagon insisted that other collateral damage most likely resulted from Libyan ordnance, which appears to be at least partially true. Some observers on the ground said that the damage caused by U. S. bombs in Bin Ashur may have been supplemented by damage from Libyan antiaircraft fire. A piece of wreckage pulled from a house, wreckage that the Libyans represented as part of a downed U. S. aircraft, was in fact identified as the booster stage of a Libyan SA–3 missile. Libyan officials displayed a house in Benghazi where a sleeping man had been killed by what they told reporters was an American bomb, but the holes in the walls appeared to have been more likely made by an antiaircraft shell, and neighborhood boys confirmed that it had been a Libyan shell before they were chased off by an official. Nearby, a lightly damaged rehabilitation center for the handicapped, which regime spokesmen had loudly declared to have been specifically targeted and destroyed by the Navy A–6s, quite likely was also damaged by antiaircraft fire. Such episodes were typical on the tours conducted for the journalists by their Libyan government "minders." While reporters from Soviet bloc and other radical countries were content to serve as mere propaganda mouthpieces for Libya, the Western reporters came to resent the heavy-handed and deceitful treatment they were receiving. They stole peeks at the strictly off-limits areas of military damage before being pulled away and reported that damage in civilian areas in the Jamahiriyah was far less extensive than they had been told. They asked questions about a bombed military helicopter hangar that an official was passing off as a "powdered milk factory" and found amusement in being told that twenty-eight U. S. planes had been shot down by Libyan defenses, with some of the pilots parachuting and changing into civilian clothes to look like Libyans.[29]

It is against this backdrop that one must view the Qaddafi regime's story that the impact of a bomb that fell outside the residence of Qaddafi's family killed the colonel's adopted fifteen-month-old daughter Hana while his other seven children survived, but two of the sons were seriously injured. From the beginning it had the appearance of a fabrication designed to win sympathy for Qaddafi in the outside world. Two regime spokesmen in the days after the attack referred to his sons being injured without making any mention of Hana. Libyan exile leader Abdul Hamid Bakoush categorically stated that Qaddafi never had an adopted daughter in remarks to *Al-Ahram* that were largely ignored by the Western press, and the CIA, which had watched Qaddafi closely throughout the years before the raid, had never found evidence of the existence of such a child. According to Libya expert Lisa Anderson, Hana's existence was previously unknown, and her supposed death was not reported to the Libyan people. The story given to reporters on April 15 was that Hana had been adopted by the Qaddafis around May 1985. In January 1986 the colonel had given Judith Miller of the *New York Times* and several other women journalists two interviews in three days, during which he sought to bolster his credentials as both a feminist and a family man, displaying his family in the second interview. The reporters were told that he had *seven* children. The only daughter was his eight-year-old, whom he said might have political potential in the Jamahiriyah, where he was working to improve the status of women. He lamented that he only had one daughter and expressed the wish for more. Surely this would have been the time for Qaddafi to mention Hana if she existed. The Hana story stands on the word of the Qaddafi regime alone: no evidence for it was ever produced, yet the Western press inexplicably has continued to repeat it as established fact.[30]

In the matter of injury to his two youngest sons, there is more likely to be some truth. Yet the Libyans had some difficulty synchronizing their story in this case: at a press conference on April 18, Majour Jalloud admitted that Qaddafi's two sons were only "slightly injured." In another hoax for the media, Western television crews had been taken to see two boys hospitalized in oxygen tents; their heavy bandages did not permit positive identification. The boys were uninjured substitutes for Qaddafi's sons.[31]

Hours after the U. S. air raid, some anonymous Western diplomats put out the grossly erroneous report that in Tripoli alone a hundred or more civilians had been killed; this figure is still cited by persons in a position to know better. In his April 18 press conference Jalloud stated that a total of thirty-seven Libyans had died, only one of them a soldier, and that ninety-three persons had been injured. Jalloud's figure of only one military death was obviously ridiculous: earlier that day four military men had been buried in a public funeral for twenty persons, mostly Bin Ashur casualties. A more realistic picture was suggested by a Filipino nurse's unauthorized disclosure to reporters that of twenty-six injured persons in Benghazi's Jalah hospital, twenty-two were soldiers. There were apparently two or more times as many military and paramilitary deaths as civilian deaths; if there was substance to unconfirmed reports of many more than thirty-seven corpses in morgues, it would clearly be explained by large numbers of soldiers whose deaths were hidden for propaganda purposes by the Qaddafi regime.[32] As for Jalloud's civilian death total, it must be noted that the Qaddafi regime could be expected to inflate and by no means understate the figure. Other estimates put the total lower than thirty-six;[33] given that the Libyan government appeared to spare absolutely no effort in publicizing civilian casualties, a good estimate of the civilian death toll from the ordnance of either side would be between twenty-five and thirty.[34]

President Reagan said concerning damage in civilian areas, "If it was one of our bombs, I'm sorry about that. . . . It's something you regret anytime children or innocent people are wounded or killed."[35] Unquestionably, the civilian casualties caused tremendous propaganda detriment to the United States, compounded by the false "hundred civilians dead" story. The Qaddafi regime cynically exploited the carnage: surgery was interrupted while journalists and television crews were brought into operating rooms; "wounded people were wheeled out into the hospital corridors and fresh wounds were exposed."[36] The anger felt by Libyan citizens was understandable to all, but the Libyan government's relentless expression of indignation over innocent loss of life and spurious allegations that U. S. jets had come to engage in carpet bombing of civilian areas were rank hypocrisy. Far less concern for avoidance of civilian casualties had been shown by the Libyan Air Force in its various African interventions,[37] and many times more Libyan civilians had been deliberately killed by the Qaddafi regime than were accidentally killed by U. S. bombs. The last time corpses had been shown over and over again on Libyan television as they were after the U. S. attack,[38] they had been the bodies of Libyans who had dared to oppose Qaddafi, serving as a grisly warning to their fellow countrymen.

THE INTERNATIONAL REACTION

The Qaddafi regime made an attempt to save face after its withering defeat by firing at 6:00 P.M. Libyan time on April 15 two land-based SS–1 Scud B missiles toward Lampedusa, an Italian island nearly as close to Libya as to Sicily, with the intention of hitting a U. S. Coast Guard Long Range Aid to Navigation station that had been moved out of Libya itself in 1972 because of the colonel's hostility. Although Qaddafi claimed to have destroyed the station, the missiles in fact fell more than two miles short of the shoreline. Italian military jets were scrambled to look for any Libyan craft that might have fired the missiles, and Italy found itself in a state of war alert, which it had not experienced since World War II.[39]

In Tripoli, Libyan state radio was issuing a continuous stream of what were probably the most bloodcurdling calls for the murder of American men, women, and children ever heard in the Middle East; to a lesser extent atrocities against Britons were also demanded.[40] Although the broadcasters stated that "we are drinking their [that is, Americans'] blood"[41] in Libya and urged Arab listeners to do the same, Qaddafi in fact had no intention of massacring the Americans who were earning him petrodollars in Libya, although his past record indicated they could have reasonable fear that he might take some hostages. The U. S. air attack, meanwhile, had left behind "utter confusion, far out of proportion to the damage incurred."[42] In succeeding days, the revolutionary committees engaged in looting, and the Libyan military in Tripoli engaged in frequent barrages of antiaircraft fire, raining yet more shrapnel on the city. These barrages were thought to stem from nervousness in some instances and in other instances from wasteful, futile efforts to shoot down the high-flying SR–71 planes by which the United States was gathering evidence for damage assessment. Fear filled the Libyan populace because of the shooting by Libyan forces and because of rumors of danger of more U.S. attacks, which were surely nurtured by Tripoli radio's repeated bogus reports of new air raids. Rather than rallying around the "leader of the revolution," multitudes of citizens fled the city, leaving Tripoli a temporary ghost town.[43]

After the air raids, the Voice of America began repeatedly broadcasting an editorial that stopped little short of calling on Libyans to overthrow Qaddafi. Contrary to the verities of the Middle East experts, the evidence points to the attack having provoked fighting among Libyans rather than having unified them. On Tuesday morning, a series of shattering explosions outside Tripoli drove Libyans indoors; European expatriates witnessed an air attack at 10:00 A.M. at Uqba bin Nafi military base (the former U. S. Wheelus airbase). One of the

Europeans stated his belief that the attacking planes were not American, and there was indeed no evidence that U. S. warplanes ever returned; diplomats on the ground believed that after failing to launch a single plane during the U. S. attack, the Libyan air force bombed a rebel convoy of the Libyan army. Unconfirmed reports also circulated in Tripoli and in Washington of a similar episode of an air attack on a column of dissident troops seeking to march on the capital from the Tarhuna military base to the southeast; the Qaddafi regime felt compelled to allege a U. S. attack on the base. Qaddafi's German advisors were reported to have quashed a minor rebellion at Bab al-Aziziyya two days after the air raid. Most observers felt that not all of the gunfire heard in Tripoli was attributable to antiaircraft fire: it was believed that much of the small-arms fire was spontaneous street fighting among Libyan forces, particularly between the regular military and the revolutionary committees.[44] Some observers opined that there was no element of anti-Qaddafi dissidence in this, but such an interpretation seems strained, particularly in view of the extremely close identification of the committees with the Libyan dictator. There were reports of executions; certainly, the demise of dissident military leaders in unsuccessful mutinies would not have enhanced the interests of the United States.[45]

Qaddafi contributed to the instability in Tripoli by remaining out of sight for nearly two full days. (One State Department analyst speculated that he did so deliberately in order to "smoke out" and eliminate opposition.) He finally emerged with a Wednesday night television speech in which he expressed gratitude to France, called for Reagan and Thatcher to be tried as murderers of children, vowed to persist in the causes of Arab unity and the liberation of Palestine and in inciting revolution, but avoided the grotesque calls for vengeance that his radio announcers were issuing.[46] He spoke in what was described as "an uncharacteristically somber and subdued voice, devoid of the passion with which he usually denounces the United States."[47]

Soon thereafter, in gestures of typical Qaddafi absurdity, it was declared that Libya had won a spectacular military victory and that the country was officially renamed the *Great* Socialist People's Libyan Arab Jamahiriyah. The Libyan people were not fooled, however. The "victory" celebrations were sparsely attended, and there were no significant anti-American demonstrations; even the normal orchestrated revolutionary fervor was noticeably lacking. The substantial amount of bitterness that the citizens of the Jamahiriyah felt toward the United States did not necessarily cause them to forget their grievances toward their own ruler, and furthermore they were stunned and angered to experience such overwhelming defeat after years of militarism, enormous expenditures on constantly displayed weaponry, and Qaddafi's hearty vows to defend Libya with every means available.[48]

The Libyan leader saw fit to retreat to the desert for the summer, shunning the publicity he was known to love so much. He failed to appear for his annual June 11 Wheelus Evacuation Day speech; instead a rambling two-hour speech by a Qaddafi with wretched facial appearance was shown on videotape, generating little interest or enthusiasm among the citizenry. Despite the cliché that pressure from the United States would only serve to force dissent and opposition in Libya further underground, Qaddafi was at the weakest and most vulnerable point yet in his seventeen-year rule. Opposition in the military intensified, and opposition mounted from Islamic fundamentalists who had previously been dismissed as a meaningful threat to the Qaddafi regime. In October the government felt compelled to close down the country's forty-eight Islamic institutes and to exercise tighter control over the mosques after Muslim militants assassinated three government officials that month and in August. Furthermore, in the wake of the U. S. air raids, criticism of Qaddafi by ordinary Libyan citizens became more bold, intense, and widespread; in just one example, in a summer 1986 soccer riot in Tripoli Qaddafi posters were defaced and for the first time derisive chants against him were heard in public.[49]

In the United States, the air raids against the Qaddafi regime were spectacularly popular: polls showed up to 77 percent approval and as low as 14 percent disapproval. Reagan's approval ratings reached a peak for his presidency, soaring as high as 70 percent. The White House reported receiving its largest outpouring of public sentiment in a dozen years, overwhelmingly supportive.[50] As the *Economist* put it, "The United States, to the grateful relief of most of its citizens, was no longer a Gulliver tormented by the Lilliputians."[51]

With only a handful of dissenters, Operation El Dorado Canyon received staunch support on Capital Hill; more complaints in connection with the War Powers Act were heard than had been heard after the Gulf of Sidra naval battle, however. Arab-American organizations and representatives of the religious left strongly condemned the air raids. Newspaper editors across the nation were mostly favorable to the action; the *New York Times* and the *Wall Street Journal* strongly supported it, while the *Washington Post* reserved judgment till the results were apparent. The conservative intelligentsia overwhelmingly endorsed the attack and considered the negative overseas reaction (described below) to be another powerful piece of evidence of the futility of preoccupation with world opinion. The bombing of Libya was highly controversial among the liberal intelligentsia, but what was noteworthy was that liberals were divided over it rather than uniformly opposed to it; there seemed to be more liberal support than had been the case with Grenada.[52] The mainstream Middle East experts were deeply disturbed by the attack. It was fairly popular with the heterodox Middle East experts, but from among their ranks Libya experts Joseph Churba and Martin Sicker considered it to be on the whole unwise, because they felt it lacked a political strategy.[53]

In great contrast to the American domestic reaction to the attack on Libya was the overseas reaction: probably not in twenty years had there been a period of such intense international criticism of the United States as in the last two weeks of April 1986. International media coverage and commentary (not neatly separated in most cases) were overwhelmingly negative. A huge number of governments condemned or criticized Washington's decision, while only a handful openly supported it. In the latter category were the governments of Great Britain, Israel, Dominica, Saint Lucia, Grenada, Honduras, Chad, South Africa, Singapore, Australia (where newspapers and politicians were said to have given qualified support), and Canada. Not only Mulroney and his administration but Liberal opposition leader John Turner supported the United States, and a week later the government called on Canadian citizens to leave Libya. Numerous other governments, including that of Japan, declined to take a public position.[54] Public and private hints left no doubt that many more governments than those named above were sympathetic to the U. S. action, but they had little to lose by not saying so publicly—far greater offenses did not result in Washington cutting aid—and perhaps much to lose by endorsing it, in view of the possibility of harm to their workers in Libya or terrorist reprisals by Libya or the organizations on its payroll. As one State Department official said concerning European allies, "A lot of them are worried that if they support the U. S. in public, they will get a grenade up their kazoos."[55]

Around the world and in the United States there were demonstrations, the great majority of them small in size, by leftists and sometimes Arab students or Muslims in protest of the U. S. retaliation. Although few opinion poll results from overseas concerning it circulated, the clear impression left was that in the great majority of countries, the majority of the populace was unfavorable to the air strikes. There were pockets of support, however. Surveys in France and Switzerland showed majority approval of the U. S. attack (which juxtaposed ironically with the damage to the French embassy and the Swiss ambassador's residence in Tripoli). It was reported that citizens of Greece were persuaded that the Arab terrorism Qaddafi was supporting was partly aimed at destroying their country's tourist industry and that most of them were pleased by or indifferent to the air raids. Even while opposition parties and their supporters heatedly denounced the action, there was said to be quiet sympathy for the U. S. action among the pro-Mubarak majority of Egyptians. A *Washington Post* correspondent found support for Reagan's decision among residents of Beijing: Qaddafi and his personality cult reminded them of the hated Mao Zedong. Another *Post* reporter found only applause and no condemnation for the attack among Lebanese Shi'ites in Tyre, who had by no means forgotten Musa Sadr. The Al-Sadr Brigades, a faction of Amal, declared support for the military strike, thanking Reagan for carrying out the "heroic operation," and issued a threat to those who would participate in a Hezbollah demonstration in Beirut to protest it.[56]

The Soviet news agency Tass termed the U. S. attack on Libya "state terrorism" and "a bloody crime";[57] the official USSR government statement called it "belligerent chauvinism, . . . an aggressive bandit action" of a sort that "cannot but affect relations between the Soviet Union and the United States."[58] Gorbachev promised Qaddafi that the Soviet Union would "fulfill its commitments in terms of further strengthening Libya's defense capacity,"[59] a warning was issued to the United States not to blockade the Jamahiriyah's ports,[60] and a planned mid-May meeting in Washington between Shultz and Soviet Foreign

Minister Eduard A. Shevardnadze to prepare the way for a second Reagan-Gorbachev summit was cancelled by the Soviets. Washington responded sharply: Speakes declared that "the Soviet decision shows where they stand on the important issue of international terrorism" and "says something about their commitment to work constructively on issues on the U. S.-Soviet agenda, including arms reductions and regional crises";[61] Kalb pointedly rebuked the Soviets for failing to prevent the La Belle discotheque bombing. The unpleasant words exchanged between the superpowers and the cancellation of the presummit meeting caused considerable wringing of hands among strong détente advocates; they found the cancellation to be sufficient evidence that the air raids against Libya were a mistake. Nonetheless various other superpower negotiations went on as planned in the wake of the Libya incident,[62] and, of course, a momentous Reagan-Gorbachev summit was held in October in Reykjavík, Iceland.

Unquestionably the U. S. attack had a souring effect on Soviet-Libyan relations. It was an embarrassment to the Soviets in the Arab world, and Swedish Prime Minister Ingvar Carlsson reported that in his talks with Gorbachev, the Soviet leader expressed "general displeasure" with Qaddafi. The Qaddafi regime, through its unofficial organ *Al-Safir* in Beirut, disclosed its great displeasure over the lukewarm support Libya had received from the Soviet Union and over the fact that the radar equipment that was supplied to Syria and Libya was not the most sophisticated in Moscow's arsenal. Jalloud's visit to Moscow in late May did not go pleasantly for the Libyans, and a Gorbachev statement quoted by Tass was interpreted by Western observers as a veiled warning to Libya to behave itself and not provoke more U. S. action with terrorist attacks. In June, the absence of an expected Soviet delegation on Evacuation Day in Tripoli was taken as a possible sign of the Kremlin's distancing itself from Qaddafi.[63]

Much milder than the criticism of Washington's actions by the Kremlin was that of China, and it was noted that the Chinese media's coverage of the matter was surprisingly even-handed. Aside from the regimes of Cuba and Nicaragua and of the emotive Alan García in Peru, Latin American governments either refrained from taking a public position on the U. S. attack on Libya or criticized it in temperate language, usually coupled with strong denunciations of terrorism, Libya, or both. Latin legislators' remarks against the United States were more heated.[64]

As expected, the reaction in the Islamic world was hostile. There were significant anti-American demonstrations in Pakistan, and the government there professed to be "deeply shocked" and condemned the U. S. action. Another of Washington's allies, Turkey, disappointed both Libya and the United States by mildly criticizing the attack. Indonesia condemned it but resisted pressure from unspecified Muslim states to cancel Reagan's visit in early May, and its troops broke up an unauthorized demonstration in front of the American embassy and tore up the demonstrators' placards; the Indonesian press was warned not to report the incident. In the Philippines, Muslim demonstrators attacked and slightly injured a Canadian whom they thought to be an American. An Afghan guerrilla leader cancelled a visit to Washington scheduled for the week after the attack on Libya, but after a short decent interval the same leader and three other Afghan guerrilla leaders met with Reagan in mid-June. Shock and anger over the attack on Libya were widespread on the streets of Tehran, and huge throngs of Friday worshippers marched and chanted against the United States and in solidarity with Libya; in Tehran's more prosperous neighborhoods, however, residents privately expressed hope that the U. S. Air Force might someday bomb the Ayatollah Khomeini's headquarters.[65]

Creating a Hero in the Arab and Third Worlds?

In a statement that provoked worry among U. S. Arabists, Chadli Klibi, the secretary general of the Arab League, on April 15 declared that the attack on Libya "compromises, perhaps irreversibly, United States relations with Arab peoples."[66] As things turned out, the reaction in the Arab world was described by one American official as harsher than the reaction to the March Gulf of Sidra battle but milder than the aftermath of the August 1981 dogfight; another official asserted that the Israeli Tunis air strike had created more problems for the United States. Some periodicals, including *Al-Akhban* and *Aker Sa'a* of Cairo, took the view that Qaddafi had reaped what he had sown. Much more typically, the Arab press raged against America and declared that the attack was not intended to be against the Qaddafi regime but against the whole Arab nation; such invective provided good catharsis, but it was probably not truly believed by most of its authors and by no means all its readers. It was noteworthy that in a region extremely prone to mob violence there was no explosion of violence against Americans, contrary to the expectations of many. Only in Sudan and Tunisia were there significant anti-American demonstrations.[67] The restrained reaction suggested that there was a grudging understanding among Arabs of why Washington had wanted to act against Qaddafi, even if they were repelled by the action, and, again, there was little evidence that offense at the U. S. air strikes translated into adulation for Qaddafi. The Middle East experts had further predicted that military action against Libya could destabilize Arab moderate governments, but nothing of the sort happened; U. S. officials would claim later that the position of the moderates had been bolstered.[68]

Two exiled Libyan opposition organizations expressed regret for the loss of civilian lives but verbally supported the U. S. air raids.[69] Bakoush, leader of the Libyan Liberation Organization, called it "an important contribution toward the overthrow of a criminal dictator."[70] By contrast, the Libyan National Movement called it a "criminal raid" and declared that "this insult to which the Libyan dignity, land, and honor were exposed would not have occurred had this filthy imbecile not been ruling our people."[71] The Libyan Committee for National Salvation, led by former RCC member Abdel Monein al-Huni, condemned the attack, held Qaddafi responsible for the harm Libya had suffered, and lamented that "the real criminal and his terrorist clique escaped unharmed."[72]

Immediately after the bombing raids, Libya demanded of Arab countries "the severance of political relations with the United States, the halting of pumping Arab oil, the withdrawal of assets, the abrogation of agreements with the United States, and the application of the same sanctions against . . . Britain";[73] additionally, Morocco, Algeria, Egypt, Jordan, and Syria were called upon to bomb the Sixth Fleet.[74] What the Jamahiriyah received was words. Syria declared that it "stands by Libya with all its strength and calls on Arab governments to perceive the dangers of this act and confront it."[75] Sudan affirmed its willingness to lend all its "material and human resources" to face America's "barbaric aggression" and recalled its ambassador to the United States for consultations,[76] the only country to do so. Saudi Arabia and the Gulf sheikdoms strongly condemned the U. S. action, but an undercurrent of relief among them was detected by delegates to the OPEC conference in Geneva as it pondered the attack.[77] Algeria denounced it as a "return to the law of the jungle";[78] Benjedid later defended his government for not having "created an atmosphere of agitations and gatherings and so on," saying, "I do not think that these things are the style of the Algerians."[79] In a remark that must have stung Qaddafi, the Algerian strongman told a Swedish interviewer, "Colonel Gadaffi is an old friend but we cannot accept the methods Libya uses."[80]

The Arab governments least enthusiastic on behalf of Qaddafi were those of Tunisia, Jordan, Iraq, and Egypt. The Bourguiba regime steadfastly refused any comment on the attack, confiscated copies of four publications with articles critical of it, and imprisoned the leading secular opposition leader, Ahmed Mestiri, for his role in a demonstration protesting the military action.[81] King Hussein had apparently not forgotten Qaddafi's several plots on his life: the Jordanian Minister of Information merely stated that "the American measure against Libya is sensitive and extremely dangerous and may lead to more dangerous results."[82] The king left the day after the attack for a private visit to Britain, and his son Crown Prince Hassan received a British trade delegation on April 19; thirty-one Jordanian university students were dismissed for their role in a rally protesting the air raids.[83]

Iraq withheld comment the first two days after the attack, and its ambassador to Washington appeared on U. S. television for commentary shortly after it without offering any hint of disapproval. Finally, Iraq did condemn the U. S. attack, but simultaneously bitterly reproached Qaddafi's effort to blackmail the Arab states and exploit the air strikes for propaganda serving him and his regime. Baghdad opposed the call for an Arab summit concerning the incident:[84] in view of its support for Iran, the Libyan regime had "the least right to demand Arab support against foreign aggression."[85] Furthermore, Iraq soon thereafter requested that the Arab League consider expelling Libya and Syria.[86] The government of Egypt issued a statement on April 15 stating, "Egypt has received with extreme worry and resentment news of the U. S. shelling of Libyan targets

... in violation of the United Nations Charter.''[87] Thereupon officials of the Mubarak regime, which was reported to be pleased in private with Washington's action, studiously avoided mention of the matter. Just two days later, the Egyptian Minister of Information, in an interview with a Kuwaiti newspaper, extensively criticized Libya and declared, ''There are no problems between Egypt and the United States.''[88]

Efforts in late April and early May to convene an Arab summit for condemning the U. S. attack foundered: Libya, Syria, and South Yemen took the position that such a meeting should be limited to discussing the attack, while Saudi Arabia and Libya's ostensible union partner Morocco wanted to include the Iran-Iraq war and other issues, and Iraq, Jordan, and the Gulf sheikdoms insisted that the Iran-Iraq war and not Libya should be at the top of the agenda. One may look to Qaddafi himself for an evaluation of the axiom that U. S. opposition would force Qaddafi's Arab enemies to come to his support. The colonel was embittered by the lack of support from his Arab colleagues; he even threatened to withdraw from the Arab League because of it, and the bitterness had still not subsided at an Arab summit two years later, when he complained of their failure on his behalf and told his fellow leaders to ''go to hell.'' The U. S. air strikes had clearly exposed Qaddafi's isolation in the Arab world, so much so that he had felt compelled in their aftermath to send a secret envoy to ask for help from the hated ''capitulationist'' regime of Egypt. Not only was the envoy's mission unsuccessful, Cairo also delivered a slap in the face to Qaddafi by deciding in late April to allow for only the second time ever transit through the Suez Canal for a nuclear-powered U. S. warship (in this instance the aircraft carrier *Enterprise*), a decision buttressed by the mild response in the Arab world to the air strikes.[89]

The Middle East experts had also stated that it was quite possible that regimes in the Middle East would find it necessary to downgrade their ties with the United States in the wake of the Libya operation. Nonetheless, the secretary general of Algeria's foreign ministry arrived as scheduled in Washington for talks in the last week of April, the Sudanese ambassador had already returned by the first week of May, and King Hussein was back for another visit in June. In addition to pro forma diplomatic complaints (which were not received from Iraq and Tunisia), the U. S. government received secret messages of congratulations from some Arab moderate governments. The Tunisians were said to be particularly gleeful, and senior Saudi air force officers were reportedly delighted by the performance of U. S. pilots and aircraft.[90] Shultz would later claim that Arab countries had quietly told the United States, ''You should have done more.''[91] This was likely a reference to the well-attested word to Washington from Arab moderates that the only major problem with the April 15 attack was that it did not kill Qaddafi.[92] Certainly, there was grumbling among America's Arab friends both before and after the attack, particularly concerning the Reagan administration's increasingly close ties with Israel, but there is little evidence of the Libya raids themselves having altered Washington's relations with Arab governments. As Robert Satloff of the Washington Institute for Near East Policy said, the episode served to "explode the myth that strategic alignments are so fragile in the Middle East that 'one false move' by Washington could turn America's strategic allies against it."[93]

The Organization of African Unity condemned the U. S. retaliation and expressed full solidarity with Libya, but the OAU's chairman, Abdou Diouf of Senegal, was criticized by opponents in his own country for maintaining silence on the matter, apparently because he was disgusted with Qaddafi for thwarting his efforts to bring peace in Chad. Prime Minister Rajiv Gandhi of India condemned the United States and Britain on behalf of the Nonaligned Movement, declaring that the air strike was especially unjustifiable because Colonel Qaddafi had after all given his most solemn word that he had nothing to do with recent terrorist operations and was opposed to skyjackings and the murder of innocents.[94] Later in September the Nonaligned Movement's representatives in Harare, Zimbabwe, listened to Qaddafi vow to undertake "'all types of terrorist acts" against the United States[95] and subsequently passed a resolution that politely ignored the Libyan leader's self-incrimination and accused the United States of "state terrorism" for attacking Libya.[96]

Nonetheless, the Middle East experts' prophecy that Qaddafi would be made a hero in the Third World was not fulfilled. The OPEC conference in April issued a statement of condemnation of the U. S. air strikes but quickly brushed aside Libya's call for an oil embargo against the United States and Great Britain; even Iran did not support the proposal. It was noted that Qaddafi's support from the Third World was rhetorical only and the minimum expected at that; the colonel was widely seen as having brought his fate upon himself.[97] At the Harare meeting Qaddafi denounced the Nonaligned Movement for its purely rhetorical support, declaring, "I want to say goodbye, farewell to this funny movement, to this fallacy, farewell to this utter falsehood."[98] Two months later Libya did win UN General Assembly condemnation of the U.S. attack as a violation of international law. However, given the fact that Third World solidarity was involved in the issue, the result was unimpressive: 79 votes for, 28 votes against, 33 abstentions (including Egypt, Greece, and Turkey), and 18 delegations absenting themselves (including Bahrain, Oman, and Tunisia). Therefore, Libya received the vote of only half the members of the UN, with a less than solid bloc of Islamic states.[99] (By contrast, the invasion of Grenada had been condemned by a 108 to 9 vote, with 27 abstentions.)

"Rambo" and the "Eurowimps"

For the United States, the most disturbing negative reaction to the retaliation against Libya was that found in Western Europe, where the response was predominantly critical among the general public and even worse among intellectuals: one survey of commentary appearing in seventy-one European newspapers found 95 percent of it unfavorable.[100] The rather imprecise statement that "the Europeans are taking to the streets against the United States" circulated in the American news media, as for nearly a week Western European cities were the sites of large anti-American demonstrations, more than in the rest of the world combined. Actually the demonstrators were far from being a cross-section of Europeans: Vernon Walters accurately called them "our professional enemies."[101] It was the same coalition of hippies, pacifists (some underwritten by Qaddafi), and leftist political party members who had long but unsuccessfully demonstrated to prevent deployment of the NATO nuclear missiles that eventually persuaded the Soviet Union to dismantle its SS–20 missiles aimed at Europe. As Walters noted, the protesters had not "suddenly become our enemies because of Libya";[102] the air strikes were a godsend for them, a new opportunity to lash out against their favorite villain, America. As before, many of the demonstrators were so consumed with their ardor for peace that they became positively violent, but, except perhaps in Italy, the demonstrations were smaller than the earlier ones. Apart from some demonstrators in Rome who condemned both Reagan and Qaddafi,[103] virtually all of them appeared to act as though the U. S. air strikes had occurred in a vacuum. Furthermore, their protests can scarcely be viewed as having been stances of principle. The same persons completely ignored the huge civilian death tolls of the War of the Cities between Iran and Iraq and the 1986–87 bombing raids against Pakistan villages by the air force of the Soviet-backed Afghan communist regime.

The European Parliament in Strasbourg unexpectedly passed a left-sponsored resolution denouncing Libya's terrorist and military threats against European states and condemning the U. S. air raids as a violation of international law and a threat to peace.[104] As Socialist party leader, Papandreou with characteristic hyperbole declared that the attack "sets dynamite to peace and destroys the independence of a nation in the name of imposing a hegemonistic United States presence in the area."[105] Greece had isolated itself within the Western alliance with its own virtually proterrorist policies, and its foreign minister's reproach of other European allies for not passing on advance warning of the attack[106] must have drawn derision in NATO chancelleries. The other Continental allies by contrast criticized or expressed disagreement with Washington's action rather than condemning it, and they made sure to condemn Libya strongly at the same time. For example, Gonzalez stated that he had "let the United States know that I do not agree with the method it used" but pronounced Libya's recent threats against Spain "intolerable and inadmissible."[107]

Belgium and West Germany expressed both understanding of and disagreement with Reagan's decision.[108] Kohl stated, "We advised against the use of force. Force is not a promising way of dealing with things," but he noted that Libya had become "a source of regional destabilization and center of international terrorism"[109] and "whoever continually preaches and practices violence, as

Kadafi does, must count on the victims defending themselves.''[110] Within his governing coalition, the Free Democratic party was more sharply critical of Washington, while Franz Josef Strauss of the Christian Social Union lambasted Europe for not supporting the U. S. policy. An opinion poll showed public disapproval of the attack in West Germany by a 70 percent to 25 percent margin.[111]

Prime Minister Craxi of Italy declared that ''far from weakening terrorism, this military action risks provoking explosive reactions of fanaticism and criminal and suicide acts.''[112] Interestingly, Giovanni Spadolini of the Republican party within the governing coalition endorsed the air strikes after having less than two weeks earlier cautioned that military action by the United States could not be effective against terrorism. Two other members of the coalition, the Liberals and the Social Democrats, rebuked Craxi and Foreign Minister Giulio Andreotti for softness on Qaddafi and Arab terrorism. The Libyan attack against Lampedusa was taken by Craxi and others in the Italian leadership as confirmation of their misgivings about U. S. military action, but for Qaddafi it was counterproductive because it substantially galvanized anti-Libyan sentiment in Rome, leading to a significant downgrading of Libyan-Italian ties. Craxi declared that Italy would retaliate with military force for any future attacks on Italian soil and responded to Qaddafi's claims of having reduced Lampedusa ''to ruins'' by asserting that if Libya's missiles had hit the island, Qaddafi would no longer be head of Libya's government. France similarly threatened a military response to any Libyan attack on southern Europe.[113] Such unprecedented tough talk against Qaddafi by the Europeans must have been enjoyed in Washington, but U. S. officials might have wondered why a hypothetical European military reprisal would not be counterproductive, as the Europeans were insisting America's reprisal would be.

French Foreign Minister Jean Barnard Raimond issued a terse criticism of the U. S. air strikes that was deftly worded to place the onus on terrorists, saying France ''deplores the fact that the intolerable rise in terrorism has led to a reprisal which itself increases the chain of violence.''[114] Former president Valery Giscard d'Estaing and his Union for French Democracy, coalition partners with Chirac, strongly endorsed the American attack and criticized the refusal of overflight. The French public, however, strongly supported the denial of overflight even as up to 70 percent supported the attack itself, and Reagan gained very high approval ratings in France. Irritation over the damage to the embassy in Tripoli even appeared to be absent. There were a number of logical explanations for the French public's reaction contrasting to that of other European NATO countries. The French were known to be resistant to pacifism—notably they held no noticeable anti-American demonstrations—and were used to viewing military force as a legitimate instrument of foreign policy because of their own governments' actions. They were involved in a long struggle with Qaddafi in Chad, they had been targeted by Arab terrorists in the 1980s on a scale similar to the United States and could therefore take some vicarious satisfaction, and France had apparently the most pro-American populace in Western Europe, which ironically is believed to be in large part the result of De Gaulle's withdrawal of his country from the military component of NATO, enabling the French to be relatively free of the fear of American dominance that bred anti-Americanism in other countries.[115] In a seeming response to public sentiment, Raimond changed the official position on the U. S. action to "neither approves or disapproves."[116]

Far different was the public response in Great Britain, where 66 percent of the public disapproved of Reagan's decision to attack Libya and 71 percent disapproved of Thatcher's decision to allow F–111s to fly from British bases. She received the most vehement and scalding condemnation from Neil Kinnock and the opposition Labour party. Thatcher was widely assailed for making Britons a target for retaliation and for alleged subservience to Washington. The political uproar was so great that across the Atlantic, James Schlesinger opined that the Libya operation was more likely to cause the downfall of Mrs. Thatcher than of Colonel Qaddafi. She faced the storm without flinching, and within a few weeks, opinion began to shift somewhat in favor of the attack on Libya; by the fall the Conservatives had regained the lead in the polls.[117]

A number of reasons were suggested for the substantial chasm in perspectives about the attack in the United States and in Western Europe, politically aligned with one another and forming together a distinct cultural region in the world. It was believed that the European leaders were fearful for their trade with Libya and the Arab world,[118] but this did not appear to have been much on the minds of the general public. Concern for the safety of the thousands of Europeans in Libya in the wake of the episode was expressed. Visceral dislike of the use of military force was more widespread among Europeans than among Americans, and in the view of the *Economist*, it tended to promote wishful thinking about the international environment:

For most Americans, the world is a dangerous place where adversaries prowl; where there are only ineffectual fragments of "international law"; where it is sometimes necessary to fight to guard one's interests. Most Europeans, on the other hand would like to believe that the world was no longer a place where force was needed. The European aversion to violence dates back to the ghastliness of the first world war, and perhaps to the humanist ideas seeping into politics even before 1914. . . . By 1945 . . . the Europeans wanted to say goodbye to all that.

    . . . This deep desire not to have to use force has created a desire to believe that force is now unnecessary, that disputes can be settled by civilised discourse, that there is a rule of law. Europe wants to see the world in the image of its own post–1945 civility.
. . . Europe, and who shall blame it, does not like war.

    . . . America's picture of the world is, of course, truer than Europe's—there are enemies out there, civilised discourse often doesn't work, there is no international arbiter.[119]

Compounding this predisposition was the fact that in 1981, Reagan and Haig— noting that Soviet leaders were openly boasting that the "correlation of forces" in the world had changed in their favor and that "the imperialists," that is, the United States, were on the run—had sought to regain Moscow's respect in part by quite bellicose rhetoric. The rhetoric had the unintended effect of frightening much of the European public, and it left such an abiding impression that, as some European commentators noted, press and public retained an exaggerated view of Reagan as a reckless "cowboy," even though events showed that he was actually fairly cautious and in no way inclined to seek a dangerous confrontation with the Soviet Union.[120] However, the *Economist* and others may have overestimated the extent of generalized opposition to military force among Europeans: certainly the British public had been willing enough to support the reconquest of the Falklands, and much of the initial European hostility to the invasion of Grenada dissipated when it became plain that the Grenadian people were overjoyed by the event. The most typical European criticism of the Libyan raid appears not to have been that it was immoral or illegal, but that rather than curbing terrorism it would lead to a great surge of terrorist reprisals, especially in Europe. The possibility of more U. S. military strikes thereby resulting and stimulating yet more terrorism in return alarmed the Europeans.

The European response to the attack on Libya generated a response among Americans that was at least equally heated. Reagan and other U. S. officials were angry in private but in public maintained a cheerful, conciliatory tone.[121] They could well afford to leave to Congress and unofficial Americans the administering of heavy criticism. An overwhelming 83 percent of Americans expressed disapproval of European weakness in dealing with terrorism,[122] and intense reproach of the Europeans poured forth alike from the common people and from "inside the Beltway" around Washington, D.C.[123] Even commentators opposed to the air strikes berated the Europeans for their refusal to take strong nonmilitary measures against states sponsoring terrorism, which refusal was undoubtedly a major factor in the overall anger in the United States. The Europeans were accused of cowardice and pusillanimity, indifference to the death of Kenneth Ford and to the past and potential deaths of other Americans, default of the obligations of allies—the *New York Times* asked, "What Are Allies For?"[124]—and wanting the NATO alliance to be a "one-way street" in which they benefited from enormous military expenditures on their behalf and gave absolutely nothing in return. Castigation of the French for refusal of overflight was particularly unsparing, and numerous local boycotts of French goods arose; meanwhile, Thatcher and her country were lionized.[125] (This juxtaposition was ironic because while France's populace was apparently more supportive than that of any other NATO ally, Britain was the scene of perhaps the most blistering censure of the Libya raids in Europe.)

In short order talk arose of the rift in NATO over the Libya air raids, and, interestingly enough, the arguments being hurled back and forth across the Atlantic involved the matter of alliance roles as much as or more than the merits of the attack itself. Both sides adopted self-serving interpretations of the obligations of alliance. Americans insisted that in accordance with the principle of teamwork, the allies should support the attack on Libya, period. (Reagan admin-istration officials, it should be noted, let it be known that they felt that the allies had shown poor judgment but did almost nothing in the way of accusing them of violating alliance obligations.) However, it was not reasonable to expect the allies as sovereign states to endorse or even permit overflight for a mission they genuinely felt to be unwise. The United States had not supported the British and French Suez intervention, had not endorsed Portugal's anticolonial wars in Af-rica, and as Walters pointed out, had not supplied crucially needed helicopters for the French in Algeria.[126] In their defense, the allies pointed out that the NATO alliance specifically applied to a fixed geographical area, and Libya was outside that area.

A more reasonable hope on the part of the United States would have been that the allies make their criticisms through private channels; the United States had been willing to suffer great damage to its image in the Third World for the sake of solidarity with Western Europe when it conveyed its misgivings about their colonial policies in the 1950s on a private basis. The spectacle of Continental Europe unified in public criticism of the United States was damaging to the struggle against terrorism and a source of comfort to Libya, and it was Libya and not the United States that was openly hostile to Europe. Anthony H. Cordes-man's assessment was that "Rather than deter American action," which the European leaders may have had in mind, "the political and public protests from Europe have tended to confirm the belief that neither the EEC nor NATO will ever be meaningful forums for out of area action and that the US has been thrust into the position of having to act alone. . . . This kind of thinking is scarcely likely to split the Alliance, but it also is unlikely to make the US take Europe seriously over any issue other than the defence of Europe."[127]

It is noteworthy that in European leaders' assertions that the United States should not have bombed Libya, the reason cited was as likely to be the simple fact that it was against the allies' wishes as it was to be the merits of the matter. Craxi on the record and other leaders off the record complained that the Europeans had been advised but not consulted. Jonathan Alford of the International Institute for Strategic Studies in London strongly disagreed that Washington could be accused of lack of consultation.[128] A problem here was the fact, not often elucidated, that in actual practice there have been two quite different forms of "consultation" in NATO: joint decision making in matters related to the defense of Europe—a classic case being the 1979 "two track" missiles decision—and polite forewarning of impending foreign policy actions in matters outside the NATO area. From the European side were heard such statements as, "How important . . . are America's European allies in Washington if the United States can afford to ignore the warning issued by the Foreign Ministers of the European Community to show restraint?"[129] and former British chief of defence staff Lord Carver's observation that "when the chips are down, the Americans do what they want, no matter what the Europeans say."[130] Behind these piteous statements was the fact that the Europeans were actually laying claim to a power of veto over U. S. foreign policy in matters outside the NATO area; while they staunchly defended their sovereign right to exercise their own judgment in foreign policy, they called upon Washington to forswear exercise of *its* judgment. No U. S. administration had ever conceded that the United States was obligated to practice joint decision making with its allies in out-of-area matters, and such decision making was no more the practice of European states than it was of Washington.

There was in effect a fallback position from the Europeans' radical claim that NATO entailed the subjection of U. S. foreign policy outside the alliance zone to the veto of its allies. In this view the United States should have bowed to European wishes, although Libya was outside the NATO area, because of its proximity to Europe—even the West Germans referred to the Jamahiriyah as "almost in our backyard"[131]—and because an attack on Libya could threaten allied security interests other than the conventional defense of Europe, specifically by stimulating more action by terrorists in Europe. Many Europeans complained that America acted and then simply "sailed home," leaving the Europeans more vulnerable to the consequences. In fact, it was myopic to argue that the aftermath of the Libya raids was likely to prove more harmful to Europeans than to Americans. America never sails home: U. S. citizens are ubiquitous in the world, easy targets for retaliation by terrorists in all areas. Depending on one's perspective, military action against Libya was either very courageous or very foolhardy from the standpoint of strictly American interests. As far as security interests were concerned, it could be argued that the air strikes against Libya came about because European inaction against Middle Eastern terrorism had threatened the security of Americans in Europe, including NATO soldiers. Regarding the proximity argument, it should be noted that the Europeans had shown very little sensitivity to U. S. wishes and interests in the Western hemisphere, particularly in giving more foreign aid to the Sandinista dictatorship of Nicaragua than to all the freely elected governments of Central America combined.

International Terrorism's Response

In the international reaction to the U. S. attack on Libya, probably the greatest interest worldwide was in seeing what the reaction of international terrorists would be. The U. S. government rushed over two hundred security police to Europe to bolster protection of its personnel. The major Palestinian groups linked to Libya and Syria announced their intention to strike American targets. The Abu Nidal group issued a public threat against Oliver North; Edward Luttwak, a defense analyst at Georgetown University's Center for Strategic and International Studies; Maj. Gen. John K. Singlaub (USA, Ret.), an activist on behalf of anticommunist insurgencies; and the Heritage Foundation, a conservative Washington think tank, which had in 1984 publicly called upon the Reagan administration to undermine the government of Libya.[132]

At 10:00 P.M. on April 15, as U. S. embassy communications officer William J. Cokals drove home from work on a residential street near the Libyan people's bureau in Khartoum, two men in another car fired five shots in his direction; one lodged in his brain, leaving his right side paralyzed. Khartoum had been near the top of the list of over thirty sites of Libyan terrorist plotting against Americans, and U. S. officials had evidence that an attack against embassy personnel was imminent the day before the air strikes. The actual gunmen might have been Abu Nidal's, it was thought, and responsibility for the attack was claimed by "Black September," one of the Abu Nidal group's cover names. The Sudanese authorities still declined to expel known Libyan terrorist agents, and the U. S. ambassador ordered evacuation of nonessential staff and dependents from Sudan. Whitehead declared on April 22 that Libya was "probably" responsible for the shooting. In a similar incident on April 25, five to seven shots were fired from a passing car at Arthur L. Pollick, another U. S. embassy communications officer, as he drove home from church in San'a, Yemen; one bullet wounded him in the left shoulder and another grazed his head.[133] The State Department later termed it an "attack believed instigated by Libya."[134]

On April 17 the bodies of Padfield, Douglas, and Kilburn were found near Beirut, each killed by a gunshot to the head, with a note beside their bodies signed by the "Arab Fedayeen Cells" claiming they were killed in reprisal for the U. S. attack on Libya. Libyan direct responsibility for the killings was strongly suspected, and they substantially inflamed the controversy in Britain over the U. S. air raids and Thatcher's role. Hours later a British television cameraman named John McCarthy was abducted from his car on the way to the Beirut airport to flee the country; his kidnapping was claimed by the "Hilal ibn al Qaddafi Organization" and the "Fedayeen Revolutionary Cells." The same day the Abu Nidal group under its cover name "Revolutionary Organization of Socialist Muslims" claimed to have hung its British hostage Alec Colett and later provided a videotape of a hanging corpse that was probably that of Collett.[135]

Also on April 17 the plot to blow up an El Al airliner leaving from London was discovered, adding greatly to public fright; it was quickly determined to be unrelated to the American-Libyan crisis, however. On April 18 a letter bomb addressed to a Jewish member of Thatcher's cabinet was intercepted and defused at the House of Commons. That evening two Libyans were arrested in Ankara, another location where the American embassy was on high alert as part of the list of targets of Libyan terrorist plotting. The terrorists were apprehended as they approached a U. S. officers' club with a bag containing six grenades that had entered the country in a Libyan diplomatic pouch and had been detected being passed to the terrorists from people's bureau personnel. The plan had been to destroy the club by placing grenades on the roof as one hundred people, including many women and children, were inside attending a wedding reception; the two terrorists confessed that club was chosen as a target because it would be crowded. The next day a bomb that had been placed at the entrance of the Koc-American Bank in Istanbul was defused; both plots were thought to relate to plans set in motion before the air strikes.[136]

On May 2 a Spaniard and a Portuguese were apprehended in Madrid as they were preparing to bomb the Bank of America headquarters; their arrest led to the seizure of eight other members of the Call of Jesus Christ, which had fallen out of French supervision and had been plotting attacks on American and Jewish targets in Spain under the direction of Libya's acting ambassador to Madrid. On May 14 a car bomb was detonated outside the Canadian embassy in Jakarta, Indonesia, and rockets were fired at the U. S. and Japanese embassies; no casualties were caused. Japanese Red Army terrorists were believed responsible, and Libyans had been seen in their company. Bombs were defused in Mexico City and Bilbao, Spain, and there were a number of other explosions in Latin America, Asia, Europe, and the Arab world seemingly related to the U. S. attack on Libya during the month after it, causing damage to property but no significant injury to humans.[137]

THE DUST SETTLES

In the days after the attack on Libya, press accounts stated that the United States had crossed a threshold into a new era of warfare against terrorists that "could easily rival Vietnam as one of America's longest and most painful military involvements."[138] Critics said that Reagan had put himself in a position to seem a fool if he did launch a reprisal strike every time terrorists attacked. However, Shultz and other officials quickly insisted both on and off the record that Washington was not going to take an "automatic pilot" approach to military retaliation against terrorism; each case would be weighed on its individual merits. The rationale would continue to be not punitive, but preemptive, oriented toward affecting the future meaningfully. Some officials said only a "particularly egregious" attack would lead to a military response, and the stringent requirement for definitive evidence of responsibility would by most accounts remain.[139] It was far from certain that U. S. officials would obtain such evidence, but even if they did there was the option of not publicly disclosing it if Washington did not consider another military venture to be wise. Even if the information leaked, the time-honored expedient of declaring such evidence "ambiguous" was available.

Despite these inhibitions, and despite the fact that the military establishment was said in private to be still not won over to the approach of military retaliation against terrorism, military planners busily prepared for another attack against Libya in case the president ordered one, and such a scenario was felt to be likely as Qaddafi sought revenge. The Ankara plot, if it had been successful, would probably have provoked another U. S. attack. A memo written by Peter Rodman of the NSC staff opined that the American public would probably support only one more strike against Libya, so it needed to be an effective one. This view was widely shared: if force was to be used again it should not be a tit-for-tat response, but rather an overwhelming blow; oil pumping and storage facilities were considered a prime target. The idea of using conventionally armed cruise missiles to avoid risk to pilots' lives and the difficulties of air-to-air refueling or seeking use of foreign bases was gaining support, especially in the NSC staff, but the Joint Chiefs of Staff were not converted to it. Administration officials were willing to go it alone without overseas support; it was understood that no more requests to Thatcher for use of the F–111s would be made after the political firestorm following the previous attack. At the same time, it was hoped that the prospect of another U. S. attack would help persuade the allies to take the kind of nonmilitary measures against Libya that could have meaning.[140]

Indeed, as one reporter noted (borrowing Samuel Johnson's expression), the attack had the effect upon the European allies of "wonderfully concentrating the mind."[141] Immediately afterward some European leaders had expressed the view that their measures of April 14 should have been viewed by the United States as an adequate substitute for military action against Libya; however, European public opinion did not back them in that notion. Washington officials had felt for some time that European governments were lagging behind their populaces in terms of willingness to take strong measures against terrorism, and the previously cited survey of newspaper commentary showed 90 percent of commentators critical of inaction by European governments against international terrorism. The fear of harm from terrorist reprisals in Europe as well as the need to dissuade Washington from more reprisals made a more serious approach essential, and political leaders became more sensitive to the problem of Libya's involvement in terrorism as they demanded and received more information from their own intelligence services. The strong popular anti-European outburst across the Atlantic made a great impression upon the Europeans, particularly the French, and this combined with Washington's military action made them realize that the United States was truly serious. The same political will to avoid a serious rift in the NATO alliance that the Reagan administration displayed was also displayed by European leaders.[142] Thus, within days of the attack the London *Times* reported, "EEC states appear to be moving away from their initial shock and dismay over the American bombing of Libya and towards a greater understanding of American motives and frustrations."[143] Both publicly and privately European officials admitted that their irresolution was partly to blame for the coming about of the air raids.

The foreign ministers of the EEC on April 21 rejected the recommendation of a monitoring group report that all Libyan people's bureaus in EEC countries should be closed but were nonetheless credited with a decisiveness they had not shown in previous such meetings. They decided to cut Libyan diplomatic representation in EEC countries and EEC representation in Libya to the minimum level necessary to maintain diplomatic relations, to limit the numbers of and extend surveillance to Libyans without diplomatic status (such as students, journalists, and employees of the Libyan airlines and of trade offices), to make Libyans expelled from one EEC country persona non grata in other EEC countries, to require Libyan diplomats to obtain special permission to travel outside the city where they were stationed, and to review sales of subsidized food to

Libya; sales of subsidized butter were soon terminated. Three days later, EEC ministers of the Trevi group agreed to increase exchange of information on terrorists among themselves and with non-EEC countries, including the United States; from now on such exchanges of information were to be done on a continuous rather than on a case-by-case basis. West Germany withdrew its ambassador from Tripoli and expelled more than half of Libya's diplomats in Bonn, including all of those who had been involved in terrorism-related endeavors. In coming months around five hundred Libyans, including over a hundred diplomats, were sent home by Western European governments; Libyan student programs were shut down in Spain, Ireland, and Great Britain, and Libyan diplomats in East Berlin were banned from West Berlin. Under U. S. prodding, some allies privately agreed to close down Libyan front groups and to monitor the Jamahiriyah's Islamic Call Societies and a variety of Libyan financial transactions with the funding of terrorist operations in mind. Western intelligence and law enforcement agencies began devoting more resources to, and cooperating more closely than ever before in, tracking and hampering the movements of terrorists; security at potential targets was strengthened.[144]

In the summer of 1986 some European governments quietly took steps to reduce imports of Libyan oil and cut off financing and guarantees for trade with Libya. Most West European airlines substantially cut service to Libya. Italy drastically reduced its trade with the Jamahiriyah, and even Malta began to distance itself from Tripoli. At the May 4–6 Tokyo summit of the seven leading industrialized democracies Craxi promised Reagan privately that he would greatly reduce the number of Italians in Libya, and the seven countries stigmatized Libya as a sponsor of terrorism in a much stronger antiterrorism declaration than had been previously expected; the statement outlined a series of measures that went beyond those adopted by the EEC on April 21. The exceptional cordiality that characterized the summit marked the definitive healing of any rift in the Western alliance over the Libya air strikes; high esteem was accorded to Reagan by the other leaders, and the meeting could be said to have marked the symbolic high point of his presidency. However, in spite of the summit statement's call for embargo of arms to terrorism-supporting states, Reagan and Poindexter were preparing even then for more of the arms shipments to Iran that would bring about the low point of his presidency. Meanwhile, Qaddafi was bitterly disappointed by the actions taken against him by the Western allies.[145]

At the same time the administration did actively seek to follow up on its attack on Libya. On April 27, when asked by the press if Washington was considering using covert action against Libya, Shultz stated that the Qaddafi regime should be made to understand that a conventional military attack was not the only possible response to terrorism available to Washington. "Covert action is something that we need to be using," he said, adding, "It is certainly intended to be disruptive."[146] From May to October, according to published accounts, small Navy Seal teams made nocturnal landings in Libya, gathering intelligence, disrupting telephone communications with Soviet-and Israeli-made dynamite charges, and leaving articles including Israeli and Syrian cigarette butts and American Kleenex tissue for Libyan patrols to find. It was in essence a scheme of pranks designed for psychological warfare to destabilize further the Qaddafi regime. The Libyans were reportedly indeed confused by the capers. It has been suggested that the NSC staff was in charge of the operation, and additionally in May Poindexter and North pursued without State Department approval a plan suggested by Iranian expatriate wheeler-dealer Manucher Ghorbanifar for a meeting with an official of the Qaddafi regime. In a striking parallel to notions in the secret Iran diplomacy, Ghorbanifar's scheme would supposedly simultaneously work toward a rapprochement with the foreign government concerned and a change in leadership of that same government. The matter reportedly went as far as booking hotel rooms in Europe for a meeting between North and the Libyan official, but doubts about Ghorbanifar's reliability, especially after McFarlane's ill-fated meeting with Iranian officials in Tehran, led to the shelving of the project.[147]

After mid-May it was abundantly clear that the flurry of terrorist activity seen after the U. S. bombing of Libya had died out; in fact, there was little of it after the first two weeks. Libya had pressured some of its African terrorist clients to mount anti-American attacks, but they made no immediate response. At least some of the plots directly guided by Libya in the period after the bombing were from the cluster originating in March, and it was not clear that a great number of new plots had been ordered after the air raids. Thus Libya and its sympathizers had been unable or unwilling to engineer the kind of incident that would remove the sting of defeat from Qaddafi. Unexpectedly, Western countries and their citizens enjoyed a quiet summer on the terrorism front, with no major lethal incidents apart from the bombing of a tourist train by Sendero Luminoso in Peru.[148]

In an incident that attracted little notice at the time, masked gunmen shot and killed a Libyan expatriate industrialist in Paris in June; the State Department later blamed Qaddafi agents. U. S. officials detected greatly reduced communications traffic and travel by Libyan agents during this period, which they interpreted as an ebbing of Libyan terrorist plotting. In a speech on July 23, Oakley described Libyan terrorism as "quiescent"; however, on that very day, authorities in Togo arrested nine citizens of Benin and Togo for plots to bomb a market place and the American embassy in Togo. The Interior Minister of Togo on August 11 made a public statement, reported in the *New York Times*, that the terrorists had confessed to receiving their explosives from the Libyan people's bureau in Benin; they also alleged participation in the plot by people's bureaus in two neighboring countries. U. S. officials took the report seriously, but did not fully and publicly embrace it until later. Also in July, weapons were purchased in Pakistan for an upcoming Libyan-sponsored Abu Nidal group skyjacking. At some point in the summer, the United States detected the reemergence in East Berlin of a senior Libyan diplomat whose presence was normally associated with terrorist plotting; American officials immediately informed

Soviet and East German authorities, and they in turn quietly obtained his departure. In Sudan U. S. diplomats reported that they were under Libyan surveillance again. Reagan was disturbed by the indications of renewed Libyan plotting and ordered his aides to warn Tripoli that Washington saw these signs and remained ready to punish Libya with military force again if necessary; a message was passed to Libya through the Soviets.[149]

In the wake of Operation El Dorado Canyon, Qaddafi had claimed that the British sovereign bases on Cyprus had been involved in the attack,[150] and demanded that Cyprus close them (despite its lack of authority to do so) or face "a new confrontation that will inflict destruction on the island."[151] On August 3 terrorists using mortars, grenades, and assault rifles launched attacks on the British base at Akotiri and on sunbathers at a crowded nearby beach; miraculously, only four people were injured. The attack was claimed as retaliation for Britain's role in the April air strikes by the obviously Libyan-oriented "Omar al-Mukhtar Martyr Group" and Lebanese Nasserites, whose mentor was Qaddafi; it was strongly suspected that the terrorists had escaped Cyprus disguised as crew on a Libyan airliner. British officials and terrorism experts believed that Libya had instigated the incident. On August 20, police in West Berlin arrested three Lebanese on suspicion of preparing a bombing attack to hit U.S. service personnel on behalf of Libya; they would later be released in early September because authorities had not been able to gather enough evidence to try them.[152]

Meanwhile, in the United States the *Wall Street Journal* had approached American and foreign officials for information for a story about Libya as the anniversary of Qaddafi's coup approached, and on August 25 it published a lengthy article that, among other things, cited unnamed U. S. and West European intelligence officials as expressing the conviction that Colonel Qaddafi was engaged in terrorist plotting again; the story also declared that the United States and Libya were on a "collision course again" and that a new U. S. attack might even come in anticipation of, rather than in response to, a Libyan terrorist attack. Soon press reports appeared citing other U. S. officials who stated that there were indeed indications of possible new Libyan terrorist activity but criticized the *Wall Street Journal's* sources for making them public before the evidence became harder. Poindexter and other administration officials warned the press that the "collision course" angle of the *Journal* story had been much overstated, and a Shultz aide attributed it to a "free-lancer" in the government pursuing a "personal agenda."[153]

Around the time of the *Wall Street Journal* article, the Federal Aviation Administration issued a general alert for possible terrorist acts to all U. S. airlines. On September 5 four terrorists of the Abu Nidal group seized Pan Am Flight 73, filled with mostly South Asian passengers, on the ground in Karachi, Pakistan. After the pilots escaped, the gunmen singled out a newly naturalized U. S. citizen of Indian ancestry for murder and many hours later opened fire on the assembled passengers, killing twenty more, including another American. The mastermind of the operation was a Libyan intelligence officer; he referred to the attempted skyjacking as a "special mission" of Libyan intelligence in an intercepted phone call to the Libyan people's bureau in Islamabad. On September 6 two Abu Nidal terrorists murdered twenty-two Jews in a synagogue in Istanbul. Libya, which quickly termed the synagogue a base of Zionist intelligence, had delivered weapons via diplomatic pouch for the killers; Syria and Iran were also believed to have been involved.[154]

On August 14 Reagan and his top advisers had approved a plan designed to destabilize Libya further as well as to intimidate Qaddafi and preoccupy him with domestic worries, both for the sake of persuading him not to carry out more terrorist attacks. It included increased support for Libyan dissidents, more of the psychological warfare measures that were already being used, such as using electronic warfare to trick Libyan radar operators into thinking that U. S. planes and ships were crossing the "line of death," altering some details of planned Air Force and Navy maneuvers in order to make them more intimidating to Qaddafi, increasing surveillance of suspected Libyan terrorist agents, and seeking increased cooperation in sharing of intelligence with allied officials.[155] Bob Woodward was able to take center stage of U. S.-Libyan relations once again by combining the administration's psychological warfare program and the disputes that had arisen between government officials in press reports in late August into a grossly overblown October 2 *Washington Post* story of a "massive disinformation" campaign by the Reagan administration. His story centered around the claim that not just the "free-lancer's" talk of imminent military action against Libya but the bulk of the August 25 *Wall Street Journal* story was "disinformation" peddled by U. S. officials; this assertion has been disputed;[156] on close examination it is quite faulty. Contrary to Woodward's assertions, "disinformation" was not discussed in the August 14 NSPG meeting, and the National Security Decision Directive signed by the president (and reviewed by congressional intelligence committees) did not mention it. Around that time, the CIA did prepare to plant more exaggerated reports concerning subversion against Qaddafi in the Arab press (but not the European press, as Woodward thought); the Washington press corps had known about and reported on this low-budget campaign in the Middle East (which was carried out under congressional oversight) since its authorization in 1981. Woodward asserted that the reports were certain to "blow back" into the American media,[157] which was not true, because the American press does not closely follow the Arab press's coverage of Libya or of anything else.

The most damaging aspect of Woodward's tale was his conversion of sincere disagreements within the government over the firmness of evidence concerning responsibility for terrorist plots and incidents, a fairly normal occurrence,[158] into an effort to promote false information concerning Libyan terrorism. He conveniently overlooked the Togolese government's public statement of August 11 and the fact that the *Wall Street Journal* story had cited European and Arab as well as American sources concerning indications of renewed terrorist activity by Libya. His prized piece of evidence on this issue was a document he called "the

Poindexter memo.'' It is difficult to imagine that Woodward was not aware that the memo was actually composed not by Poindexter but by Elaine Morton, an opponent of active U. S. opposition to Qaddafi who was soon forced to resign from the NSC staff under suspicion of being the source of Woodward's leak.[159] Morton's memo, believed to have been written in a manner she hoped would torpedo the psychological war project, claimed that "the current intelligence community assessment is that Qaddafi is temporarily quiescent in his support of terrorism, [though] he may soon move to a more active role."[160] Though seized upon as gospel by Woodward, this assertion was far from the truth: among U. S. officials who were fully convinced that Qaddafi was sponsoring terrorism again, those who saw reasons to suspect it, and those who thought he was quiescent, the latter were by far the least numerous. How did Woodward cope with the fact that the Karachi incident proved correct the assessment of the officials he was accusing of "disinformation"? He found some officials who speculated, without any evidence, that the Karachi incident was a response to U. S. officials' press comments of a week and a half earlier. Such an idea would not have been taken seriously by terrorism experts, who insist that complex terrorist operations such as skyjackings are not prepared on short notice, and, indeed, investigators soon established that the plot went at least as far back as July.[161] The disinformation story was very detrimental for the United States in the long term; it encouraged visceral opponents of pressure against Qaddafi to make irresponsible, ill-founded allegations against Washington. In the short term, it forced the administration to take a low public profile concerning Libya, which actually accorded well with the next phase of the confrontation with Qaddafi: support for the Chadians in their successful struggle against the Jamahiriyah, without distracting the Libyan people from the fact that they were being defeated by the people they had once raided for slaves with impunity.

CONCLUSIONS

The question of how much of a success the April 15, 1986, air strikes against Libya were will probably long be controversial. It was inevitable that it be so, barring outcomes of unmitigated catastrophe or of miraculous accomplishment beyond the planners' wildest dreams. Since the attack was such an unusual event, no generally accepted criteria for measuring its success exists, leaving the choice of criteria a subjective matter. Many commentators view foreign policies and foreign policy actions as failures if they are anything short of 100 percent successes, but such thinking is surely misguided. It might be appropriate to keep in view that both in public and in private, members of the Reagan administration did not express hope that Operation El Dorado Canyon would dramatically change the world all by itself. It would be absurd to say the attack was a failure because it did nothing to prevent Sikh terrorism in the Punjab or even the autumn 1986 campaign of bombings in France, the country conspicuous for its nonparticipation; on the other hand, if the only effect was a lull of a few months in Arab terrorism, followed by an enduring return to previous levels, that would not have constituted much of a success.

In early autumn 1986 it appeared that the latter scenario might prove true, with the Karachi and Istanbul massacres, the Paris bombings, and the kidnapping of three more Americans in Lebanon, but fortunately it did not. The lull in terrorist spectaculars resumed; the Abu Nidal group, which had been apparently inactive between April and its horrid actions in September, went back into a period of inactivity that lasted through 1987. International terrorist incidents in Western Europe dropped 28 percent, and Middle Eastern terrorism in Europe dropped almost by half in 1986, from seventy-four to thirty-nine incidents, the decline being accounted for by the portion of the year after the attack on Libya; the lowered level continued for both categories in 1987. To the great relief of Americans, bloody anti-American episodes became less common: international terrorist incidents directed at U. S. targets declined by over 25 percent from 1986 to 1987, and terrorism fatalities for Americans dropped from thirty-eight in 1985 to twelve in 1986 to seven in 1987.[162]

The U. S. attack on Libya was acknowledged widely, particularly among European security officials, to have made an impact on terrorism by encouraging allied governments to take stricter measures in opposition to terrorism.[163] The expulsions of Libyans from Europe, including what a State Department official called "some of the real bad apples . . . in the Peoples [*sic*] Bureaus,"[164] was believed to have had a severe effect on Qaddafi's terrorist infrastructure.[165] Operation El Dorado Canyon was undoubtedly responsible to a significant extent for creating the atmosphere in which Great Britain and West Germany publicly stigmatized Syria in 1986 for the two Hindawi brothers' cases. They were certainly not the first instances in which European governments had solid evidence of complicity of a state in terrorist acts in Europe; such evidence had in the past been downplayed or deliberately concealed.

Aside from these indirect effects, the issue of the direct effect of the Libya raids for counterterrorism is more difficult. Obviously, it is impossible to divine with certainty the motives behind the action or inaction of terrorist groups and their state sponsors, but that does not mean that hypothesizing is improper. Some analysts attributed the improvements in the terrorism picture in 1986–87 entirely to the enhanced defensive measures adopted by Europe after the attack, but others believed that there was also some deterrent effect upon state sponsors. The latter proposition seems plausible when one considers that Middle Eastern terrorist groups, including the Abu Nidal group, were quite capable of operations in regions other than Europe, but there was no pattern of simply channeling anti-Western terrorist spectaculars to different regions. Although he seemed to have forgotten his lesson in late summer of 1986, Qaddafi pulled back in the realm of terrorism after the Karachi and Istanbul incidents; perhaps the fact that his intelligence officer in Pakistan was arrested less than a week after the Pan Am Flight 73 massacre reminded the colonel of his vulnerability to retaliation. Libyan terrorism, especially against American targets, was drastically down during the rest of 1986 and 1987.[166] The long quiescence of the Abu Nidal group could well have been related to pressure for restraint from Libya and Syria. Certainly, it appears that in 1986 (apart from the plots performed on the weekend of Sept. 5 and 6) and 1987, Abu Nidal's sponsors were not pressing him to carry out a campaign of new attacks, since his track record suggested that had they done so he would have gladly obliged.

The much-cited fact that Qaddafi personally "went into a hole" after the U. S. attack was in and of itself a minor victory. His agents continued to pursue his globalist policies: for example, the Libyan air force enabled government troops in Sudan to retake the town of Rumbek from insurgents the month after the U. S. raids, and Libyan "diplomats" continued to increase their involvement in Oceania and the Caribbean, particularly long-term building of terrorist infrastructure. Activities likely to bring a direct confrontation with the United States tended to be avoided, however, and Libya has not professed to find so much need to imprison Westerners for espionage in recent years. It was reported that Qaddafi withdrew his support from some terrorist groups after the U. S. attack. Regarding Abu Nidal, some reports had it that Qaddafi had found it expedient to pressure him to leave Libya for Syria shortly before or after the U. S. air strikes, but other reports contradicted that; in any case, the FRC's strong operational ties with Tripoli were not interrupted. Libya received the FRC officials who were expelled from Damascus in a June 1987 Syrian crackdown. And in October, the *Eksund II* was intercepted by French authorities bearing 150 tons of Libyan weapons intended for the IRA and probably other European terrorist groups. In 1988, Libyan terrorism was on the rise again, most notably with the Japanese Red Army's April car bombing in Naples and a bomb plot aborted in New Jersey, linked as a Libyan conspiracy in a U. S. district court in 1989.[167] The Abu Nidal group reemerged with several major armed assaults in 1988.

It was well attested that Syria was greatly shaken by the U. S. attack in Libya, immediately going into a sustained high military alert, and was embarrassed by the arrests of the Hindawi brothers; observers felt they perceived greater caution from Damascus. Nonetheless, the Syrians seem to have made one last effort before giving up at blowing up an Israeli airplane: a Fatah Uprising bomb exploded at a Madrid airport on June 26, 1986, having been intended to detonate aboard an El Al airliner; Syria was implicated, although Spain chose to bypass this angle in the captured terrorist's trial in 1987.[168] Syria's motivation for better behavior was greatly reinforced in October and November 1986 when it was publicly condemned for sponsorship of terrorism in trials in London and West Berlin and subjected to Western sanctions that were symbolic but nonetheless worth the effort. From the time of those trials to this writing Syria has been implicated in no new anti-Western terrorist attacks. The entirety of Western pressure against state-sponsored terrorism seems therefore to have had a deeper effect upon Syria than upon Libya. This should come as no surprise: it was always felt that Assad was more concerned about having a respectable image than was Qaddafi and that the Syrian dictator viewed terrorism not as an end but as a tactic useful only for its immediate service to Syrian foreign policy goals, whereas Qaddafi has appeared to have an ideological attachment to terrorism itself.

Iran's motivation for holding back Shi'ite terrorism against the United States in the periods both before and after the attack on Libya was clearly its secret deal with Washington. Iranian-backed terrorism increased substantially in 1987, directed at exiled dissidents and Arab states supporting Iraq. Interestingly, after the Iran-*contra* revelations brought the collapse of the secret deal, periodic kidnappings in Lebanon continued—the safest variety of terrorism in the world from the terrorist's perspective—but the fierce anti-American Shi'ite terrorist campaign of 1983–85 did not resume. There were no Iranian-sponsored attacks against U.S. citizens other than the Lebanon kidnappings in 1987.[169] Some Shi'ite terrorist plotting was aborted, but given the overwhelming advantage of offense over defense in terrorism, the failure of Iran to bring about lethal attacks against Americans even when it was expected to during the period of Kuwaiti tanker escorts suggests a lack of political will for it in Tehran. It is possible that the U.S. bombing of Libya, reinforced by the naval buildup in the Persian Gulf, increased Iranian respect for U.S. power so as to induce restraint. However, the *Vincennes* disaster of July 1988 appeared to have overridden Iranian restraint.

The U. S. attack on Libya damaged Qaddafi's prestige in the Arab world and on a broader international basis, and weakened his position in Libya as well, but it did not by itself or in combination with other factors lead to a successful move against the colonel by his domestic foes. More surprising and disappointing to Washington officials must have been the fact that he was able to survive the discontent provoked by his humiliating defeat in Chad; those defeats nonetheless privately delighted the Reagan administration as they further weakened Qaddafi's regional position. It is possible that the Libyan dictator will view all terrorism he sponsors against the United States from now on as revenge for the April 15 air attack, but that does not mean that without it he would have ceased from such activities. In a matter beyond any control of Washington, Qaddafi may have helped prolong his tenure in Libya by belatedly scaling back the repression of the revolutionary committees and allowing renewed private enterprise in hopes of ameliorating the Jamahiriyah's economic situation.

Shultz stated, "We must make it clear that while we are not looking around for ways to use force, and we seek other means of putting pressure on and denying terrorists their objectives, . . . there are situations where we will use force and we will have the will and the ability."[170] Terrorism expert Brian Jenkins observed, "Clearly the bombing of Libya changed the equation. It suggested to nations that use terrorism as an instrument of policy that they risk retaliation. They may choose to dismiss that risk or to accept it, but they're going to have to take it into account."[171] The Reagan administration wanted to send such a message to America's violent enemies in the Middle East, and a message was indeed delivered; its value is obviously intangible.

In the realm of military tactics, it may be noted that proportional response as applied in the March 1986 battle of the Gulf of Sidra failed to serve its objectives, while escalation as represented by Operation El Dorado Canyon had at least some degree of success. Conversely, U. S. political objectives were realized in the Persian Gulf in 1987–88, where escalation was eschewed and proportional response again was applied. It must also be noted that the analysis of the mainstream Middle East experts fared poorly in the matter of the U. S. attack on Libya. Rather than becoming a larger-than-life figure, Qaddafi was never less prominent than in the years after the attack. He was weakened rather than strengthened in Libya; opposition to him did not subside. American ties with Arab governments remained unchanged, Arab moderates did not crumble, and they did not meaningfully rally behind Qaddafi. (Interestingly, although Syria was considered to be far less isolated in the Arab world than Libya, when Western countries publicly condemned and imposed sanctions upon Damascus for terrorism in autumn 1986, the response in the Arab world was close to silence.) Middle Eastern diplomacy was not crippled, as witnessed by the Israeli-Moroccan summit and the Taba arbitration accord between Israel and Egypt in 1986.[172] Libya did not become a Soviet satellite. Over against the rigid assertion that military force cannot possibly accomplish anything against terrorism, and in fact will only create a cycle of worse violence, it appears that the U. S. attack may have helped break the cycle of accelerating Middle Eastern terrorism dating from 1983. If any more evidence was needed to discredit the portrayal of Middle Eastern terrorism as uncontrollable outbursts of desperation, it was provided by the aftermath of the U. S. attack.[173] While not denying that the mainstream Middle East experts have worthwhile contributions to make, until they emancipate themselves from their groupthink and dogmatic clichés, U. S. policies toward Libya and toward terrorism should not be tailored to conform to their views.

On the other hand, the U. S. attack on Libya is still an isolated event and does not provide a sufficient basis for a doctrine of U. S. military retaliation against terrorism. The Libya strikes and the clashes with Iran in the Persian Gulf demonstrated that there can be situations in which the United States can use military force in the Middle East without catastrophic consequences for its interests. However, it is certainly an open question as to what effect an escalatory retaliation would have when applied to Iran or Syria. It is not even certain what effect another attack on Libya would have; one can only speculate as to how much of the impact on Libyan behavior was due to Qaddafi's apparently having personally experienced the roar of the F–111s overhead, which would presumably not be the case in another U. S. attack. A far harsher reaction in the Arab world than was seen in the cases of Libya and the Persian Gulf could be expected in the aftermath of a U. S. strike against a Palestinian terrorist base in Lebanon, more so against a group other than the Abu Nidal group. It would be foolish for any administration to renounce publicly the option of military retaliation against terrorism, but abstaining from the empty threats such as Reagan uttered on a number of occasions would be wise; Washington should not paint itself into a corner on the issue. For the United States to engage in reprisal strikes with a regularity even approaching that of Israel would be a nightmare from a logistical standpoint as well as a number of other standpoints, but it should be abundantly clear by now that there was never any chance of that happening for the following reason: the smoking gun criterion. Although relevant government agencies have good success at tracing the responsibility for many terrorist acts, they are usually not able to do so instantly, and a retaliatory strike would not likely be launched long after a terrorist incident, when the public outrage over it had abated.

All this points to something even the strongest believers in military retaliation against terrorism agree upon: the high desirability of finding nonmilitary means of making state support for terrorism costly, which again turns the attention to America's allies. There has definitely been progress in the willingness of the Western Europeans to stand up to Middle Eastern terrorism, but the improvement is to a mixed record from a positively miserable record. Discouraging signs include several European nations' renewed economic flirtation with Libya in 1988 just as signs of its reemerging involvement in terrorist activities surfaced; West Germany's 1987 acceptance as ambassador from Iran a participant in the holding of American diplomats as hostages in Tehran in 1979–80; Bonn's attempted cover-up concerning the Libyan chemical weapons plant (thwarted by the West German press); and the continuing Achilles' heel regarding hostages, to which Reagan also succumbed in 1985–86. Encouraging signs include the increased momentum of governmental cooperation described above and the fact that, contrary to predictions, the Iran-Contra affair did not derail it; longer jail sentences for Arab terrorists; the willingness of several NATO allies to brave the wrath of Iran and join the U. S. Navy in the Persian Gulf; and the EEC's swift response to Khomeini's death threat against Salmon Rushdie, a far less serious matter than the holding of fifty-two American hostages (under threat of trial and execution) in Tehran, which had drawn such a sluggish response from Europe nine years earlier.

However, there is still room for doubt as to whether the West European governments will be willing to apply stiff sanctions, especially economic sanctions, in response to murderous state-sponsored terrorist assaults against U. S. citizens, even though much of the rationale for such reluctance was undercut by the EEC's sanctions against South Africa in September 1986. There is a possible avenue that could give the United States another option besides doing nothing and using military force. In the wake of European failure to implement meaningful punitive measures after an especially appalling terrorist attack linked to a state or to a terrorist organization whose sources of state support are well known, private U. S. citizens could organize an American tourist boycott of Europe aimed at forcing a change in EEC policies. It would openly state that Americans were staying away from Europe not out of fear but out of disgust over the priority being given to commercial interests (and pleasing the Arab world at all costs) over imposing costs upon governments that support bands of murderers who prey upon U. S. citizens and others in the streets of Europe, among other places. Such a boycott could also be undertaken against individual European countries that commit egregious actions such as releasing from jail men whose occupations are to plant explosives aboard airplanes. The U. S. government would, of course, have to disavow such a campaign, but the possibility of mass private foreign policy initiatives having significant effect is demonstrated by the de facto process of U. S. disinvestment in South Africa wrought without endorsement from the executive branch and, as of this writing, the legislative branch. Naturally such tactics would bring much gnashing of teeth and tension between the United States and Europe, but it could not be much worse than what was seen in 1986, and it is foolish to think that painless methods can be found for combatting state-sponsored terrorism.

As terrorism expert Ariel Merari has written:

Terrorism is useful for its sponsors as long as it does not become counter-productive in strategic and political terms. As a rule of thumb, the state sponsors of terrorism wish to remain below the threshold of punishment that is set by the states against which terrorism is directed. In this sense, it is the target countries of state-sponsored terrorism that determine the scope and form of this kind of warfare by their responses or lack of responses to it.

By early 1987 the threshold of punishment appeared to be direct involvement of the sponsoring states in the actual perpetration of international terrorist attacks. The mere harboring, training, and arming of terrorist groups, on the other hand, were, according to the standards set by those western countries that are the main targets of these groups, manifestations of international conduct that however deplorable, did not justify a strong response. These criteria, in turn, undoubtedly determined the form of state-sponsored Middle Eastern terrorism to be expected in the near future.[174]

This smoking gun emphasis has been promoted by the U. S. government as a politically realistic criterion for military action and has been favored by European governments as an excuse for avoiding any action, military or nonmilitary. Clearly this emphasis plays into the hands of the members of the Middle Eastern terrorism network, and beyond that it has intrinsic absurdity: governments selecting specific targets for terrorist groups or having their intelligence officers at the actual scene of the crime are not the most crucial forms of state involvement in terrorism in any case. If the struggle against state-sponsored terrorism is to go any farther, Washington must take the lead in shifting the emphasis away from state links to specific acts to state links to the groups that carry out the acts. Even this shifting of the focus of debate will not be easily accomplished, but efforts must be made to impose heavy costs on this form of aggression, particularly before the stakes become higher.

NOTES

1. Konrad Alder, "An Eye for an Eye, A Tooth for a Tooth . . . : The US Airborne Strike against Libya," *Armada International*, Jan.-Feb. 1987, pp. 37–40; Rick Hornung,

"Air Tankers Aid in Raid on Libya," *Military Logistics Forum* 2 (June 1986): 11; interview with Brig. Gen. Sam Westbrook, 30 June 1989; *Washington Post* (hereafter cited as *WP*), 20 Apr. 1986; "U. S. Demonstrates Advanced Weapons Technology in Libya," *Aviation Week & Space Technology*, 21 Apr. 1986, p. 18; David C. Martin and John Walcott, *Best Laid Plans: The Inside Story of America's War Against Terrorism* (New York: Harper & Row, 1988), pp. 301, 307.

2. Larry Speakes with Robert Pack, *Speaking Out: The Reagan Presidency from inside the White House* (New York: Charles Scribner's Sons, 1988), pp. 181–82; "Hitting the Source," *Time*, 28 Apr. 1986, pp. 26–27.

3. Speakes with Pack, p. 182; *Los Angeles Times* (hereafter cited as *LAT*), 15 Apr. 1986; "Hitting the Source," p. 27; *Washington Times* (hereafter cited as *WT*), 18 Apr. 1986; *Wall Street Journal* (hereafter cited as *WSJ*), 18 Apr. 1986; *NYT*, 14 Apr. 1986.

4. Martin and Walcott, pp. 303, 304; Alder, p. 40; Dave Lee and Chris Holmes, "Operation El Dorado: The Men behind the Headlines," *All Hands*, no. 831 (June 1986), pp. 25–26.
Daniel P. Bolger, *Americans at War: 1975–1986, An Era of Violent Peace* (Novato, Calif.: Presidio Press, 1988), p. 417; *Times* (London), 14 Aug. 1986; *NYT*, 6 Aug. 1986.

5. *WT*, 28 Apr. 1986; *NYT*, 15 Apr. 1986; Bolger, pp. 422–23; "U. S. Demonstrates," p. 18; Martin and Walcott, p. 306; John Lehman, address before the National Press Club, Washington, D.C., 2 Apr. 1987, LEGI-SLATE, 220042.

6. Bolger, p. 422; "So Close, Yet So Far," *Time*, 28 Apr. 1986, p. 33.

7. Bolger, p. 421.

8. *NYT*, 15, 16 Apr. 1986; Martin and Walcott, pp. 305–6; W. Hays Parks, "Crossing the Line," U. S. Naval Institute *Proceedings* 112 (Nov. 1986):51; "Hitting the Source," p. 17; David Blundy and Andrew Lycett, *Qaddafi and the Libyan Revolution* (Boston: Little, Brown, 1987), pp. 9–10; "Qaddafi—O.K. for Now," *U. S. News & World Report*, 28 Apr. 1986, p. 27; David Evans, "The Inevitable Attack on Libya," U. S. Naval Institute *Proceedings* 112 (June 1986), p. 32; *Foreign Broadcast Information Service, Daily Report*, Middle East and Africa (hereafter cited as FBIS-MEA), 11 Apr. 1986, p. Q3.

9. Bolger, pp. 415, 424; Parks, p. 51; *Air Force Times*, 28 Apr. 1986.

10. Parks, p. 51; "US Airpower Hits Back," *Defence Update International* 73 (July 1986), p. 31.

11. Lehman, address before the National Press Club.

12. Joseph S. Bermudez Jr., "Libyan SAMs and Air Defences," *Jane's Defence Weekly*, 17 May 1986, pp. 880–81; "U. S. Airpower Hits Back," p. 31; Aharon Levran and Zeev Eytan, *The Middle East Military Balance, 1986* (Boulder, Colo.: Westview, 1988), p. 163; "Reagan's Raiders," *Newsweek*, 28 Apr. 1986, pp. 28, 31; "In the Dead of the Night," *Time*, 28 Apr. 1986, p. 30; Bolger, p. 422; *WP*, 16 Apr. 1986; Martin and Walcott, pp. 295, 305, 307, 309; New Orleans *Times-Picayune*, 17 Apr. 1986; Bolger, pp. 421–22, 424.

13. Martin and Walcott, p. 295.

14. Department of Defense, "Results of US Military Operations against Libya on April 15, 1986," 8 May 1986, LEGI-SLATE, 110130.

15. Martin and Walcott, pp. 228, 295, 305, 309; *NYT*, 19, 24 Apr. 1986; interview with Brig. Gen. Sam Westbrook, 30 June 1989; Bolger, p. 424.

16. Martin and Walcott, pp. 296, 309; *Air Force Times*, 28 Apr. 1986; "In the Dead of the Night," p. 31; *LAT*, 17, 19 Apr. 1986; Blundy and Lycett, pp. 9, 11; FBIS-MEA, 17 Apr. 1986, p. Q2; FBIS-MEA, 22 Apr. 1986, p. Q2; *NYT*, 24 Apr. 1986; "Hitting

the Source,'' p. 18; *WT*, 15 Apr., 15 Aug. 1986 (UPI); ''Targeting Gaddafi,'' *Time*, 21 Apr. 1986.

17. *NYT*, 21 Apr. 1986; Bolger, p. 411; Martin and Walcott, pp. 272, 308; Blundy and Lycett, p. 11; *Sunday Times* (London, hereafter cited as *ST*), 27 Apr. 1986; Dept. of Defense, ''Results of US Military Operations.'' A significant amount of damage at the secondary naval school took place the night after the U. S. attack in a series of explosions that some foreigners in the area believed were due to an outbreak of internal fighting among the Libyans (*NYT*, 21 Apr. 1986, *ST*, 27 Apr. 1986).

18. Dept. of Defense, ''Results of US Military Operations''; *Air Force Times*, 28 Apr. 1986; Bolger, p. 415; interview with Brig. Gen. Sam Westbrook, 30 June 1989; *LAT*, 16 Apr. 1986; ''In the Dead of the Night,'' p. 31; *Atlanta Journal and Constitution*, 20 Apr. 1986.

19. Parks, pp. 47–48, 51; ''How the Blows Went In,'' *Economist*, 19 Apr. 1986, p. 18; ''US Airpower Hits Back,'' p. 31; Bolger, p. 423; *WT*, 22 Apr. 1986.

20. Bolger, pp. 409, 423, 425, 427; Alder, p. 38; interview with Daniel P. Bolger, 11 Mar. 1989; Dept. of Defense, ''Results of US Military Operations''; *Air Force Times*, 28 Apr. 1986; Blundy and Lycett, p. 11; Martin and Walcott, p. 311; *WT*, 22 Apr. 1986; *Memphis Commercial Appeal*, 21 Apr. 1986.

21. Martin and Walcott, p. 306; interview with Capt. Daniel P. Bolger, 9 Mar. 1989: Speakes with Pack, p. 182.

22. *NYT*, 15, 16 Apr. 1986; ''Intelligence Gathering—At a Price,'' *National Journal* 18 (10 May 1986): 1104.

23. *NYT*, 15 Apr. 1986.

24. Ibid.

25. Bolger, pp. 425, 427, 430; Alder, p. 40; interview with Brig. Gen. Sam Westbrook, 30 June 1989; *WP*, 18 Apr. 1986; Bolger, pp. 427, 430; Adam M. Garfinkle, ''The Unspoken Success of the Libyan Raid,'' *The World & I* 2 (Jan. 1987): 144; Martin and Walcott, p. 380.

26. Anthony H. Cordesman, ''After the Raid: The Emerging Lessons from the US Attack on Libya,'' *Armed Forces* 5 (Aug. 1986):360; Bolger, pp. 411, 432–33; *WP*, 22 Apr. 1986; *WT*, 22 Apr. 1986; *NYT*, 20 Apr. 1986; interview with Brig. Gen. Sam Westbrook, 30 June 1989; FBIS-MEA, 15 Apr. 1986, p. Q9.

27. *LAT*, 15, 16, 20 Apr. 1986; *WP*, 16 Apr. 1986; *WT*, 16 Apr. 1986; ''A View from the Bull's-eye,'' *Newsweek*, 28 Apr. 1986, p. 30; *NYT*, 16 Apr. 1986.

28. *NYT*, 16 Apr. 1986; ''Reagan's Raiders,'' p. 27; Parks, p. 47; Martin and Walcott, pp. 287, 309–10; Dept. of Defense, ''Results of U. S. Military Operations''; ''USAF's Role in Libyan Raid,'' *Air Force*, November 1986, p. 26; Bolger, p. 424. In his memoir, former Secretary of the Navy John F. Lehman, Jr., (who candidly admitted that Weinberger entirely excluded him and the other civilian chiefs of the military departments from the planning of the Grenada and Libya operations) presumed that the Libyan intelligence center had been targeted, citing as his source a book expressing such suspicions coauthored by a journalist who participated in the April 15 tour of Bin Ashur. (*Command of the Seas* [New York: Charles Scribner's Sons, 1989], pp. 297, 374).

29. Dept. of Defense, ''Results of U. S. Military Operations''; *LAT*, 16, 22 Apr. 1986; Parks, p. 52; Blundy and Lycett, p. 13; FBIS-MEA, 15 Apr. 1986, p. Q4; *WT*, 22, 24 Apr. 1986; *Chicago Tribune*, 22 Apr. 1986.

30. FBIS-MEA, 17 Apr. 1986, p. Q12; FBIS-MEA, 15 May 1986, p. Q1; *WT*, 18 Apr. 1986; Lisa Anderson, ''Libya's Qaddafi: Still in Command?,'' *Current History* 86

(Feb. 1987):86; *NYT*, 11 Jan., 16 Apr., 14 June 1986; AP NEWS, 13 Jan. 1986; David Blundy, "The Man We Love to Hate," *Sunday Times Magazine*, 2 Mar. 1986, p. 30. After the second interview, Qaddafi made passes at three of the women (*NYT*, 14 June 1986).

31. FBIS-MEA, 21 Apr. 1986, p. Q6; "So Close, Yet So Far," p. 33; Bolger, pp. 131–32; "Waiting for Muammar," *Newsweek*, 10 Nov. 1986, p. 42; Terrell E. Arnold, *The Violence Formula* (Lexington, Mass.: Lexington Books, 1988), p. 98; interview with Terrell E. Arnold, 9 June 1989.

32. FBIS-MEA, 21 Apr. 1986, p. Q6; *NYT*, 19 Apr. 1986; *WT*, 22 Apr. 1986; Edward Schumacher, "The United States and Libya," *Foreign Affairs* 65 (Winter 1986/87):335; *Times* (London), 17 Apr. 1986.

33. FBIS-MEA, 15 May 1986, p. Q2; Schumacher, p. 335; Memphis *Commercial Appeal* 5 Jan. 1989.

34. Libyan television had on the night of April 17 shown six corpses of persons said to have been killed in the attack on Benghazi (*NYT*, 19 Apr. 1986). Four days later when the reporters were flown to Benghazi, they were told that twenty-four persons, all civilians, had died there. This was clearly an inflated figure: from the information the correspondents were able to gather, about a half dozen civilians had died in the area (*NYT*, 22 Apr. 1986; *WP*, 22 Apr. 1986; *WT*, 22 Apr. 1986; *LAT*, 22 Apr. 1986; *Chicago Tribune*, 22 Apr. 1986).

35. *WT*, 22 Apr. 1986.

36. Blundy and Lycett, p. 11.

37. For example, William Gutteridge, ed., *Libya: Still a Threat to Western Interests?*, Conflict Studies, no. 160 (London: Institute for the Study of Conflict, 1984), p. 12–13.

38. "So Close, Yet So Far," p. 33. That the Qaddafi regime viewed Libyan civilians as propaganda pawns rather than with genuine concern was demonstrated well by its moving of five thousand civilians, including many school children, into tents near the Rabta Chemical Factory in 1989 so that they would be killed in a possible U. S. attack (" 'Human Shield' Guards Libyan Chemical Plant," *Insight*, 6 Mar. 1989, p. 39; *WSJ*, 17 Feb. 1989.

39. *WP*, 16, 17 Apr. 1986; "Libyan Scud B Attack on Lampedusa Island," *Jane's Defence Weekly*, 26 Apr. 1986, p. 739; *NYT*, 27 May 1986; FBIS-MEA, 17 Apr. 1986, p. Q2; Bolger, p. 425.

40. FBIS-MEA, 15 Apr. 1986, pp. Q4–Q8; 16 Apr. 1986, pp. Q12–14; 17 Apr. 1986, pp. Q14–15; 18 Apr. 1986, pp. Q6–Q7.

41. FBIS-MEA, 15 Apr. 1986, p. Q7.

42. Bolger, p. 425.

43. Anderson, "Libya's Qaddafi," p. 87; *WSJ*, 16 Apr. 1986; *WP*, 23 Apr. 1986; *Chicago Tribune*, 16 Apr. 1986.

44. *WT*, 16 Apr. 1986; *Chicago Tribune*, 16 Apr., 18 Aug. 1986; *ST*, 27 Apr. 1986; Blundy and Lycett, p. 12; *NYT*, 17, 24 Apr. 1986; *LAT*, 25 Apr. 1986; Martin and Walcott, p. 314.

45. *LAT*, 25 Apr. 1986; *WSJ*, 25 Aug. 1986; *Middle East Policy Survey* (hereafter cited as *MEPS*), no. 151 (2 May 1986).

46. *MEPS*, no. 150 (18 Apr. 1986); FBIS-MEA, 17 Apr. 1986, pp. Q2–Q4.

47. *LAT*, 17 Apr. 1986.

48. *Times* (London), 26 Apr. 1986; *WSJ*, 25 Apr. 1986; *WT*, 21 Apr. 1986; *NYT*, 15 June, 7 Sept. 1986; Schumacher, p. 339; Alder, p. 39.

49. *NYT*, 9 Apr. 1987, 14, 15 June 1986, 7 Sept. 1986; *Focus on Libya*, Aug. 1986;

WT, 5, 26 Feb. 1987 (NewsBank [Microform], International Affairs and Defense, 1987, 23:A5, A6); François Burgat, "Koran Challenges Green Book in Libya's Ideological Shifts," *Manchester Guardian Weekly*, 1 Feb. 1987, p. 12; FBIS-MEA, 21 Apr. 1986, p. Q15; Schumacher, p. 339; *WT*, 22 Aug. 1986. A Jamahiriyah official privately told a Libyan exile that economic conditions in Libya after the U. S. attack were "terrible" and suggested that Reagan might be the most popular man in that country for having acted against Qaddafi (ibid.). While it seems safe to treat the latter observation as a major exaggeration barring substantial corroboration, it reflected the reality of Qaddafi's unpopularity.

50. *NYT*, 17 Apr., 4 May 1986; *WSJ*, 16 Apr. 1986; *WP*, 30 Apr. 1986; Memphis *Commercial Appeal*, 16 Apr. 1986.

51. "Reagan Decides It Had to Be Done," *Economist*, 19 Apr. 1986, p. 17.

52. *NYT*, 15 Apr. 1986; *WP*, 15 Apr. 1986; *WSJ*, 16 Apr. 1986; "Liberals Surrender and Rejoice with Reagan," *New Statesman*, 25 Apr. 1986, p. 18. As time went on, most of the U. S. liberal support, especially outside Congress, for the attack on Libya dissipated because of a variety of factors, particularly the October 1986 allegation of a disinformation campaign concerning Libya, the Iran-contra scandal, and Hersh's scurrilous *New York Times Magazine* piece (22 Feb. 1987).

53. *Focus on Libya*, Apr. 1986, Jan 1987.

54. *Foreign Broadcast Information Service, Daily Report*, Latin America (hereafter cited as FBIS-LA), 18 Apr. 1986, p. S1, 21 Apr. 1986, pp. S1–S3, 23 Apr. 1986, p. 4; FBIS-MEA, 16 Apr. 1986, p. S1; *Facts on File*, 18 Apr. 1986, p. 260; *WT*, 17, 18 Apr. 1986; Richard Mackenzie and Adam Platt, "Furor Explodes over NATO as U. S. Bombs Fall on Libya," *Insight*, 28 Apr. 1986, p. 28; "The Fury of Khadafy," *Maclean's*, 28 Apr. 1986, p. 22; "The Anger and the Expectation," *Maclean's*, 28 Apr. 1986, p. 27; *Times* (London), 23 Apr. 1986; *NYT*, 22 Apr. 1986.

55. *WT*, 16 Apr. 1986.

56. *NYT*, 23 Apr., 1 May 1986; *WT*, 16 Apr. 1986; *WSJ*, 16, 17 Apr. 1986; *WP*, 16, 23 Apr. 1986; FBIS-MEA, 16 Apr. 1986, p. G2, 17 Apr. 1986, p. G3.

57. *WP*, 15 Apr. 1986.

58. *LAT*, 15 Apr. 1986.

59. *NYT*, 17 Apr. 1986.

60. *Chicago Tribune*, 20 Apr. 1986.

61. *NYT*, 16 Apr. 1986.

62. *LAT*, 16 Apr. 1986; *WP*, 27 Apr. 1986.

63. *WP*, 23 Apr., 28 May 1986; *NYT*, 6 May, 15 June 1986; *Middle East Contemporary Survey*, vol. 10:*1986*, ed. Itamar Rabinovich and Haim Shaked (Boulder, Colo.: Westview, 1986), p. 516.

64. *NYT*, 16 Apr. 1986; *WP*, 23 Apr. 1986; FBIS-LA, 15–24 Apr. 1986.

65. *WP*, 17, 25 Apr., 16 May 1986; *Foreign Broadcast Information Service, Daily Report*, South Asia, 15 Apr. 1986, p. F1, 17 Apr. 1986, p. E2; *WT*, 21 Apr. 1986 (UPI); *NYT*, 19 Apr., 18 June 1986; *WSJ*, 21 Apr. 1986; *Christian Science Monitor* (hereafter cited as *CSM*), 25 Apr. 1986. In January 1987, Iraq boasted that its air force had bombed Khomeini's house in Tehran; the claim was not confirmed by Iran (*NYT*, 18 Jan. 1987).

66. *NYT*, 21 Apr. 1986.

67. *MEPS*, 18 Apr. 1986; *MEPS*, 2 May 1986; "Gaddafi and Terrorism," *World Press Review*, June 1986, p. 25; *NYT*, 9 May 1986. The most severe public reaction was in Sudan. This apparently related to the backdrop in which allegations that Washington

was not honoring its aid commitments were prominently aired in Khartoum, and the Sudanese public felt that the United States was abandoning it in the war against black insurgents in southern Sudan, while Libya provided direct military assistance. Additionally, there was long-term resentment over Washington's former links with Nimeiry. Libyan radio accused the government of Tunisia of granting overflight rights to the United States and called upon Tunisians to arise and overthrow Bourguiba's regime. The Tunisian demonstrators protested this imaginary cooperation by their government as well as the U. S. attack itself (*WP*, 17 Apr. 1986; *NYT*, 29 Apr. 1986).

68. *Chicago Tribune*, 17 Aug. 1986.

69. *Times* (London), 16 Apr. 1986; FBIS-MEA, 17 Apr. 1986, p. Q8.

70. *WT*, 16 Apr. 1986.

71. FBIS-MEA, 21 Apr. 1986, p. Q10.

72. FBIS-MEA, 15 May 1986, p. Q2.

73. FBIS-MEA, 15 Apr. 1986, p. Q4.

74. *NYT*, 16 Apr. 1986.

75. Ibid.

76. *NYT*, 17 Apr. 1986.

77. FBIS-MEA, 18 Apr. 1986, p. C4, 16 Apr. 1986, pp. C1–C2, C5; *NYT*, 16 Apr. 1986.

78. *NYT*, 9 May 1986.

79. FBIS-MEA, 22 Apr. 1986, p. Q1.

80. *Times* (London), 23 Apr. 1986.

81. *WP*, 17 Apr., 4 May 1986; FBIS-MEA, 21 Apr. 1986, p. Q19.

82. FBIS-MEA, 16 Apr. 1986, p. F1. In Washington, the Jordanian ambassador to the United States went somewhat further, saying, "As an Arab state and a member of the Arab League, we have in principle to condemn any attack on any Arab country coming from any source. . . . The United States would not have attacked today," he continued, if Arab states had managed to "work together to resolve this [i.e., terrorism]" (*WP*, 16 Apr. 1986).

83. FBIS-MEA, 16 Apr. 1986, p. F2, 21 Apr. 1986, p. F1; *NYT*, 21 May 1986.

84. FBIS-MEA, 16 Apr. 1986, p. i, 18 Apr. 1986, p. E1, 21 Apr. 1986, p. E4.

85. FBIS-MEA, 21 Apr. 1986, p. E4.

86. FBIS-MEA, 2 May 1986, p. A2.

87. *NYT*, 16 Apr. 1986.

88. "Revenge and Anger Resound in Arab World," *U. S. News & World Report*, 28 Apr. 1986, p. 28; FBIS-MEA, 22 Apr. 1986, pp. D5–D6.

89. FBIS-MEA, 18 Apr. 1986, p. A1; *Times* (London), 3 May 1986; Salah Nour, "Libya after the Air Raids," *Arabia: The Islamic World Review* 5 (June 1986):26–27; *WP*, 29 Apr., 3, 8, 16 May 1986; *NYT*, 10 June, 1988; *WT*, 11 Apr. 1986; *MEPS*, 2 May 1986.

90. *MEPS*, 2 May 1986; *NYT*, 9 May, 10 June 1986; *WP*, 29 Apr. 1986; *WT*, 16 Apr. 1986; *WSJ*, 16 Apr. 1986; "Hitting the Source," p. 26.

91. George P. Shultz, address before Trustees of Community Colleges, 23 Feb. 1987, LEGI-SLATE, 200300.

92. "Hitting the Source," p. 26; *WP*, 29 Apr. 1986.

93. *NYT*, 9 May 1986. Ironically, far greater difficulties in relations with Arab governments were caused by the Reagan administration's capitulation to terrorism in the arms-to-Iran-for-hostages transactions when they were exposed.

94. *Times* (London), 16 Apr. 1986; FBIS-MEA, 22 Apr. 1986, p. T5; "Chad Conference Off," *Arabia: The Islamic World Review* 5 (May 1986):14; *NYT*, 16 Apr. 1986.

95. *NYT*, 5 Sept. 1986.

96. *NYT*, 8 Sept. 1986.

97. *NYT*, 16 Apr. 1986; *WP*, 16 Apr. 1986; *WSJ*, 16 Apr. 1986; *Times* (London), 19 Apr. 1986; Schumacher, pp. 344, 346; Anderson, "Libya's Qaddafi," p. 87.

98. *NYT*, 5 Sept. 1986.

99. *NYT*, 21 Nov. 1986; Provisional verbatim record, United Nations General Assembly, 78th plenary meeting (A/41/PV. 78).

100. Robert Oakley, "International Terrorism," *Foreign Affairs* 65 (1987):618.

101. *LAT*, 16 Apr. 1986.

102. Ibid.

103. *NYT*, 25, 27 Apr. 1986; *WP*, 17, 20 Apr. 1986; "We Love You, We Love You Not: Gosh, Isn't Life Confusing," *Economist*, 26 Apr. 1986, p. 45; Mackenzie and Platt, pp. 28, 32. Perhaps the Rome demonstrators had the Lampedusa attack in mind; it was conveniently overlooked by the peace activists elsewhere in Europe.

104. *WT*, 18 Apr. 1986; *NYT*, 18 Apr. 1986 (national edition). In September 1988 the European Parliament condemned the United States for butchering Latin American babies to provide organ transplants for American citizens, an allegation stemming from malicious Soviet disinformation and not taken seriously by many responsible observers (Memphis *Commercial Appeal*, 25 Oct. 1988).

105. *NYT*, 16 Apr. 1986 (national edition).

106. *NYT*, 16 Apr. 1986.

107. *WT*, 16 Apr. 1986. Some Washington officials spoke privately to reporters after the attack about European leaders having privately expressed support for the decision but warning they would not support it publicly (Cf. *WT*, 22 Apr. 1986; *NYT*, 22, 23, 24). It must be noted that this goes against a great body of evidence. However, a senior French official did say beforehand, "Some would love the Americans to strike; they would secretly jump for joy. But because of Europe's vulnerability, no European leader wants to be seen as publicly sanctioning such a strike" (*NYT*, 14 Apr. 1986).

108. *WT*, 16, 17 Apr. 1986.

109. *NYT*, 16 Apr. 1986.

110. *LAT*, 16 Apr. 1986.

111. *NYT*, 25 Apr. 1986; *German Tribune*, 4 May 1986; Oakley, "International Terrorism," p. 618.

112. *LAT*, 16 Apr. 1986.

113. Karin Santoro et al., "Italian Attitudes and Responses to Terrorism," *Terrorism* (New York) 10 (1987):301–3; *WT*, 3 Apr. 1986; *Times* (London), 14 May 1986; *WP*, 16 Apr., 24 May 1986; George Armstrong, "Italy," in *Britannica Book of the Year, 1987* (Chicago: Encyclopedia Britannica, 1987), p. 502; *NYT*, 16, 24 Apr. 1986.

114. *WSJ*, 16 Apr. 1986.

115. *WP*, 17, 19 Apr. 1986; *WT*, 18 Apr. 1986; *WSJ*, 30 Apr. 1986; *NYT*, 23 Apr., 1, 20 May 1986.

116. *Times* (London), 22 Apr. 1986.

117. *Times* (London), 16, 17 Apr., 4 May 1986; *WT*, 17 Apr., 9 June 1986; *WSJ* 21 Apr. 1986; Peter Jenkins, "United Kingdom," in *Britannica Book of the Year, 1987* (Chicago: Encyclopedia Britannica, 1987), p. 509.

118. *WT*, 17 Apr. 1986; *Times* (London), 21 Apr. 1986; "In Western Europe, Strains among Friends," *U. S. News & World Report*, 28 Apr. 1986, p. 24.

119. "Bill and Ebenezer," *Economist*, 26 Apr. 1986, p. 14.

120. Ibid., p. 13; "We Love You," p. 46; Edward Pearce, "Transatlantic Differences: Getting Things Right & Wrong," *Encounter*, July-August 1986, pp. 34–35.

121. According to reporter R. W. Apple, Jr., the restraint shown by administration officials by their account partially reflected " 'a much more complex reality' than was readily apparent in the attitude of European nations" (*NYT*, 16 Apr. 1986).

122. Oakley, "International Terrorism," p. 618.

123. Europe and Middle East expert Robert Hunter declared then, "I haven't seen so much anger, bitterness and contempt toward the European allies in this town since 1967, during Vietnam" ("A New War—And New Risks," *U. S. News & World Report*, 28 Apr. 1986, p. 22).

124. *NYT*, 17 Apr. 1986.

125. *NYT*, 26 Apr. 1986.

126. Mackenzie and Platt, p. 31.

127. Cordesman, p. 357.

128. *LAT*, 16 Apr. 1986.

129. *German Tribune*, 27 Apr. 1986.

130. "Why Europe is Angry," *Newsweek*, 28 Apr. 1986, p. 34. Americans felt taken for granted by the Europeans no less; Sen. Pete Domenici (R.-N.M.) fumed, "It is inconceivable to me that our European allies should disagree with us 100 percent of the time and still expect to be treated as allies" ("A New War," p. 22).

131. *NYT*, 12 Apr. 1986.

132. *Air Force Times*, 26 May 1986; *WP*, 30 Apr. 1986; *NYT*, 20 Nov. 1984.

133. *WT*, 16, 17 Apr. 1986; *LAT*, 16 Apr. 1986; *NYT*, 17, 26, 27 Apr. 1986; "Khartoum: An Embassy under Siege," *Newsweek*, 28 Apr. 1986, p. 33; FBIS-MEA, 18 Apr. 1986, p. Q11; *WP*, 27 Apr., 12 Dec. 1986; U. S. Department of State, *Counterterrorism Policy*, Current Policy No. 823 (1986).

134. U. S. Department of State, *Libya's Qadhafi Continues Support for Terrorism* (1989), p. 18.

135. *NYT*, 18, 19, 24 Apr. 1986; FBIS-MEA, 17 Apr. 1986, p. G2, 18 Apr. 1986, p. G1; U. S. Department of State, *Patterns of Global Terrorism: 1986* (1988), p. 35.

136. *NYT*, 19, 20, 29 Apr., 7 June 1986; Oakley, "International Terrorism," p. 617; *WP*, 29, 30 Apr.; Judith Miller, "The Istanbul Synagogue Massacre: An Investigation," *New York Times Magazine*, 4 Jan. 1987, p. 19.

137. *WP*, 29 Apr., 11 May 1986; *ST*, 25 May 1986; U. S. Department of Defense, *Terrorist Group Profiles*, 1989, p. 119; *NYT*, 15 May 1986; *Times* (London), 21 Apr. 1986. The fatal shooting of British tourist Paul Appleby in East Jerusalem on April 27 was believed not to be a reprisal for the Libya air strikes, but the latest in a series of random attacks on tourists by a cell of the Abu Musa terrorist group (*NYT*, 28, 30 Apr. 1986).

138. "A New War," p. 23.

139. *NYT*, 16, 18 Apr. 1986; "Reagan Ordered Air Strikes to Preempt Libyan Terrorists," *Aviation Week & Space Technology* 124 (21 Apr. 1986):22; *WT*, 17 Apr. 1986; *WSJ*, 28 Apr. 1986; *WP*, 22 Apr. 1986.

140. Cordesman, p. 355; *Jerusalem Post*, 12 Sept. 1986; *MEPS*, 18 April, 2 May, 30 May 1986; Martin and Walcott, p. 315; *WP*, 11 May 1986; "Hitting the Source,"

p. 27. During deliberations over contingencies for a follow-up attack against Libya, one NSC staffer is said to have suggested that the United States spur a friendly foreign leader to make a phone call to Qaddafi, intercept the call, and send jets immediately to bomb the location where the Libyan dictator received the call. The idea was swiftly shouted down by officials who declared that such an operation would almost certainly violate the ban on assassinations (Martin and Walcott, p. 315).

141. *NYT*, 27 Apr. 1986.

142. *NYT*, 16, 29 Apr. 1986, 14 Apr. 1987; *MEPS*, 18 Apr., 2 May 1986; Oakley, "International Terrorism," p. 618; *Chicago Tribune*, 19 Aug. 1986; *Times* (London), 21 Apr. 1986.

143. *Times* (London), 21 Apr. 1986.

144. Geoffrey M. Levitt, *Democracies against Terror: The Western Response to State-Supported Terrorism*, The Washington Papers, no. 134 (New York: Praeger for the Center for Strategic and International Studies, 1988), p. 135; *WT*, 22 Apr. 1986 (*Daily Telegraph* [London]), 22 Apr. 1986; *NYT*, 22, 25, 26 Apr., 27 Nov. 1986; *WP*, 22 Apr., 6 May 1986; *Times* (London), 23 Apr. 1986; "Bonn's Ambassador Will Cultivate Tripoli," *Insight*, 24 Oct. 1988, p. 37; *Jerusalem Post*, 7 Sept. 1986; Oakley, "International Terrorism," p. 620; *Chicago Tribune*, 19 Aug. 1986; Schumacher, p. 341; *ST*, 19 Apr. 1987; *LAT*, 12 Apr., 11 Oct. 1987. After having resisted implementation of the EEC sanctions with much fanfare, the Greek government sent fifteen to twenty Libyan diplomats home in July (*NYT*, 10 July 1986; *Chicago Tribune*, 19 Aug. 1986).

145. *NYT*, 6, 7 May, 13 June, 1 July, 10 Aug. 1986; *Chicago Tribune*, 19 Aug. 1986; Oakley, "International Terrorism," p. 620; Schumacher, p. 341; *WP*, 5, 6, 8, 24 May, 1986; "Malta's Testing Time," *World Today* 47 (Jan. 1987):17.

146. *NYT*, 28 Apr. 1986.

147. *WT*, 18 Sept. 1987; *NYT*, 16 Aug. 1987; Samuel Segev, *The Iranian Triangle: The Untold Story of Israel's Role in the Iran-Contra Affair*, trans. Haim Watzman (New York: Free Press, 1988), pp. 259–60. At North's direction, his cohort businessman Albert Hakim had purchased the Danish freighter *Erria* on April 28 to provide a floating radio station off the Libyan coast for anti-Qaddafi propaganda, but the CIA and the Navy refused to take up the project, in part because the ship would be an easy target for retaliation by the Qaddafi regime (Segev, p. 258; Martin and Walcott, pp. 314–15).

148. Dept. of State, *Patterns: 1986*, pp. 8, 16; *NYT*, 23 May 1986.

149. Dept. of State, *Libya's Qadhafi Continues*, pp. 17–18; *NYT*, 12 Apr. 1987, 12, 29 Aug., 29 Oct., 20 Nov. 1986; Robert B. Oakley, "Terrorism and Tourism," *Department of State Bulletin* 86 (Oct. 1986):56.

150. Dept. of State, *Patterns: 1986*, p. 6.

151. FBIS-MEA, 15 May 1986, p. Q1.

152. *NYT*, 5, 27 Aug. 1986; Dept. of State, *Patterns: 1986*, p. 6; *WT*, 8 Aug. 1986 (Reuters); Ariel Merari et al., *Inter 86: A Review of International Terrorism in 1986* (Boulder, Colo.: Westview, 1987), pp. 101–2; Martin and Walcott, pp. 320–21; *WP*, 4 Sept. 1986.

153. *WP*, 2 Oct. 1986; *WSJ*, 25 Aug. 1986; *NYT*, 27 Aug. 1986; " 'Real and Illusionary Events,' " *Time*, 13 Oct. 1986, p. 43; "Kaddafi: A War of Leaks," *Newsweek*, 8 Sept. 1986, p. 29. The latter assertion was later in effect confirmed by the primary author of the *Wall Street Journal* story, who stated that "past experience with" the official responsible for the story's "collision course" spin "dictated that those remarks should have been discounted more heavily than they were" (Martin and Walcott, p. 380).

154. *NYT*, 11 Nov. 1986; 6 Sept. 1987; Bob Woodward, *VEIL: The Secret Wars of the CIA, 1981–1987* (New York: Simon & Schuster, 1987), p. 475; CBS, "CBS Evening News with Dan Rather," 6 Mar. 1987; Miller, p. 16; *WT*, 8 Sept. 1986.

155. Martin and Walcott, pp. 317–21; *WSJ*, 2 Sept. 1986; *Jerusalem Post*, 3 Oct. 1986 (AP); *WT*, 22 Oct. 1986.

156. Speakes with Pack, pp. 184–85; Michael Ledeen, review of Bob Woodward, *VEIL: The Secret Wars of the CIA, 1981–1987*, in *Commentary* 84 (Dec. 1987):68; Martin and Walcott, p. 380.

157. Martin and Walcott, pp. 318, 321; *WSJ*, 2 Sept. 1986; Woodward, p. 475.

158. A parallel instance was described in *NYT*, 3 June 1988.

159. *WSJ*, 25 Aug. 1986; Martin and Walcott, p. 320; *WP*, 25 Oct. 1986. *Time* confirmed the *Wall Street Journal's* assertion that Western intelligence agencies outside the United States were detecting signs of Libyan terrorist plotting ("Shadowboxing with Gaddafi," *Time*, 8 Sept. 1986, p. 25). There were no indications that the stories the CIA was planning to place in Arab media had anything to do with Qaddafi's terrorist plotting.

160. *WP*, 2 Oct. 1986.

161. Ibid.; *NYT*, 29 Oct. 1986. For more on the Morton memo and the Libya "disinformation" controversy, readers should consult Martin and Walcott, pp. 317–21, 380.

162. Dept. of State, *Patterns: 1986*, pp. 13, 16, 27; Merari, et al., p. 31; U. S. Department of State, *Patterns of Global Terrorism: 1987*, 1988, pp. 1, 16.

163. *NYT*, 14 Apr. 1987.

164. State Department Background Briefing: Situation Report on Libya, 9 Apr. 1987, LEGI-SLATE, 220166.

165. *NYT*, 13 July 1986.

166. *NYT*, 12 Sept. 1986; Dept. of State, *Patterns: 1987*, p. 6; Dept. of State, *Libya's Qadhafi Continues*, pp. 14–17.

167. *Middle East Military Balance 1986*, pp. 43, 166; *ST*, 19 Apr. 1987; *LAT*, 1 Feb. 1988; Dept. of State, *Patterns: 1987*, p. 37; Memphis *Commercial Appeal*, 4 Feb. 1989.

168. *NYT*, 10, 15 May, 14 June 1986; Dept. of State, *Patterns: 1986*, p. 13.

169. Dept. of State, *Patterns: 1987*, p. 36.

170. G. Shultz, address before Trustees of Community Colleges.

171. *LAT*, 11 Oct. 1987.

172. Garfinkle, p. 142.

173. Terrorism expert Ariel Merari noted, "Changes in the pattern of state-sponsored terrorism in the period that followed the American raid on Libya indicate that the use of terrorism by the states in question is not a matter of fanatic frenzy, but rather a calculated tool of foreign policy. . . . Although many of the individuals recruited for missions are zealots, and some are indeed psychological and social deviates, the states that use their services to promote ideological and strategic objectives do so in a calculated manner subject to cost-benefit analysis" (Merari et al., pp. 33–34).

174. Ibid., pp. 34–35.

Appendix

The Qaddafi Regime on Terrorism: A Sampling

June 11, 1972. In his annual speech commemorating the American evacuation of Wheelus Field in Tripoli, Qaddafi declared "Britain and the United States will pay dearly for the wrongs and perfidy they inflicted on us" and announced his intention to "fight Britain and United States on their own lands" (*New York Times* [hereafter cited as *NYT*], 12 June 1972). He boasted, "We are helping the Irish to put a thorn in Britain's flesh and make her pay dearly" (*NYT*, 13 June 1972). "At present we support the revolutionaries of Ireland, who oppose Britain and are motivated by nationalism and religion. . . . There are arms and there is support" (Shlomi Elad and Ariel Merari, *The Soviet Bloc and World Terrorism*, Jaffee Center for Strategic Studies Paper, no. 26 [Tel Aviv: Jaffee Center for Strategic Studies, Tel Aviv University, 1984], p. 24). Furthermore, said Qaddafi, "We declared here today that any Arab from the Atlantic Ocean to the Gulf wishing to volunteer . . . [for Palestinian terrorist groups] can register his name at any Libyan embassy and will be given adequate training for combat" (*Washington Post*; [hereafter cited as *WP*], 12 June 1972); financial aid for such groups was also promised (*NYT*, 12 June 1972).

October 7, 1972. Referring to the Japanese Red Army's Lod Airport attack, in which mostly Christian pilgrims from Puerto Rico were massacred, Qaddafi in a speech stated, "Indeed, feda'yin [guerrilla] action must be of the type of the operation carried out by the Japanese feda'yin. . . . We demand that feda'i action be able to carry out operations similar to the operation carried out by the Japanese. Why should a Palestinian not carry out such an operation?" (Steve Posner, *Israel Undercover: Secret Warfare and Hidden Diplomacy in the Middle East* [Syracuse: Syracuse University Press, 1987], pp. 82–83).

Early 1970s. In the hagiography *Gaddafi: Voice from the Desert* by Mirella Bianco (London: Longman, 1975), Qaddafi was quoted as saying, "If we assist the Irish people it is simply because here we see a small people still under the yoke of Great Britain and fighting to free themselves from it. And it must be remembered that the revolutionaries of the Irish Republican Army are striking, and striking hard, at the power which has humiliated the Arabs for centuries" (quoted in John Wright, *Libya: A Modern History* [Baltimore: Johns Hopkins University Press, 1982,], p. 174).

1976. Qaddafi stated, "Those bombs which are convulsing Britain and breaking its spirit are the bombs of the Libyan people. We have sent them to the Irish revolutionaries so that the British will pay the price for their past deeds" (Samuel T. Francis, "Libya's Empire of Terror," *Africa Insight* 12 [1982]:9–10).

April 27, 1980. In an address to students of the military academy in Tripoli, Qaddafi declared that "all persons who have left Libya must return by this June 10. . . . If the refugees do not obey they must be inevitably liquidated, wherever they are" (Dennis Pluchinsky, "Political Terrorism in Western Europe: Some Themes and Variations," in *Terrorism in Europe*, ed. Yonah Alexander and Kenneth Myers [New York: St. Martin's Press, 1982], p. 61). The same message was repeated in a press conference in Rome by a visiting member of the Libyan People's Committee in early May (ibid.).

June 6, 1980. "Ahmed Shehati, the head of Libya's Foreign Liaison Committee, said dissidents who did not return to Libya by June 11 would be 'in the hands of the revolutionary committees,' over which the Libyan government claimed to have no control."

"Asked why Qaddafi was treating his political opponents so harshly, Shehati said if the late President Gamal Abdel Nasser of Egypt had killed his opponents while they were in exile, then Anwar Sadat would not be in power there now" (*Facts on File*, 20 June 1980, p. 451).

June 11, 1980. In his Evacuation Day speech, Qaddafi rejoiced that "the revolutionary committees have confirmed that the arm of the revolution is long and strong, and that they can reach any place in the world to strike at the enemies of the revolution.

" . . . [T]hey were capable of striking with bravery and with a steel fist everywhere, and . . . the enemies of the revolution became convinced that the hotels of London, the brothels of Italy, and the winehouses of Beirut could not protect them from the verdict passed on them by the revolutionary committees." Qaddafi then asked the revolutionary committees to await convictions by revolutionary courts before carrying out any further killings, except against those who "have had dealings with . . . the Egyptian, Israeli, and U. S. authorities," which persons "deserve death everywhere" (*Foreign Broadcast Information Service, Daily Report*, Middle East & Africa [hereafter cited as FBIS-MEA], 12 June 1980, p. 15).

June 12, 1980. On the steps of the London Libyan people's bureau, its chief Musa Kusa told a London *Times* reporter that the revolutionary committees had the previous day decided "to kill two more people" in Great Britain. Kusa said, "I approve of this" (P. Edward Haley, *Qaddafi and the United States since 1969* [New York: Praeger, 1984], pp. 129–30).

Mid–1980. In recent months, Qaddafi had "publicly called upon Palestinian groups to attack Egyptian, Israeli, and American targets in the Middle East," according to Under Secretary of State for Political Affairs David D. Newsom in testimony before Congress on August 4, 1980 (U. S. Department of State, *U.S.-Libyan Relations since 1969*, prepared by David D. Newsom, Current Policy No. 216 [Washington, D.C.: Government Printing Office, 1980], p. 2).

January 14, 1981. In the context of Libya's occupation of Chad, Qaddafi declared, "If France interferes with the security of the Libyan people, the Libyan people will enter the battle with all its weapons, the oil weapon, the political and economic weapon, and the revolutionary weapon [i.e., terrorism]. France will then suffer heavy losses" (FBIS-MEA, 15 Jan. 1981, p. I2).

1981? Upon being asked by British journalists Christopher Dobson and Ronald Payne about Libyan hit squad activities in Great Britain, Qaddafi asserted that "this is a purely Libyan matter . . . the new Libya is getting rid of the old Libya" (Christopher Dobson and Ronald Payne, *Counterattack: The West's Battle against the Terrorists* [New York: Facts on File, 1982], p. 183).[1]

October 1982. Qaddafi warned Libyan exiles to "repent" and return to the Jamahiriyah. "We will not allow any trivial person to give Libya a bad reputation abroad. Such people are charged with high treason because of their collaboration with the Israelis and Americans. They should be killed not because they constitute any danger, but because of their high treason. It is the Libyan people's responsibility to liquidate such scums who are distorting Libya's image" (FBIS-MEA, 12 Oct. 1982, quoted in "The Libyan Problem," *Department of State Bulletin* 83 (Oct. 1983), p. 78).

June 11, 1984. In his Evacuation Day speech Qaddafi blamed the United States for the dramatic coup attempt by the National Front for the Salvation of Libya the previous month—he also on other occasions blamed Great Britain, Tunisia, Sudan, the Muslim Brotherhood, and the Fatah faction of the PLO for it—and in this context he stated, "We are capable of exporting terrorism to the heart of America. We are also capable of physical liquidation, destruction, and arson inside American. . . . As for America, which has exported terrorism to us, we will respond likewise" (FBIS-MEA, 12 June 1984, pp. Q6, Q11).

June 29, 1984. In a speech Qaddafi told Libyans that " it is the duty of every able young person who goes to Hajj to take responsibility [for] fighting and liquidating the enemy and stray dogs [Libyan dissidents] . . . if they are found there between Safa and Marwa" in the holy city of Mecca (Mohamed A. El-Khawas, *Qaddafi: His Ideology in Theory and Practice* [Brattleboro, Vt.: Amana Books, 1986,], p. 108). In August a Libyan plot to seize the Grand Mosque during the Hajj was thwarted.

March 3, 1985. In a speech before the General People's Congress in Tripoli, Qaddafi declared, "We have the right to take a legitimate and sacred action—an entire people liquidating its opponents at home and abroad in plain daylight" (Ariel Merari, et al., *Inter 86: A Review of International Terrorism in 1986* [Boulder, Colo.: Westview, 1987], p. 20).

March 1985. In an interview with the pro-Libyan daily *Al-Safir*, Qaddafi said: Would not they [that is, the Arabs] stand up for themselves for once and divorce the United States for good. I am telling them: Unless you do this, I who am already blacklisted and branded as an international terrorist, swear by Almighty God that I will take it upon myself to thwart this defeatism and make the Arabs dignified for once. By God Almighty, I will take up my responsibility and start terrorism against Arab rulers. I will threaten and terrify them. I will sever relations and sever their heads one by one, if I can. I am a terrorist when the dignity of this people is at stake" (FBIS-MEA, 22 Mar. 1989, p. Q3). In the same interview Qaddafi stated, "Nabih Birri and his group do not meet with any Libyan, but I still consider him the hero of the liberation of southern Lebanon. . . . The Shi'ite proves his heroism when he falls martyr. Nobody else except the Shi'ite would load a car with explosives and blow it up himself. . . . There may be a Hezbollah party, but the fact is that they are all Shi'ites. . . . Nabih Birri is a hero, and so are other leaders such as Al-Musawi [the leader of the terroristic faction Islamic Amal]'' (FBIS-MEA, 29 Mar. 1985, p. Q2).

March 31, 1985. Before the terrorist convention of the Pan-Arab Command for Leading the Revolutionary Forces in the Arab Homeland, Qaddafi stated, ''Even the individual suicidal operations which took place against the American, French and Israeli forces in Lebanon are in fact an expression of the fact that there are no capabilities and methods other than suicide and death. . . . There is no alternative to confronting the enemy with violence. . . . [O]ur task here in this command is to see to it that individual operations are transformed into an organized . . . action which will reap fruit, defeat the enemy, and liberate the nation. . . . When a Fida'i said I want to die in exchange for 300 Americans in Lebanon, it was carried out and America, with all its might, with 50 warships close to Lebanon's shores could not prevent this. . . . We want to resurrect this spirit in this [Arab] nation, the spirit of martyrdom. We want every one of us to say: I have decided to die just to spite America, because this decision is one that America can not veto'' (FBIS-MEA, 1 Apr. 1985, pp. Q10–Q11, Q13).

April 1, 1985. Qaddafi's deputy Major Jalloud in a Land Day speech declared, ''Greetings . . . to the fighters and militants of Amal movement and Hezbollah fighters, to the militants of Fatah movement and all the organizations which had fought, to the unidentified heroes who drove car bombs and spread terror and fear for Reagan in the White House. . . . We kneel in awe and glory before the heroic Lebanese national resistance. The shoe of a hero from the resistance in the south or from the brave martyrs who drove car bombs is for us more sacred than Arab reaction with its money, oil and palaces. . . . [T]he Lebanese national resistance, however, decided that its only communication with the Zionists, the Americans, and the enemies of the Arab nation will be through T.N.T. and car bombs. However we try to glorify this sacred, noble phenomenon, words will not be enough to give this rave resistance its due honor.

''. . . As from next year, after the announcement of the nationalist command of revolutionary forces, celebrations of Land Day will be different. We shall ourselves drive the car bombs and carry out heroic operations'' (FBIS-MEA, 2 Apr. 1985, pp. Q2–Q3).

April 10, 1985. Qaddafi warned Reagan not to interfere in Sudan in the aftermath of the overthrow of Nimiery, and stated, ''We will have to carry the battle to the very heartland of those who are interfering'' (WP, 11 Apr. 1985).

May 7, 1985. Speaking at the dedication of a mosque in Rwanda, Qaddafi declared, ''Mobutu is a Zionist agent, and you must incite Muslims in Zaire and urge them to engage in the *jihad* so that Mobutu may be toppled, together with his regime. *He who kills this agent will go to paradise.* . . . Killing him is the duty of every Muslim, and so is the killing of all his infidel aides who have allied themselves with the Jews'' (*Middle East Contemporary Survey*, vol. 8:*1983–84*, ed. Haim Shaked and Daniel Dishon [Tel Aviv: Dayan Center for Middle Eastern and African Studies, The Shiloah Institute, Tel Aviv University, 1986], pp. 60–62).

June 11, 1985. In the wake of Amal beginning its long siege of Palestinian camps in Lebanon, Qaddafi declared, "This man called Nabih Birri, it is right to kill him. . . . Nabih Birri is a Zionist, a non-Muslim and a non-Shi'ite and non-Sunni. His death is permitted. The one who kills him will enter heaven" (FBIS-MEA, 12 June 1985, pp. Q6, Q10). Additionally, he asked, "Why do the rulers of Egypt not go to prison for life for publicly shaking the hands of the Israelis? They should be executed. . . . The sentence was executed in the case of Al-Sadat, and it will be executed with the others. Anybody who puts his hand in the hand of the Israelis should be executed. . . . This is your mission and the mission of all Arab revolutionaries" (ibid., p. Q6).

September 1, 1985. Qaddafi declared: "The Western states—all of them—are now conspiring against us; they have been transformed into arenas for training in terrorism against us—to export terrorism to us [a reference to Western countries giving asylum to Libyan dissidents, who were responsible for very few acts of violence]. Until now we have not established alliances with the Red Brigades, the gangs in Germany or in Spain, or the rest of the gangs. Until now we have not openly established alliances with these, despite the fact that we are victims of injustice and have the right to establish alliances with these gangs. If others export terrorism to us, then we have the right to export terrorism to them—tit for tat. . . .

"We are always wronged. Therefore we have the right to fight Zionism, we have the right to fight America, and we have the right to export terrorism to them because they have done everything to us. . . .

"We are destined to be a base for liberation. Even the Palestinian guerillas' action, if they have not ability to act from Lebanon, Syria, Jordan and Egypt, it must act from Libya. . . . This is self-defense. Until now it is possible to begin studying the possibilities of basing the guerilla action in Libya" (FBIS-MEA, 3 Sept. 1985, p. Q9).

November 21, 1985. Radio broadcasts announced that the "Libyan Revolutionary Officers" were "anxious to clash with the enemies of the revolution" and "determined to settle accounts with our enemies, the enemies of the revolution and to chase them wherever they may be." The officers called for "striking of American interests in the Arab homeland" and "continuation of chasing the stray dogs, the dogs of the CIA, and their physical elimination." They warned that "any harm that might come to" Qaddafi, "whether material or moral, constitutes harm to us, to which we will reply by most ferociously turning ourselves into suicide squads to destroy everything. [Chants: 'All revolutionaries are Mu'ammar and anyone who antagonizes him must be destroyed.']" (FBIS-MEA, 21 Nov. 1985, pp. Q2–Q3).

December 29, 1985. The Libyan state news agency JANA commented on the Rome and Vienna massacres: "A number of Arab regimes have condemned the daring operation undertaken by the sons of the martyrs of Palestine from the Sabra and Shatilah camps against the Zionist El Al company desks in the Rome and Vienna airports. . . . The fact that these Arab officials condemn the sacrificial [fida'iy] action of the sons of the martyrs of Sabra and Shatilah will carry more significance than the well-known positions of the submissive Arab regimes. Furthermore, such heroic operations, which are considered to be a direct result of the Sabra and Shatilah massacres, are in themselves a condemnation of the Arab regimes and the world public opinion" (FBIS-MEA, 30 Dec. 1985, p. Q1).

December 31, 1985. A statement by the People's Bureau for Foreign Liaison declared that Libya "denounces and rejects every action that harms the innocent and threatens their lives" (FBIS-MEA, 2 Jan. 1986, p. Q3).

January 1, 1986. In a press conference Qaddafi stated, "I firmly reject the claim that the Palestinian action should be accused of terrorism. The Palestinian action is the most sacred action on earth in this era because it concerns fighting by people who have been wronged. . . . " Asked about Libyan assistance to Abu Nidal, he said, "The Libyan people have decided that all they have is at the disposal of the Palestinian people"; he also asserted, "There are a million Abu Nidals among the Palestinian people." Referring to Israeli and American hints of striking against the Abu Nidal group in Libya, the colonel declared, "If they [Palestinians] are pursued in Libya . . . we shall pursue U. S. citizens in their country and streets. We shall pursue Jews in the streets of occupied Palestine" (FBIS-MEA, 3 Jan. 1986, pp. Q1–Q2, Q4).

January 2, 1986. "An English language report on Libyan television Thursday said Libya was forming suicide squads to attack American and Western European interests in Libya" (*NYT*, 4 Jan. 1986).

January 3, 1986. In a letter to UN Secretary-General Javier Perez de Cuellar, Libya's foreign minister Ali Treiki denied Libyan involvement in the Rome and Vienna massacres, calling them "deplorable blood outrages" (*WP*, 4 Jan. 1986). Nonetheless, during the two weeks after the attacks, JANA continued to praise them as "heroic acts" (*NYT*, 11 Jan. 1986).

January 5, 1986. In another press conference Qaddafi declared, "We support the Palestinians and their right to liberate Palestine, but at the same time we are not responsible for the method which the Palestinians adopt toward this end. *They are free to adopt what they consider appropriate*. They do not have aircraft or submarines. They only have rifles and light weapons and they have to assert their struggle and express their opinion to the world. They are compelled to do this and it is their responsibility (FBIS-MEA, 6 Jan. 1986, p. Q1; emphasis added).

" . . . [A]ttacking passengers at airports is an unlawful action as far as we are concerned as an independent state. However, as far as the Palestinians are concerned some believe that it is a legitimate action. . . . [y]ou in America, during the days of George Washington carried out such actions against British colonialism. In the era of Abraham Lincoln, the Americans carried out numerous actions similar to what the Palestinians carry out today. Mao Zetung did the same for the unification of China and Garibaldi also did the same for the liberation and unification of Italy" (ibid., p. Q4).

He said Palestinians could have training camps in Libya if they requested them (ibid.) and said Abu Nidal "comes to visit us" (*WP*, 6 Jan. 1986). He declared that "with regard to what happened in Rome and Vienna, in the final analysis, it concerned the Israelis. So why should America interfere and speak about threats and reprisals? . . . Although we do not possess B–52 bombers or aircraft carriers that could reach the shores of America, we possess fedayeen people. . . . Our bombers and aircraft carriers are the fedayeen who are capable of entering anywhere. . . . America believes that it can enter any place, but we can also reach any place, not with aircraft carriers or with bombers but with suicide squads" (FBIS-MEA, 6 Jan. 1986, pp. Q5–Q6).

January 6, 1986. JANA cited a fresh publication by the Libyan revolutionary committees declaring "that is the right of the Arab Palestinian people to revolt, retaliate, avenge themselves, and throw the Zionists, wherever they are, into a red hot inferno. This is because it is the Zionists who pushed them and forced them to carry out legitimate field fida'i operations which the Zionists wrongly describe as terrorist, irresponsible, and against international law. . . . [t]he Arab Palestinian people carry out sacred, revenge-seeking operations in retaliation for what was done by the racist Zionists, and it is for this reason an indisputably legitimate action. . . . [s]tupid, amusing voices which describe . . . these actions as 'terrorism' . . . should support those actions'' (FBIS-MEA, 7 Jan. 1986, p. Q4).

January 8, 1986. Qaddafi told a gathering of seven Western European ambassadors, "If they [the United States] attack me, I'll become a madman'' (Memphis *Commercial Appeal*, 10 Jan. 1986). If attacked from American bases in Europe, "then we have to close our eyes and ears and hit indiscriminately. We are going to react with suicide squads against towns, ports, etc., wherever the threats are—while at the same time the Americans are far away. If it comes to war, we will drag Europe into it'' (*WP*, 10 Jan. 1986).

January 9, 1986. Salim Huweidi, Libya's cultural representative in Moscow, justified the Rome and Vienna massacres as "actions of a partisan war, committed by revolutionaries'' and said, "We are not responsible for these acts, but we support them because in our view they are acts in the struggle for freedom. . . . Libya is in no way a source of terrorism,'' but "we are in support of the acts perpetrated in Rome and Vienna'' (*WP*, 10 Jan. 1986).

January 9, 1986. Qaddafi in a press conference stated concerning the Rome and Vienna massacres, "As independent states we do not condone such acts. But as for the Palestinians—it may well be necessary for them'' (*WP*, 10 Jan. 1986). In an interview with five women reporters afterwards he retreated and said the "Palestinian 'freedom fighters' had hurt their cause by killing civilians . . . and called upon Palestinians to limit their struggle to 'military Israeli objectives' '' (*NYT*, 10. Jan. 1986).

January 15, 1986. Referring to radical Arab groupings present in Libya, Qaddafi stated, "I accept all their resolutions. I announce that they will be trained for terrorist and suicide missions. We shall allocate trainers to train them and place all the weapons needed to perform those missions at their disposal. . . .

"If the Israelis pursue the Palestinians outside of Palestine, it is the right of the Palestinians to pursue the Israelis anywhere in the world. The Rome and Vienna attacks targeted the Israeli airline counters'' (*WP*, 16 Jan. 1986).

Early 1986. When asked by *Sunday Times* reporter David Blundy about the overseas murder campaign against Libyan dissidents termed "stray dogs,'' Major Jalloud stated, "That policy is over, . . . they are all dead'' (David Blundy, "The Man We Love to Hate,'' *Sunday Times Magazine*, 2 Mar. 1986, p. 26).

March 4, 1986. The General People's Congress in Libya called for "working for forming suicide squads to wreck U.S.-Zionist interests everywhere'' and for "wrecking U.S.-Zionist embassies in the Arab homeland'' (*WP*, 5 Mar. 1986).

March 5, 1986. Qaddafi declared, "Any person who left Libya is now in the hostile ranks on America's side. He is finished. He will receive no mercy or compassion at home or abroad. All traces of him should be wiped out. Even his house should not remain'' (Larry Pressler, "Libya,'' *Department of State Bulletin* 87 [Jan. 1987]: 88).

March 15, 1986. Hosting a sizable convention of guerrillas, terrorists, pacifists, and other leftists, Qaddafi warned that the United States might attempt to deal with Libya as it had with Grenada. He urged "a collective struggle against the joint enemy," suggesting attacks on "communication routes in the vital regions of the world," (*WP*, 27 Mar. 1986) and declared, "We will go out of control in defending ourselves" (Rod Nordland and Ray Wilkinson, "Inside Terror, Inc.," *Newsweek*, 7 Apr. 1986, p. 26).

March 25, 1986. In the wake of Qaddafi's losing battle with the United States in the Gulf of Sidra, Libyan radio declared, "The American bases in the Arab homeland should now be stormed. American spies who were pushed forward as experts and consultants should now be executed, wherever they might be in the Arab homeland" (*NYT*, 26 Mar. 1986).

March 26, 1986. Libyan radio "urged that the Arab nation transform itself 'in its entirety into suicide squads and into human bombs. . . . Let your missiles and suicide cells pursue American terrorist embassies and interests wherever they may be' " (*Times* [London], 27 Mar. 1986).

March 28, 1986. Libyan radio called it "the duty of all Arabs to 'make everything American . . . a military target' " (Memphis *Commercial Appeal*, 29 Mar. 1986).

April 1, 1986. Qaddafi said he would order no terrorist attacks, "but you must know many, many people in the world support us, and they are angry. They may do anything, but we are not responsible for this. . . . Americans are a good people. . . . But they must also know I am ready to fight. I do not support terrorism, but I am a revolutionary man" (*Washington Times*, 1 Apr. 1986 [UPI]).

April 9, 1986. The Libyan dictator told reporters: "It is axiomatic that if aggression is being staged against us, we shall escalate the violence against American targets, civilian and noncivilian, all over the world" (*NYT*, 10 Apr. 1986).

April 15, 1986. After the United States air raids, Libyan radio addressed Arabs: "Attack everything American. . . . [R]ip apart the bodies of the Americans, be they military or civilians. Drink their blood. Set ablaze their interests because they are now shelling Libyan Arab cities and they are destroying population centers over the heads of their civilian residents. Brothers in Tunisia, Algeria, Morocco, Egypt, Sudan, the Arab Peninsula, and the Gulf: Come forward toward American embassies, companies' premises and military bases in your countries. . . . Set fire to American embassies and companies in Tunisia, Morocco, Sudan and Syria. Set ablaze any American embassy, factory or military base in the greater Arab world as a reply to the treacherous attack against the people of the Jamahiriyah, the conscience of the Arab nation and its beating heart" (FBIS-MEA, 15 Apr. 1986, p. Q5).

In another broadcast: "We are drinking their blood. But every one of you can in his own place also drink the Americans' blood: There are their embassies, consulates and companies' offices in the Arab capitals; there are Americans living in the Arab capitals and towns. Say God is great, O Arab, and slaughter them like sheep. . . . Come out against the Anglo-Saxons, Americans and British, and pour out your wrath on them . . . " (ibid., p. Q7).

In yet another radio broadcast: "Strike at the U.S. embassies and individuals. Tear them with your teeth, with your daggers, with your bombs, with your guns, and with your planes, O proud Arabs" (ibid., p. Q8).

April 16, 1986. Tripoli radio continued: "Is an American citizen, whether he is a civilian or military person, [one] who deserves to remain alive one single moment when you, the Arab compatriot in all the regions of the homeland can reach him?... Arabs, kill them, slaughter them in the streets and highways.... [K]ill them and kill them only after you kill their children in front of their own eyes.... [T]he Americans are to be found within easy reach of you. Strangle them. Cut up their bodies as punishment for their deeds against your women and children" (FBIS-MEA, 16 Apr. 1986, pp. Q12–Q13).

In another broadcast: "Shame, curse, and disgrace be upon the agents of the United States in the Arab homeland who welcome the U.S. fleets... who welcome the envoys and the dogs of the mad terrorist Reagan... and even open to them the bedrooms of their wives!... [T]hose agents and their masters will pay the price for their treachery! We will destroy their thrones and tear up their bodies.... [T]he masses and the revolutionary forces of these countries... must now kill every American, civilian or military, without mercy and ruthlessly and without any compassion and pursue them everywhere. He who kills an American enters heaven; he who slaughters an American creates a new glory for the Arab nation with blood" (ibid., p. Q14).

September 5, 1986. In his address before the Nonaligned Movement, Qaddafi stated, "I am fully convinced that we should counter this empire [the United States] in defense of the whole of humanity with an international army. We shall undertake then all types of terrorist acts and I shall declare that this is the action of my army" (*NYT*, 5 Sept. 1986).

Late October 1986. Richard Z. Chesnoff of *U.S. News & World Report* and author Barbara Victor interviewed Qaddafi.

Have the events of the last six months altered your support of what the U.S. considers terrorist movements?

Qaddafi: We have increased our support for the liberation movements of the Palestinians and for all liberation movements throughout the world. To react to this aggression we have doubled our efforts with the liberation movements....

Do the Abu Nidal and Georges Habash groups [both linked to terrorism] use Libya as a base for their operations?

Qaddafi: Libya is open for the Palestinians....

Is it conceivable that Americans will face attacks by "liberation movements" inside the United States? Would you support the activities of such groups?

Qaddafi: Peoples have the right to defend themselves and to react to aggression

(" 'I Am a Mixture of Washington and Lincoln,' " *U.S. News & World Report*, 10 Nov. 1986, p. 32).

Late October 1986. Qaddafi told Ruth Marshall of *Newsweek* that he did "not approve of killing civilians anywhere," even Israel. He financed, armed, and trained terrorist groups "so they can liberate their homelands," though "it is not our concern or our responsibility what they do." He asserted that the attempted bombing of an El Al plane taking off from London "is a matter for the Israelis. It has nothing to do with the English." Even an attack on an American check-in desk in Rome "has nothing to do with America.

It is a question for the Arabs and the Israelis.'' Furthermore, he asserted that after the April U.S. attack on Libya, ''freedom fighters all over the world avenged me on my behalf. They hit American targets all over the world and killed a record number of Americans.'' Although he admitted that this development had somehow escaped the attention of the press, he said ''the American government knows'' (''Waiting for Muammar,'' *Newsweek*, 10 Nov. 1986, p. 42).

NOTE

1. Cf. Karl Marx in the *Neue Rheinishe Zeitung* of November 5, 1846: ''There is only one way to shorten the murderous death agonies of the old society, only one way to shorten the bloody birth pangs of the new society . . . only one means—revolutionary terrorism'' (quoted in Shlomi Elad and Ariel Merari, *The Soviet Bloc and World Terrorism*, Jaffee Center for Strategic Studies Papers, no. 26 (Tel Aviv: Tel Aviv University, 1984) p. 58).

Bibliographical Essay

Information on developments relating to Libya can be found in the several leading prestige newspapers of the United States and Great Britain, as well as the *Washington Times*, which takes a special interest in Libya and terrorism. The *Foreign Broadcast Information Service Daily Reports*, Middle East and Africa (since mid-1987, Near East and South Asia), are an excellent primary source; included are many of Muammar al-Qaddafi's speeches, a rich resource (in contrast to his frequent interviews with Western correspondents, in which he seldom says anything new or different). The International Security Council (Washington, D.C.) publishes *Focus on Libya*, a monthly newsletter. Intriguing coverage of Libya was found in the Islamic fundamentalist monthly *Arabia: The Islamic World Review* (London, 1981–87), including a June 1984 cover story. In the pages of *Arabia* (which was funded by the government of Saudi Arabia, but was far more enamored of the theocratic regime of Iran) Qaddafi was detested for his heresies and his persecution of conservative Muslims in Libya and his downfall was hopefully awaited.

Two useful Department of State white papers are "The Libyan Problem," *Department of State Bulletin* 83 (Oct. 1983):71–78, and *Libya under Qadhafi: A Pattern of Aggression*, Special Report No. 138 (1986), the latter containing appendices on Abu Nidal and on selected violent incidents attributed to Libya from 1979 to 1985. The following are two pertinent congressional hearings: U. S. Congress, Senate Committee on the Judiciary, Subcommittee on Security and Terrorism, *Libyan-Sponsored Terrorism: A Dilemma for Policymakers*, 19 Feb. 1986, 99th Cong., 2d sess.; and U. S. Congress, House Committee on Foreign Affairs, Subcommittee on Arms Control, International Security, and Science, *War Powers, Libya, and State-Sponsored Terrorism*, 29 Apr.–15 May 1986, 99th Cong., 2d sess.

Extensive Defense Department testimony on the April 15, 1986, air strikes is found in U. S. Congress, House Committee on Appropriations, *Department of Defense Appropriations for 1987*, 99th Cong., 2d sess., 1986, pp. 680–725. Detailed military accounts of the 1981 Gulf of Sidra dogfight, the January and February 1986 naval maneuvers north of Libya, the March 1986 battle and Operation El Dorado Canyon in April are contained in Daniel P. Bolger, *Americans at War: 1975–1986, An Era of Violent Peace* (Novato, Calif.: Presidio Press, 1988). An informed account of the attitudes of the policy community, especially the military, concerning the Libya air strikes in their aftermath is found in Anthony H. Cordesman, "The Emerging Lessons from the U. S. Attack on Libya," *Armed Forces* 5 (Aug. 1986):355–60. A good account of the planning of the April attack is provided in David C. Martin and John Walcott, *Best Laid Plans: The Inside Story of America's War Against Terrorism* (New York: Harper & Row, 1988); *Best Laid Plans* greatly surpasses for accuracy a more ballyhooed work that covers much of the same material: Bob Woodward, *VEIL: The Secret Wars of the CIA, 1981–1987* (New York: Simon & Schuster, 1987). An adaptation of an interview with Martin and Walcott's F–111 pilot "Fred Allen" (pseudonym) is given in " 'How I Bombed Qaddafi,' " *Popular Mechanics*, July 1987, pp. 111–14, 153.

A collection of essays, some quite vituperative, assembled by British anti-NATO activists in the wake of the air raids is found in Mary Kaldor and Paul Anderson, eds., *Mad Dogs: The US Raids on Libya* (London: Pluto Press for European Nuclear Disarmament, 1986). Undoubtedly the most overrated contribution on the U. S. and Libya is Seymour M. Hersh, "Target: Qaddafi," *New York Times Magazine*, 22 Feb. 1987, pp. 16–22. It is a very poor source, remarkably tendentious and replete with misinformation from the beginning to the end.

For legal aspects one may consult Michael Rubner, "Antiterrorism and the Withering of the 1973 War Powers Resolution," *Political Science Quarterly* 102 (Summer 1987):193–215; Yehuda Z. Blum, "The Gulf of Sidra Incident," *American Journal of International Law* 80 (July 1986):668–77; David L. Larson, "Naval Weaponry and the Law of the Sea," *Ocean Development and International Law* 18 (1987):125–98. References to numerous other useful books and articles on Libya and on terrorism may be found in the chapter endnotes of this book and in *PAIS Bulletin* (New York).

Index